Once Upon a Virus

AIDS Legends and Vernacular Risk Perception

Once Upon a Virus

AIDS Legends and Vernacular Risk Perception

•••••

Diane E. Goldstein

Utah State University Press
Logan, Utah

Utah State University Press
7800 Old Main Hill
Logan, Utah 84322-7800

Manufactured in the United States of America
Printed on acid-free paper

Library of Congress Cataloging-in-Publication Data

Goldstein, Diane E.
    Once upon a virus : AIDS legends and vernacular risk perception / Diane E.
Goldstein.
        p. cm.
    Includes bibliographical references and index.
    ISBN 0-87421-586-2 (hardcover : alk. paper) -- ISBN 0-87421-587-0 (pbk. : alk.
paper)
    1. AIDS (Disease)--Newfoundland. 2. Risk perception. 3. Health behavior. 4.
AIDS (Disease)--Folklore. I. Title.

    RA643.86.C22N494 2004
    614.5'99392'09718--dc22

                                                                2004010414

To

the memory of

Kenneth S. Goldstein

and

David Buchan

and to

the people of Conception Bay North

and people everywhere

who have been stigmatized by illness

Contents

Acknowledgments

More than any other part of the writing process for this book, the part that I have dreaded the most has been the acknowledgments. When one has felt so continually surrounded by supportive and helpful people, it becomes nearly impossible to feel confident that everyone who deserves to be thanked will make it safely onto the pages of appreciation. To those whom I should have mentioned here and did not, I extend my apologies. Please know that I am nevertheless indebted to you for your insights, encouragement, and assistance. Those who are mentioned here should in no way, however, be held accountable for any errors (of fact or judgement) these pages may contain.

I am grateful to a number of agencies that generously helped to fund this research. The Institute for Social and Economic Research funded the early years of the AIDS project and provided seed support for the fieldwork and media analysis. The Social Science and Humanities Research Council funded the latter years of this work and continues to support my ongoing study of legends and vernacular health discourse. The Office of the Dean of Arts and the Office of Research at Memorial University provided assistance with travel funding, which allowed me to discuss these issues with other scholars in both folklore and public health. The Folklore Department at Memorial provided occasional graduate research assistants, which made an enormous difference in my ability to handle the large amounts of material that ultimately became part of this project.

An earlier version of chapter 5 was published in Contemporary Legend 2 (1992): 23–40. Thank you to editor Cathy Preston for permission to reprint portions of that article here. Thank you also to Kevin Tobin (KT) for granting permission to reprint his editorial cartoon originally published in the *Evening Telegram*. I wish to express my appreciation to John Alley and the staff at USU Press for expertly guiding this manuscript through the review and publication process.

This book would not have been written without the help of those individuals who allowed themselves to be interviewed, filled out questionnaires, and passed on e-mail messages, newspaper clippings, jokes, stories, and letters. Due to the sensitive nature of much of the material, I do not mention most of these individuals by name, but their anonymity is in no way a measure of my gratitude. Without them there would have been no AIDS project.

My colleagues at Memorial University were characteristically generous with their time, expertise, and support. For several years hardly a week went by when Paul Smith did not put some relevant bibliographical item or popular culture tidbit in my office mailbox. Paul taught me much of what I know about legend through endless conversations and patient responses to my questions and by making his massive legend library always accessible. Martin Lovelace and Philip Hiscock helped me to find missing pieces of information while I was writing. Peter Narváez, Diane Tye, Neil Rosenberg, Gerald Pocius, Pat Byrne, Gerald Thomas, Larry Small, Wilf Wareham, Giovanna Del Negro, and John Ashton all at one time or another passed on something they had seen or heard about AIDS and in general provided departmental support. Colleagues in other departments were also helpful supports, especially Susanne Ottenheimer, Mark Tate, Wayne Fife, Robert Paine, Bert Riggs, Ian Bowmer, Linda Philips, and Terry Murphy. Sharon Roseman supported me in every way a friend and colleague could, from reading drafts, to listening as I worked my way through ideas, to pulling me out for coffee when the going got tough.

Jill Blackwood, Krista Browne, Brenda Carew, Lorna Griffin, Michelle Hart, Adam Hayden, Paula Hayes, Scott Kelly, Kevin Martin, Nicole Parisi, Robert Penney, Debbie Ryan, Gertie Sheppard, Lorna Griffin, Marie-Annick Desplanques, and John Harries were wonderful research assistants over the years. Jon Lee, my assistant on the legend and health project, provided a variety of supports, not the least of which has been his incredible facility with computers and software. Lynn McNeill provided invaluable editorial and bibliographic assistance. She has been my right-hand person in getting this manuscript finished. I have learned not only to trust her eye for detail but also her comments on content. Barbara Reddy, transcriber extraordinaire, brought her considerable transcribing skills to many of the interviews. Sharon Cochrane, Cindy Turpin, and Karen O'Leary provided excellent office support with their incredible ability to solve almost any problem. Their willingness to help, their networking, their technical skills, their friendship, and their always interesting office stash of good things to eat made every problem easier to manage.

Many people in the community outside the university provided assistance, support, and information. Tom Mills provided me with access to the public documents pertaining to HIV-related cases, answered my endless questions about the law, read several drafts of chapter 6, and always demonstrated an interest in what I was doing. Gerard Yetman, former director of the AIDS Committee of Newfoundland and Labrador continually answered my questions and was always willing to discuss the issues.

Colleagues and friends in other provinces and countries also deserve to be thanked. Cindy Patton's work on AIDS has long served as an inspiration to me, and our personal discussions of some of these issues have been crucial to my thinking. Sally Peterson, my sister in every way except biology, cheered me on at every turn. Participants in the International Society for Contemporary Legend Research taught me a lot about this material and continually sent me things they thought would be of interest. I would especially like to thank Bill Ellis, Gillian Bennett, Sylvia Grider, Elissa Henken, Cathy Preston, Michael Preston, Jan Brunvand, and Mark Glazer. Elaine Lawless, Joe Goodwin, and Glenn Hinson have been particularly supportive over the years. My good friends, Jeannie Thomas, Carl Lindahl, Sally Peterson, Sharon Roseman, Tom Mills, and Lori Fritz, have helped me process ideas or have read early drafts of chapters and provided me with invaluable commentary. They are all very special people to me.

David Hufford has built a community of scholars interested in lay perspectives in health care. His impact on the fields of belief, folk medicine, and applied folklore cannot be overestimated, and his impact on my thinking has been substantial. Bonnie O'Connor, another important member of that scholarly community and my friend for many years, has never stopped inspiring me with her brilliant work on traditional medicine and on AIDS. Since our time together as graduate students, Bonnie and her husband, Mal O'Connor, have nurtured my spirit and my work.

My family's unreserved love and interest in my work have been nothing short of extraordinary. I am grateful to my mother, Rochelle Goldstein, for her incredible strength, her support, and, most of all, for her friendship. I am blessed by the love of my siblings, Rhoda, Scott, and Levi, and the laughter of my nephews, Russell and Matthew. I regret that this work could not come to fruition during the lifetime of my father, Kenneth S. Goldstein. Everything good that is in this book and in me I owe to him and to my mother. My husband, David Buchan, also passed away, too young and too soon. Not a day goes by that I do not yearn for his wisdom, his love, and his smile.

Introduction

Philosophizing in a War Zone

AIDS activist and cultural theorist Paula Treichler once commented that speaking of AIDS as a symbolic and linguistic construction "may seem politically and pragmatically dubious, like philosophizing in the middle of a war zone" (1999:4). She continued,

> But . . . making sense of AIDS compels us to address questions of signification and representation. . . . Language is not a substitute for reality; it is one of the most significant ways we know reality, experience it, and articulate it; indeed language plays a powerful role in producing experience." (1999:4)

Once Upon a Virus is a book about how AIDS discourse, in the form of narrative, shapes and creates vernacular responses to the disease. But like Treichler, I wish to go further, to argue that AIDS narratives don't just create responses to illness but in fact come to constitute the disease itself. In the pages that follow, I shall demonstrate that narrative both provides compelling insight into cultural concepts of risk and also socially constructs and reconstructs those risks, making them powerful disease realities.

By titling my book *Once Upon A Virus*, I had hoped to capture exactly the dilemma of the philosopher in the war zone mentioned by Treichler. The kinds of stories addressed here rarely use the "once upon a time" opening suggested by the title, but the image of story worlds conjured up by the familiarity of that opening, juxtaposed with the hard realities of the scientific term virus, provided me with a microcosm of exactly the relationships I wished to highlight. Story and science are interrelated, interactive, and ultimately constitute each other. This is not to say that T cells, test tubes, and retroviruses don't exist but, rather, that the natural world and the cultural world share the burden of creating disease realities.

As I write this introduction, another deadly disease, SARS (Severe Acute Respiratory Syndrome) has hit the world stage. In these initial weeks of the outbreak of the disease, one cannot help but notice that epidemiologists and the general public alike have become obsessed with story making. While members of the public engage in rumors about who has the disease, places and people to avoid, mandatory quarantines, and government health conspiracies, epidemiologists create and recreate plots that they hope will establish links of transmission. Both sets of stories mirror the narratives discussed in this volume. They explore notions of animal origins, superinfectors, hidden carriers, and numerous other themes entrenched in our stories about AIDS but also seen in reaction to virtually any devastating disease we have experienced historically. Already, only a few weeks into the SARS outbreak, we can see how story comes to define risk. And therein lies the subject of this volume.

Once Upon a Virus is organized as a series of case studies, each centered around a cluster of contemporary legends about AIDS and each exploring a different constellation of issues concerning official and vernacular notions of risk. In the first chapter, I will introduce disease folklore and its relationship to the cultural construction of illness through a general discussion of various types of popular expression concerning epidemics. I begin with children's folklore to highlight how early our folkloric constructions of risk take hold in our thinking. "Tag, you've got AIDS," the phrase I have chosen for the title of the chapter and the name of a game I describe at the onset, is in many ways a representative anecdote (to borrow from Kenneth Burke), a story that sets the tone for everything else to come (Burke 1945:60). The second part of this introductory chapter locates my study in its ethnographic context, the Canadian province of Newfoundland and Labrador. While most of the narratives discussed in this volume appear elsewhere in the international reaction to AIDS, they are best understood in situ, as responses to real world situations taking place in local cultures. The understanding of legend as an index to risk perception requires contextualization among a people, within a place and set in time. Proper contextualization, however, requires that we not simply match bits of social information with bits of narrative but rather that we try to understand those narratives, those perceptions, and those aspects of health as having meaning only in relation to cultural worlds.

Chapter 2 introduces the reader to the genre of contemporary legend and traces the use of narrative as a means of understanding health worldviews. As a type of narrative that captures the extraordinary in the ordinary, the unbelievable twists in daily life, legends provide an index to what intrigues us, concerns us, frightens us, and puzzles us about quotidian reality. They capture our thoughts and understandings of health, illness, risk, life, and death and turn those thoughts outward in ways that are not otherwise easily seen. Perhaps most importantly, this chapter begins to establish the relationship between narrative and emergent action, setting the stage for exploring the role of legend in personal health decision making.

Chapter 3 examines approaches to the development of culturally appropriate and culturally sensitive health education and introduces some of the crucial differences between expert and vernacular constructions of risk. Primary among the goals of this chapter is to convey the commonsense basis of vernacular perceptions of risk and the means by which risk perception evolves in response to cultural as well as health realities.

Chapter 4 is the first of four narrative case studies. This first study focuses on AIDS-origin narratives as they are found in both official discourse and vernacular culture. Science and folklore seem to have a common obsession with establishing origins, a shared sense that knowing where something began is to understand it. This chapter explores the means by which such narratives establish concepts of cultural otherness, control, and distrust.

The second case study, in chapter 5, traces localized variations of one AIDS legend, examining how the narrative adapts to and comes to reflect regional, social, and cultural understandings. Tied to notions of geographic vulnerability, the protection of community social networks, and local cultural taboos, the legend becomes a powerful means of articulating risk perceptions unlikely to be captured through standard knowledge, belief, and behavior studies.

Case study number three follows in chapter 6, demonstrating the central role of legend in official responses to the disease and examining relationships between legend and reality. This chapter explores a legal case of HIV-status nondisclosure, which became intertwined with legendary tradition in a rural community devastated by a high incidence of infection. The chapter shows how legend moves from being told as narrative to being enacted.

Chapter 7 provides the final case study, focusing on legends of HIV-infected needles encountered in public venues. This chapter explores the evolution of deliberate-infector narratives and the creation of nameless, faceless infectors, which move risk out into the public and away from personal responsibility. Ultimately, this chapter addresses vernacular concerns about the increasing medicalization of our lives and the intrusion of medicine into our homes and personal relationships.

The final chapter in this volume provides a more general discussion of vernacular risk perception in this particular ethnographic context based on the narrative articulation of AIDS beliefs and worldview. Chapter 8 primarily provides some thoughts about the relationship of vernacular theory to public health education, exploring the methods and pragmatic use of narrative in combating disease.

And so, having established a general map for what follows, the time has come to explain what a folklorist, and a narrative specialist at that, is doing in the dubious place of this particular war zone. As is appropriate for a folklorist, I will begin with a story.

1

"Tag, You've Got AIDS"

HIV in Folklore and Legend

One Sunday afternoon as I worked in the garden of my house in St. John's, I was distracted by five children playing tag in the neighbor's yard. The game didn't seem to be very different from the one I had played as a child. In that game, the one whom we called "it" ran around trying to catch the others, ultimately gaining on someone enough to touch them and thereby transfer "itness." This would then free up the former "it" to run and require that the new person in that role be the chaser. When the transfer happened, the chasing child would yell, "Tag, you're it, now catch me." Because I always thought it was interesting that we were such slaves to narrating what was taking place at the moment of transfer, I moved my gardening closer to the fence where I could overhear the children. To my surprise I heard the oldest child, who was around seven or eight years of age, say, "Tag, you've got AIDS." Part of me was pleased that a seven-year-old child knew what AIDS was, that public awareness had hit even the youngest sectors of society. But another part of me was terrified to see that the stigmatization of AIDS had drifted into the popular culture of one so young.

AIDS Folklore and Disease in Popular Discourse

I had never thought about "tag, you're it" as a contagion and immunity game, but the addition of the AIDS tag line reminded me that a number of children's games are about fear of infection.[1] We played several "cooties" games as children and created a paper fortune-teller that we called a "cootie catcher." Getting "cooties" was an enormous thing to us children, although I don't think any of us had the slightest idea what a "cootie" was. We did know, however, that "cooties" was something you caught and something you didn't want to have. Children's folklorist Simon Bronner notes that cooties came into play among children in the early 1950s, the time of the polio epidemic in the United States. Bronner goes on to say,

> The polio epidemic was especially disconcerting to many Americans because the healthy and wealthy, who it was thought should be immune to such affliction because of their clean and honorable living, contracted it, and distrustful, blaming eyes turned toward lower classes. It turned out that the disease probably spread from person to person (the virus normally attaches to living tissue cells) by intimate human contact although unsanitary conditions, especially fecal and sewage contamination, could support the virus. . . . During the scare, children were pulled out of swimming pools in fear of contagion and told to avoid touching other children because of dread for the debilitating polio virus which could paralyze or kill its victims. The cooties complex became among children a way to playfully dramatize the dread of the disease while also bringing out social relations underlying the modern emphasis on cleanliness and appearance, relations important to adult ways of dealing with one another. (1990:107)

The historical emphasis in children's folklore on fears of infection, childhood obsessions with body parts, fluids, and emissions and concerns about diversity and conformity suggest that AIDS would quite naturally be a focus of children's play. Bronner reports in relation to AIDS games (1990:109) one played with three bowls filled with ketchup, mustard, and water, which are placed in a box. Players were to blindly reach over the box and put their fingers into

---

1.   British children's folklorists Iona and Peter Opie have written extensively on the topic of contagion in children's games. The most often asserted connection of games to disease is the legendary origin of the singing game "Ring around the Rosy" as commentary on the plague. The plague-origin hypothesis argued that "rosy" referred to the rash associated with the plague, posies referred to protective herbs, and the sneezing was symptomatic. The Opies point out that this connection, while possible, has no real evidential basis (Opie 1985:220–222).

one of the three bowls. If they put their fingers in mustard, they had rabies. If they touched ketchup, they had AIDS. If they touched water, they were "immune"[2] from all diseases. Like the polio epidemic in the 1950s, AIDS affects the lives of children as well as adults, through the experience of friends and family members with the disease, through fear and prejudice expressed in and around the home, and through media coverage.

It should not surprise us that AIDS has entered children's popular culture, not just through games, but in songs and rhymes as well. In their book on children's subversive folklore, Sherman and Weisskopf include a rhyme sent to them by the father of a sixth-grade girl, who was overheard with her friends singing the following parody of a song from the 1988 children's television show "Barney." Barney was a stuffed purple dinosaur, who opened every show with a song that said, "I love you, you love me, we're a happy family / With a great big hug and a kiss from me to you / Won't you say you love me too?" The girls sang,

> I love you, you loved me
> Barney has got HIV
> Barney jumped on Baby Bop[3] one time
> That's called rape and that's a crime.
>
> I hate you, you hate me
> Barney died of HIV
> Tripped on a skate and fell on a whore
> No more purple dinosaur
>
> I hate you, you hate me
> Baby Bop fucked with Barney
> He gave a hop and she said to stop
> Now they have to see the DOC.[4] (Sherman and Weisskopf 1995:198)

---

2. One of the things that is most interesting in children's contagion games is the extent of focus on immunity. From a biomedical point of view immunity is an incredibly complex and not well-understood process (Haraway 1991; Martin 1994). From a child's point of view one simply wins exemption from disease.

3. Baby Bop is another smaller (and younger) dinosaur that visits Barney every day on the show.

4. The father who sent in the parody commented, "It seems that AIDS awareness training does work" (Sherman and Weisskopf 1995:199).

As was the case with the AIDS games and older epidemic concerns expressed through children's play, the Barney parody takes its
place next to a host of disease rhymes favored in children's folklore.
Tuberculosis rhymes, for example, were common throughout the
1940s, 1950s, and 1960s and are occasionally still collected. In 1960
the following song, sung to the tune of "My Bonnie Lies over the
Ocean," was collected from a twelve-year-old girl from Montana.

My Bonnie has tuberculosis,
My Bonnie has only one lung,
My Bonnie coughs up slimy green stuff
And dries it and chews it for gum.

Come up, come up,
Come up, dear dinner, come up, come up,
Come up, come up,
Come up, dear dinner, come up.

I'm coming, I'm coming,
Though my head is hanging low.
I hear those gentle voices calling
(Spoken)
Hasten, Jason, fetch the basin,
Oops, flop. Fetch the mop. (Sherman and Weisskopf 1995:67–
68)

Interestingly, adult folklore concerning tuberculosis is not commonly found in collections and archives. Sometimes called the "un-
mentionable disease," the "folk" association of tuberculosis with
poverty and squalor created a silence that worked against the development and preservation of adult verbal traditions concerning the
epidemic.[5] Children's traditions, however, provide a special kind of
insight and a special commentary on issues, which take a different

5.   A few years ago I attempted to track down archived tuberculosis folklore for
      comparative purposes as the current TB epidemic affected more and more of the
      population. At that time, I was told by three different archivists that such material
      was scant, because of the secrecy surrounding the disease. TB had a devastating
      effect on the Newfoundland population in the previous epidemic, and yet neither
      the Memorial University Folklore and Language Archives nor the Center for
      Newfoundland Studies Archives had any significant holdings related to community
      experiences of the disease.

form (or which are absent altogether) in adult culture. Children have license to speak the unspeakable. Furthermore, the fact that something is spoken in children's folklore suggests that an issue has truly taken hold in society. In many ways, what makes children's folklore so interesting to adults is that we recognize children as a wildly original, too loud, too truthful version of us. As children's popular culture expert Kathleen McDonnell observes, "Children don't recognize the distinction between high and low culture, they embrace it all equally" (1994:18). In this sense, children's folklore articulates attitudes and understandings internally censored by their more mature adult counterparts. In the play, in the games, and in the rhymes are expressions of health beliefs and attitudes held on some level by the children and perhaps also, despite the internal censorship of maturity, held by their parents. Complex themes of the "infecting Other," morality and illness, blaming victims, stereotypes of the correlation of economic class with illness, concerns about contagion and sanitation, and health fatalism pervade the games and rhymes of children, who in some cases aren't old enough even to have lost their first tooth.

Adult folklore contains the same themes and concerns but chooses slightly different means of expression. Our jokes, sayings, songs, stories, and even our material ways of expressing ourselves[6] can become what illness-narrativity theorists call "illness representations." Beyond obvious referential statements, traces of explanatory models for illness are embedded in our multiple forms of discourse. To create distance from disease and illness, we "construct boundaries between ourselves and those categories of individuals whom we believe (or hope) to be more at risk than ourselves" (Gilman 1988:4). The means of distancing, the boundaries we create, the risks we construct and destruct can be read in our expressive choices.

While games and rhymes appear to be the genres of choice for such articulations from children and adolescents, adult illness

---

6. We express our concepts of health and illness through the construction and use of buildings, objects, costume, and art. The so-called care-cottages associated with the treatment of tuberculosis are a good example of architectural expressions of attitudes toward health and illness. The cottages had large porches built so that patients could spend long hours taking "the fresh-air cure." Material culture related to AIDS is a vast and relatively untapped resource for exploring disease understandings and constructions. A number of interesting and important studies of representations of AIDS in artistic renderings have been published, however (see, for example, Gilman 1988, Crimp and Rolston 1990, and Miller 1992).

representations make use of what are understood in our culture as more mature vehicles of expression. AIDS beliefs and commentary certainly appear in adult games (including risk-taking games) and rhymes (particularly in graffiti, Xerox lore, and slogan making), but by far the most vital adult forms for AIDS-related expressions are jokes and narratives.[7] Furthermore, since tradition is dynamic, these expressive forms reflect the changes in beliefs and attitudes that come in response to new scientific developments, new understandings of transmission patterns, public health education programs, media coverage, current events, and so forth. The traditions, however, do not simply follow a specific trajectory chosen by public health or other officials but rather reflect the processing of a vast quantity of different and sometimes competing messages, all affecting disease understandings.

Jokes about AIDS followed slowly after the documentation of the first cases in 1981, but became gradually more popular as the disease entered public consciousness. As epidemiologists continually refined notions of who was most vulnerable to the new disease, jokes followed suit, always distancing the teller from the population currently understood as "at risk." Early jokes focused on the gay population and the association of AIDS with drugs, eventually incorporating other notions of risk groups. These initial jokes focused on what came to be known as the 4 Hs: Homosexuals, Heroin users, Hemophiliacs, and Haitians. Like most health folklore, they assigned the disease to a group understood as distant from the teller.

> Question: Do you know what the hardest thing about having AIDS is?
> Answer: Convincing your mother that you are Haitian.[8]
> Question: Do you know what gay stands for?
> Answer: Got AIDS yet?

---

7.   Genre choice for the expression of specific topics is, of course, extremely culture bound. Wallman has noted that AIDS expressions in Uganda show preference for proverbial forms (see Goldstein 1993). Clearly, within a culture, specific peer groups may demonstrate a preference for other forms (for example, professional musicians may choose musical expressions). My assertion of a Western adult preference for jokes and narratives as AIDS expressions is meant only as a general observation based on years of following AIDS popular culture.

8.   This joke was told in gay and straight communities. Joe Goodwin, writing on gay folklore, observed that its popularity in the gay community reflected concerns about being "outed" by the disease (Goodwin 1989). In this case, the joke is self-consciously about assigning "otherness."

As AIDS affected more and more of the population, the jokes became increasingly homophobic and racist, with many focusing on famous figures known to be infected with the disease. Liberace and Magic Johnson jokes affirmed stereotypes of risk and deviance, collapsing notions of risky behaviors with notions of risky people. Like all folklore, the jokes changed as public health and public education became more refined, evolving in response to emerging understandings of the disease. By the mid-1980s it became clear to health educators that the general public was concerned about issues of casual transmission, generating fears of social contact[9] with members of groups dubbed as "high risk." In 1988, in response to these concerns, the United States issued the Surgeon General's Report on AIDS,[10] which, as Cindy Patton notes, "assumed that while risk reduction knowledge was nice, the general population, never imagined to be at risk, should be educated about the impossibility of contracting HIV through casual or social contact" (Patton 1994:15). Jokes again followed suit. Goodwin reports one joke involving a little boy telling his mother about the AIDS discussion in his sex-education class.

> So she said, "Well, what did you learn about AIDS?" He said, "well, you can't get it from a toilet seat, and you can't get it from kissing, and you really have to watch those intersections"[11] (Goodwin 1989: 84).

The emphasis in the Surgeon General's Report on the "facts" as they were known and constructed at the time began to move AIDS jokes into new areas of focus on risk behaviors and safety.

> Did you hear about the two junkies? They were sharing needles. A friend said, "Don't you know you could get AIDS?" The junkies replied, "It's OK, we're wearing condoms."

AIDS jokes of the early 1990s (in addition to the ever-present

---

9. Casual contact includes fears of viral transmission through toilet seats, drinking glasses, shaking hands, hairbrushes, and other means that do not involve any real exchange of body fluids.

10. The U.S. Surgeon General's Report had an impact in Canada as well as in the United States, in part because the resulting educational campaigns in the American media were broadcast continually in Canada.

11. Goodwin notes that the joke is an apparent conflation of "homosexuals," "injections," and "intercourse" and a seeming play on the standard parental warning to look both ways (Goodwin 1989:84).

themes of racism and homophobia) asserted fool figures, like those in the joke just cited, who were too stupid to understand safe-sex messages. The jokes were, in their own way, educational.[12]

As Patton argues, however, health educators and education projects showed little agreement on whether to decrease risk by modifying the behavior of an entire population or by targeting only those (subgroups) believed to be at the highest risk. For the most part, public health chose the targeted approach, focusing educational campaigns on "at risk" subcultures (Patton 1996). Even as the global AIDS picture began to make it clear that whole populations were at risk, public health accommodated information on the potential for heterosexual transmission through "Choose Your Partner Wisely" campaigns. These campaigns continually underscored notions of AIDS "otherness" even in attempts to be inclusive. As AIDS became more and more an issue through increasing numbers of infections and deaths, moving beyond subcultural boundaries, AIDS jokes began to drop off,[13] becoming fewer in number and tending to flare up only in reaction to specific media events, such as new-treatment news or celebrities announcing that they tested HIV positive.

Where AIDS jokes began to drop off, narrative took over. This is not to say that AIDS rumors and legend only began to circulate in the late 1990s as the disease took hold in staggering epidemic numbers. To the contrary, stories were circulating from the beginning. But over time legends and rumors flourished, producing more than the nervous laughter or outrageous biting social commentary associated with humor. Instead, rumor and legend revealed a deep-seated sense of concern, fear, distrust, and even resistance. In some sense, while AIDS jokes focused on what was known about the disease (or believed to be known at that moment regarding, for example, risk groups and safe sex),[14] AIDS legends focused on what was still unknown, unproven, unspoken, and, most of all, uncomfortable.

Legends were the perfect tool for dialogue. They were not personal since they tend to be stories about what happened to someone else. The risk of telling was minimal because the narratives take a

---

12.   See Goldstein 1991 on the responsible folklore of AIDS.
13.   As one of my students noted, "It's hard to think it's funny once you know someone who's died—and we all know someone who's died from AIDS."
14.   Jokes tend to follow public familiarity with an issue. If there is not a degree of shared understanding, the joke will not work. For this reason, jokes often appear after issues have become mundane. See Goldstein 2001.

"believe it or not" position, opening up discussion but not really requiring that one reveal one's own stance in relation to the narrative's truth or falsity. But the stories were not completely distanced either; they brought the issue closely into the teller's sphere through the legend's characteristic "friend of a friend" protagonist. These stories did not happen to the teller or even to anyone the teller knows. Rather, they happened to the friend of someone with whom the teller was familiar—close enough for concern, distanced enough for comfort. Legends put the issue out there, created dialogue, but allowed the teller to mask personal fear or curiosity.

AIDS Folklore in Newfoundland

In 1986, as it became clear that AIDS was not only not going to go away but was beginning to have a devastating global affect, I began to collect AIDS folklore in Newfoundland. At that time, Newfoundland had not yet reported its first cases.[15] Nevertheless, AIDS folklore was everywhere. Jokes, slogans, cartoons, graffiti, and even songs were circulating about the disease; but, by far, the most interesting material was in the form of contemporary legend. I began with a questionnaire distributed to the students in my classes at Memorial University. I included very general questions about jokes, stories, and other kinds of expressive lore concerning AIDS, asking that the respondents write down their recollections of what they had heard. This information was accompanied by a series of bare-bones biographical questions and a couple of questions asking the respondent to reflect on the material they reported and on the AIDS epidemic in general. Each questionnaire was anonymous[16] but included a tear-off sheet, which the respondents could fill out if they were interested in a follow-up interview. At around the same time as I began to administer the questionnaire, I also started a survey of local newspaper, radio, television, and health brochures to enable complementary study of media and public health information coverage. I began the survey initially to point out to my students the contemporary nature of folklore and the manner in which folklore responds to current events. But my longtime interest in the relationship between health folklore and health information soon

15.   Later in 1986 the first two cases were reported to public health.
16.   Because of the sensitivity of much of this material, both the questionnaires and
      follow-up interviews are presented anonymously, unless otherwise stipulated.

took over, and the project began to grow. Interviews led to other interviews, and once AIDS cases entered the local scene, I began to focus on specific events reported in the media and specific rumors that were making the rounds. As the Internet became an increasing part of my students' lives,[17] I also began to include AIDS folklore communicated through e-mail and the Web.

As the largest university in Newfoundland, Memorial's student population of between sixteen thousand and eighteen thousand clearly represented a huge sample of the age group seen at the time as most potentially "at risk" in the province (ages eighteen to twenty-nine). Further, the cohort came from all over Newfoundland and Labrador, since the University serves the entire province. It was not long before students began to come back to me with things they had heard at home on semester breaks or from friends in other places, further widening the research sample. Over the years, numerous graduate and undergraduate students voluntarily initiated and conducted their own interviews on my behalf, turning over tapes, transcripts, e-mails, Xerox lore, and a great variety of other materials to the project. I am indebted to them for their enthusiasm and hard work. What their generous additions to the research did, in addition to seizing the "ethnographic moment," was to provide additional access to other age and educational groups, other networks and cohorts, and a wider scope of the provincial population. In that sense, this study is based on material that began with the university population but ultimately evolved to include a portion of the larger body of non-university-related Newfoundlanders.

The People and the Place

Newfoundland and Labrador is located in the most northeastern corner of North America. After a long period as an autonomous colony of Great Britain, Newfoundland joined Canada in 1949, becoming one of the ten provinces and three territories[18] that make up the country. The vote to join Canada was won by an incredibly narrow margin of 51 percent, a result that is still the

---

17.   Regular use of the Internet came relatively late to Newfoundland due to the province's disadvantaged economic situation. Consultation with the Computer Help Center at the University confirmed that full e-mail and Internet access for every student occurred sometime around 1994.

18.   The country added the third territory of Nunavut in April 1999.

subject of controversy and of a fledgling separatist movement. The province officially carried the name of Newfoundland until 2001, when an amendment to Canada's federal Constitution Act changed the name to Newfoundland and Labrador, in recognition of Labrador's[19] status as a full provincial partner (Rosenberg 2003). Even with its two geographical parts, Labrador and the island of Newfoundland, the population is small (estimated by Statistics Canada in July 2002 at 531,600)[20] and is spread over an extremely large land mass (405,720 square kilometers).[21] Despite the fact that well over half of the land mass belongs to Labrador, the vast majority of the provincial population lives on the island portion of the province; only about 30,000 of the total population reside in Labrador. This book is based primarily on research from the island portion of the province.

The majority of Newfoundlanders live along the picturesque coastline. Referred to fondly as "the rock," Newfoundland is extremely rugged, featuring jagged cliffs and rocky beaches along the coast and a largely unpopulated interior, thickly covered in forest and brush, bog land and ponds. The approximately one thousand communities along the coast and small islands around its edges are referred to locally as "outports." Many of these communities were traditionally accessible only by sea until the middle to late twentieth century when the provincial government began campaigns to centralize and resettle isolated communities and to expand the roads.[22] As part of the resettlement program, the Newfoundland government offered one thousand dollars per household to families from isolated communities who agreed to move to larger growth centers. In some communities, the government also restricted access to ferries, teachers, and other essential services, in attempts to force

19. Labrador had traditionally been considered a part of Newfoundland, a relationship that was solidified in 1927 when the British Privy Council defined Newfoundland's "territorial jurisdiction" over the coast of Labrador (Baker and Cuff 1993).
20. Statistics are from Statistics Canada, Population, 2003. (Online at http://www. statcan.ca/english/Pgdb/demo30a.htm/.)
21. Newfoundland and Labrador has an area more than three times the total land mass of the maritime provinces of Nova Scotia, New Brunswick, and Prince Edward Island. Compared to land size in the United States, Newfoundland and Labrador ranks fourth in size behind Alaska, Texas, and California. It is nearly two times the size of Great Britain. (See Government of Newfoundland and Labrador, 2003, Provincial Economy. Online at http://www.gov.nf.ca/nfld&lab/economy.htm/.)
22. Donna Davis writes about "the Road" in Newfoundland communities as a metaphor for the comparative merits of traditional versus modern ways of life (1995).

the population to relocate. Promises of "two jobs for every person," "the good life," and modernity in these new homes didn't, however, pan out for the large numbers of fishermen, with no formal education, who found it impossible to compete for employment. Feelings of betrayal by the government resulting from the resettlement initiative continue to this day and are the topic of a wealth of songs, poetry, short stories, plays, novels, and artwork.

The population of the island sprang mostly from English and Irish migrants who came in the late eighteenth and early nineteenth centuries hoping to make their fortunes or at least sustain their families through the traditional cod fishery. Some have estimated that 95 percent of Newfoundlanders are of Irish or British stock (Hanrahan 1993). Early cultural influences were also provided by Scottish immigrants who settled on the West coast and the French, who maintain a culturally strong Francophone community. The province is also home to three native groups: the Innu and Inuit in Labrador and the Mi'kmaq on the island (see Dettmer 2001). In the early part of the twentieth century small Chinese, Lebanese, and Eastern European Jewish communities sprang up in and around St. John's. While the population has been, for the most part, remarkably homogeneous, there is a small and growing ethnic diversity in the province. The university, industry, mineral resource development (particularly oil and gas), and a series of refugee waves to Canada in the 1980s and 1990s have created a degree of pluralism. In contrast, however, to other parts of North America, Newfoundland's diversity is extremely limited.

The province's religious makeup is similarly lacking in heterogeneity. Approximately 37 percent of the population are Roman Catholic. Of the remainder of the population, all but 2 percent are Protestant, primarily Anglican, United Church, and Pentecostal.[23] The beginnings of ethnic diversity in the province in this century are reflected in the establishment of Jewish, Muslim, and Hindu places of worship; but numbers of adherents are small, and those communities continually struggle to retain their buildings and organizations. Newfoundland has traditionally been religiously conservative, boasting a denominational school system, which was only abolished (by referendum) in 1998.

---

23.   Statistics are from the 1991 census, published by Statistics Canada, Population by Religion. (Online at www.statcan.ca/english/Pgdb/demo30a.htm/.)

Resources and Their Management

Traditionally, it was the fishery that drew residents to Newfoundland, considered at one time to be among the greatest fishing grounds in the world. Cod was, for centuries, the sole basis of
the Newfoundland economy. Everything about Newfoundland was
organized around the sea and the fishery. As one historian of Newfoundland wrote, "With the Greeks, ocean was a synonym for bar-
renness, land alone being life-giving. To the Newfoundlander the
land is a forest or a 'barren,' the ocean a mine or harvest field" (Rogers 1911:190). Rogers, along with numerous more contemporary
historians, argued that the land, for Newfoundlanders, was simply
a platform for access to the sea (Baker 2001:9). The land in Newfoundland is rough, boasting little in the way of soil, flora, or fauna.
The growing season is short, and the climate is challenging, with a
reputation for the most rain, fog, wind, and snow in Canada. For a
long time, the sea made up for the seemingly scarce resources of the
land—but that was to change.

The cod fishery remained the central feature of the Newfoundland economy until 1992, when, in hopes of rebuilding dwindling
fish stocks, the federal government imposed a moratorium on the
cod fishery off Newfoundland's east coast. The decision put thirty
thousand Newfoundland fisher people out of work (Baker 2001:9)
and created enormous spinoff unemployment.[24] In 1995, all commercial ground stocks around Newfoundland were closed to fishing
indefinitely. The government created a compensation package for
displaced fisher people, with funding tied to enrollment in counseling and retraining programs (Sinclair 2001). Nevertheless, in a
culture so strongly oriented toward the sea, the effects of the collapse of the fishery were devastating. Out-migration escalated and
numerous fishing communities, traditionally thriving with activity,
began to resemble ghost towns.

Despite the continued devastating effects of the collapse of the
fishery on Newfoundland society and culture, economic forecasters
argue that due to new growth sectors, the financial outlook for the
province has never been brighter. Government statistics indicate that
in the period between 1997 and 2001, the Newfoundland economy

---

24. Primary among the spinoff effects was the closure of a large number of fish plants.
The collapse of the fishery, however, could be felt in virtually every sector of the
economy, from transportation to real estate.

expanded by more than 24 percent.[25] The fishing industry has diver-
sified, focusing more on crab and shrimp, and secondary processing
in the province has increased. Non-resource-based manufacturing
and service industries are constantly being developed and expanded.
By far, however, the brightness of Newfoundland's economic future
is seen to rest on oil and gas offshore developments.

While the advent of the oil industry has meant new wealth, jobs,
and opportunities for the province, many Newfoundlanders are not
convinced that they will benefit from the industry. The province's
take in royalties has been seemingly small compared to the profits of
oil companies; and the benefits have not appeared to spread to rural Newfoundland, where unemployment is most significant. Newfoundlanders are concerned about the resources being exported to
be processed elsewhere, about the employment of the local labor
force on oil projects, about the impact on the environment, and,
more than all else, about the impact on local culture (House 2001).
Traditionally referred to as a "have not" province in Canada, Newfoundland now leads the other provinces in predictions for financial growth. Ironically, however, Newfoundland still maintains the
highest unemployment rate in the country (over 16 percent)[26] and
one of the lowest income rates per capita (McGrath 2001).

Newfoundlanders are not strangers to concerns about receiving minimum benefit from the sale of their rich resources. Numerous deals made by successive governments on everything from
hydropower to forestry to fishery have been decried by the public,
historians, and economists alike as primarily benefitting outside
interests (McGrath 2001). The themes addressed repeatedly in
the narratives discussed in this book—themes of government distrust and "otherness"—are perhaps resulting from, or exacerbated
by, decades of feeling "ripped off" by leaders who claimed to be
working on behalf of the population.

The issue of the exploitation of the province's natural resources
took on an even more dramatic and bizarre twist recently through
the discovery of the desirability and profitability of Newfoundland's
genetic legacy. Due to geographic isolation and the fact that early

---

25.   Taken from Government of Newfoundland and Labrador, Provincial Economy,
       2003. (Online at http://www.gov.nf.ca/nfld&lab/economy.htm/.)
26.   This figure does not include the "hidden unemployed," such as those who have
       enrolled in school or have entered retraining programs for the purpose of receiving
       loans and grants to sustain themselves and their families.

immigrants came from a limited number of British and Irish communities, Newfoundland has been called "a gold mine for the study of human genetics" (Staples 2000:117). The province has an isolated gene pool, meaning that 95 percent of the population can be traced to the first twenty thousand people who settled the province. This so-called founder effect is of enormous interest to genetics researchers, pharmaceutical manufacturers, and biotechnology companies who invest heavily in genetic research. For several years, Iceland has been working toward control over its unique isolated genetic heritage, fighting off multinational companies that are intent on turning that heritage into a tradable commodity.

In 1998, Newfoundland had its own run-in with the issue of biopiracy (as some have dubbed genetic trading). A group of scientists from Texas's Baylor College of Medicine flew into St. John's to study an extended family who suffer from ARVC, a congenital disease that renders individuals prone to cardiac arrest at an early age. The scientists spent their time in Newfoundland collecting DNA samples from family and community members and then left the province without offer of the customary follow-up treatment or genetic counseling. Access to the resulting data was not shared with local physicians or researchers, and participants in the study were never informed if they were or were not at risk for ARVC (Staples 2000). The Texas group (locally referred to as the "Texas Vampires" for "taking the blood and running") made local medical researchers aware of the need for stricter genetic-research guidelines. The response, however, from the lay population was, once again, a sense of vulnerability to, violation by, and distrust of the very authorities that are supposed to protect the population.

Trust and Community

The ARVC study, of course, did not pop up into a vacuum but rather into a culture that already had good reason to distrust authority figures, cultural elites, and foreigners. The historical events cited above—confederation, resettlement, weak resource management, and poverty—contributed to that sense of distrust, but centuries of isolation had also built a culture that looked inward for support and was wary of outsiders and those in positions of political power. Despite the fact that well over half the Newfoundland population today lives in the cities, the vast majority of families came from

the outports, generally in search of employment or education.[27] As
people acculturated to urban lifestyles, they nevertheless retained
networks of trust they brought with them from the outports. Due
to isolation and the small, rarely changing population in rural Newfoundland, social life was intimate—you knew everyone and everything about everyone. St. John's, Corner Brook, and the other cities
were bigger and more impersonal, but the population continued to
value the predictability of local social networks. Searching to place
those you meet by last name, family or friendship connections, and
home community is commonplace across Newfoundland, as is the
labeling of outsiders as "CFAs" (come from away)[28] or "mainlanders."

Numerous older ethnographies of Newfoundland continually
identified social intimacy and the threat posed by strangers as significant features of outport life (Dinham 1977; Firestone 1969, 1980;
Faris 1972; Szwed 1966). Paul Dinham wrote,

> In outport life, the epitome of unpredictability and thus threat is
> the stranger. Although treated with overt hospitality and warmth,
> the stranger is covertly feared, or at least is the focus of suspicion
> and apprehension. A stranger is someone about whom the com-
> munity knows little or nothing (his origin, what type of person he
> is, or his reason for being in the community). Community resi-
> dents depend upon each other to hold the same norms attitudes
> and values, thus insuring the predictability, the continuity and the
> coherence of social interaction. In the case of the stranger, the
> outport community has no knowledge of the degree to which he
> shares or fails to share their values. (1977:67)

Contemporary ethnographies of Newfoundland stress the incredible changes of the last three or four decades in terms of the
effects of increased mobility, out-migration, urbanization, and
tourism on social networks; but even while noting the expansion

---

27.   In fact, it is said that if "you take all the 'baymen' out of St. John's, there will be no
      one left." As Maura Hanrahan points out, this notion puts a new twist on the much-
      written-about dichotomy between "townies" (those from St. John's) and "baymen"
      (those from rural communities) (Hanrahan 1993).

28.   Novelist Jane Urquhart noted in her address to convocation at Memorial University
      in June 1999, after serving a period as artist in residence, "During the course of
      that first day [here] at least a dozen people either asked me if I was from away or
      informed me that I was from away"(quoted in Bella 2002:i).

of those networks, they emphasize the insider/outsider dichotomy[29] (McGrath 2001; Durdle 2001; Davis 1995; Bella 2002). In her 2001 study of women's roles in one community after the downsizing of the fishery, for example, Jodi Durdle wrote, "The dynamics of small town Newfoundland, with greater exposure (via travel and television) to outside influences, are such that most people today are much more tolerant of the behavior of *strangers or outsiders*" (139; emphasis in the original). Although the norms have changed for how many people one might see in a given day and where they might be from, Durdle's choice of the word "tolerant" betrays the continuing relevance of distinctions of "us" and "them," of who can be trusted and who can't. In the chapters that follow, those culturally significant distinctions can be seen to combine with natural boundary-making responses to disease, stranger-danger themes common to legend, and the dichotomy-making mistakes of public health. The natural human tendency to externalize disease risk combines in the Newfoundland legends with centuries of evidence that strangers and outsiders are, indeed, unpredictable and threatening. While many of these legends appear cross-culturally, they take on a different resonance when understood in the context of local Newfoundland history and experience.

Medical Care and Public Health in Newfoundland

The history of medical care and public health in Newfoundland has also been traditionally a story of coping with isolation and poverty. Much of the history of health care in Newfoundland did not involve physicians or hospitals. While the first civilian hospital on the island opened in 1814 in St. John's (Pitt 1984), most health care—both before and after— was community based, handled through home remedies or local folk practitioners, particularly midwives. The establishment of a hospital in St. John's had little impact on the lives of most Newfoundlanders at the time, located, as they were, great distances from the city. During the 1890s and early 1900s a number of small cottage hospitals, inspired by Dr. Wilfred Grenfell, were created in a variety of places in Labrador and on the

---

29.   Despite this emphasis on insiders and outsiders, Newfoundlanders are often referred to in travel literature as the kindest, most generous, most hospitable, friendliest people you will ever meet; and most visitors would agree that this is not a false stereotype.

island (Pitt 1984). Cottage hospitals were small facilities set up in strategic places around the island and Labrador, staffed initially by nurses imported from Britain. In 1949 air ambulance service was introduced in Newfoundland to transfer patients from isolated communities to larger medical centers. One year later the government purchased four boats to enable doctors and nurses to visit isolated communities. In 1958 the Hospital Insurance Act came into effect, providing free health-care coverage for all residents of the province (Pitt 1984). The challenge of cost and accessibility of health care had been at least partially addressed.

Over the years numerous modern hospitals have been created in the province, both inside and outside St. John's. Some of these facilities were meant to be temporary, established in reaction to needs resulting from specific epidemics, especially cholera and tuberculosis. Tuberculosis hit Newfoundland hard, particularly in the first decade of the twentieth century and again in the period between 1945 and 1955 (O'Brien 1994). It is not unusual to meet couples in Newfoundland who met and married in the sanatorium or families who raised other people's children while the biological parents were "in the san."[30] In 1972 the last of the sanatorium beds were closed (O'Brien 1994), leaving behind memories, for those who were old enough, of the stigma, poverty, death, and devastation caused by the epidemic.

While modern health care and hospitals are accessible today for most Newfoundlanders, there is still a shortage of physicians in rural Newfoundland, dependence on air ambulances, and some procedures that require sending patients to the mainland. As is the case in most parts of North America, government cuts have meant the closure of beds in some facilities, reduction in staff, and an insufficient supply of medical equipment. Nevertheless, Newfoundland continues to try to find innovative ways to serve its urban and rural population. The province has become a North American leader in the development and provision of telemedicine, using telecommunications links in both the delivery of health care and the education of health professionals in remote areas.

---

30.   TB had a lasting impact on the lives and relationships of Newfoundlanders. One couple I knew (now deceased) "reared" twenty-one children from their community while the children's parents were confined to the sanatorium. These children, now adults, were still a regular fixture in the household until the time of the couple's deaths and continued to call them "Mom" and "Dad," despite the fact that their guardianship lasted only a few years.

AIDS in Newfoundland

AIDS got a slow start in Newfoundland relative to the rest of North America, perhaps in part because of the geographical isolation. It wasn't until 1984 that the first two people in the province tested positive for HIV (MacKinnon 1993). Two years later the first case of AIDS was reported.[31] The slowness of the epidemic in hitting Newfoundland, however, was not indicative of the pace the disease would eventually take in affecting the population. While numbers of positive HIV tests still register as low in the province (210 reported from 1985 to 2002[32]), public health officials are in agreement that the figures do not present anything even close to an accurate picture of the current extent of HIV infection on the island. It is estimated that fifteen thousand people in Canada are HIV positive without knowing about their HIV status (*The Compass* 2001).

Numerous issues about the disease itself work against the accuracy of surveillance reports: individuals may be infected but symptom free, thus reducing the likelihood of testing; individuals may test HIV negative despite being positive, due to the recentness of infection; and anecdotal evidence suggests that some may donate blood as a way to assess HIV status, assuming that any problems detected will be flagged and they will be contacted.

In Newfoundland a series of specialized issues affecting statistical accuracy appear to take on significance. Fear of loss of anonymity is generally recognized by public health as a tremendous factor in the choice of individuals not to test. The relationship between anonymity and confidentiality of report and the rules of public-health reportage in Newfoundland have continually been cited as problematic for practitioners and the public alike (Goldstein 1991:2). Two types of tests are available, one that supplies a written report linked to your name and another non-nominal coded test in which the individual checks back for results. All positive tests, however,

31. HIV is the virus that causes AIDS. It attacks the T cells in our immune system, making us vulnerable to a series of opportunistic infections (such as Kaposi's sarcoma and pneumocystis pneumonia). AIDS is used to refer to the syndrome itself. One can be HIV positive for some time without developing the constellation of opportunistic infections that are associated with the disease. The distinction is important for a number of reasons but most especially because, as AIDS activists have argued, AIDS is the last stage of a much longer chronic viral process.

32. From Health Canada, *HIV and AIDS in Canada: Surveillance Report to June 30, 2002.* Division of HIV/AIDS Epidemiology and Surveillance, November 2002.

are reportable for statistical surveillance purposes. The nature of this "mandatory reporting" in terms of anonymity issues is confusing and causes concern in the lay population. Statistical reporting, contact tracing, partner notification, and other similar issues made public through the media create a level of distrust and discomfort with the true anonymity of the testing mechanism. Numerous individuals interviewed as part of this project expressed serious doubt concerning the availability of completely anonymous tests in the province. Discomfort with the anonymity of the testing mechanism, of course, is not particular to Newfoundland, but the nature of small community lifestyle with little opportunity for any type of anonymity highlights the concern. I was told repeatedly by interviewees, "I would never go to those test sites. You don't know what they do with the information, and anyone could see you going in." It is common for individuals wishing to check their HIV status but fearing loss of anonymity to test while visiting other provinces (McKinnon 1993; Jackson 1992b). This practice, while ensuring a greater level of comfort in terms of identity protection, means the positive result will be reflected in the statistics of the province that provides the test, not the province of residence.

What convinces public health officials that Newfoundland rates of infection are much higher than surveillance data suggest are the results of a Department of Health study done in the early 1990s across Canada, in which blood samples were collected from pregnant women between the ages of fifteen and twenty-nine for anonymous HIV testing (Ratnam 1994). Newfoundland rates of seropositive blood samples were by far the highest in the country, with one in every 900 samples testing positive. These rates compared with one in 1,600 in Quebec, one in 3,700 in British Columbia, and one in 9,100 in Manitoba. Figures released from the study in 1992 indicated that Newfoundland had the highest number of pregnant women with HIV, per capita, in the country (Jackson 1992a).

Rates of infection in Newfoundland show much higher ratios of women to men than are reported elsewhere in North America (Bartlett 2001). While average North American ratios stand at about 8:1[33] (meaning that for every eight males who are HIV positive, one

---

33.   Ratios of male to female infection are changing in North America in general, indicating that women are far more at risk than they were earlier in the epidemic. For a discussion of global male/female ratios, see Marge Berer and Sunanda Ray (1993).

female is infected), in Newfoundland the ratio stands at 3:1 (for every three males infected, one female is HIV positive). The high ratio of HIV-positive women in a province with relatively low IV-drug-user and blood-product infections suggests a high incidence of heterosexual transmission.

The high incidence of HIV infection among women in the province is consistent with the information revealed in surveys of sexuality and risk behaviors among Newfoundland youth. Several of these surveys indicate that Newfoundland and Labrador youth are more sexually active, earlier, with more partners than other teens in Canada and that protected sex is not the norm (King 1989; Cregheur, Casey, and Banfield 1992; MacKinnon 1993; Donovan 1995). Sixty-three percent of grade-eleven students in the province report being sexually active (Cregheur, Casey, and Banfield 1992). Follow-up studies administered in 1988 (King 1989) and 1992 (Cregheur, Casey, and Banfield 1992) indicate that this percentage is not in decline in the face of HIV but, rather, is on the rise.

The surveys also indicate that Newfoundland youth are not likely to be taking precautions for HIV. The live-birth rate among fifteen- to nineteen-year-olds in Newfoundland is 1.3 times the national rate (MacKinnon 1993). In 1988 (King 1989) the Canada Youth and AIDS national survey found that Newfoundland youth conveyed strongly negative attitudes toward condom use. In a follow-up study done of Newfoundland youth sexuality in 1991, Cregheur, Casey, and Banfield found that 35 percent of the teens surveyed reported that they would be embarrassed to buy condoms, and an additional 54 percent indicated that carrying a condom suggested a willingness to have sex. While survey information of this type is patchy in Newfoundland,[34] it paints a picture of high-risk sexual activity. This, combined with high incidence of chlamydia, genital warts, and other sexually transmitted diseases in the province[35] (Donovan 1995; MacKinnon 1993), indicates a situation that, as MacKinnon notes, is ripe for HIV transmission.

---

34.   Unfortunately, knowledge, belief, and behavior studies in the province privilege teen responses and do not focus with the same detail on comparative adult data. While the population seen as most at risk falls into the fifteen to thirty-five age group, less is known about the upper age brackets.

35.   The presence of other sexually transmitted diseases creates a positive environment for HIV transmission through the presence of inflamation and small lesions. Women infected with chlamydia have a substantially increased risk of acquiring HIV if exposed to the virus.

In the early 1990s the province discovered it had cause for alarm. Public health officials began to detect a clustering of HIV-positive individuals within a twenty-five kilometer stretch of communities along the Conception Bay North Coast. By 1995, thirty-one women, nine men, and three infants tested positive for HIV in an area that has a population of only 27,000, including just over 8,600 in the fifteen to thirty-five age range (Donovan 1995). All of the adult women and eight of the nine men reported no identifiable risk factor other than heterosexual sex (Donovan 1995). Case studies failed to identify the reason for the clustering in the area, but it was clear that the presence of such high numbers of HIV-positive individuals in such a small geographic area indicated the likelihood of numerous others who were unaware of their HIV status but capable of transmitting the virus. The AIDS crisis in Conception Bay North meant that the province had to seriously, and quickly, alter its approach to the disease.

The Conception Bay North situation was complicated by the rural nature of the communities involved. Rural communities, by virtue of their geography, can provide the perfect conditions for wildfire transmission. Further, access to education, information, and treatment is more limited outside urban areas, and mobility for treatment is not easily afforded in communities that relied so heavily on the (now-defunct) fishery for employment (Bartlett 2001). Federal funding and support are difficult to muster when the crisis, clearly seen in the province, amounts to less than 1 percent of the total national HIV situation. Rural health care, by definition, affects small numbers of people spread over large distances—an expensive and difficult undertaking and one that finds little sympathy across a large country dealing with larger numbers of infection.

Comprehending what is going on with AIDS in Conception Bay North and in Newfoundland in general requires understanding how risk is constructed by both the lay public and those responsible for public health. Surveys, like those that have provided some of the data used here, arise out of official perceptions of risk. Oriented toward teenagers and focused on age of first sexual activity (although neither factor in and of itself constitutes risk), the surveys come from and construct a story of HIV transmission—young people, impulsive, screwing around before they are mature enough, afraid to buy condoms, and exercising the mind/body disconnect that adults attribute to youth. The story is one we have heard before and is perhaps a narrative that has some truth to it. But it is a flattened story, one without orientation, complicating action, or narrative depth. Certainly, the story-making process is unavoidable. But what is problematic about that process is that it doesn't necessarily have the capacity to hear or to record alternative perceptions or alternative stories. It simply touches the person running and says, "Tag, you've got AIDS." The idea behind the chapters that follow is to hear some alternative stories and explore some alternative perceptions of risk. Who's "it," who's not, and why might be far more instructive than initially meets the eye.

2

Bad People and Body Fluids

Contemporary Legend and AIDS Discourse

In 1989, versions of a story circulating around St. John's asserted that a local teenager was covertly but deliberately causing damage to the condoms on display in local drug stores. One woman told the story as follows:

> My friend Marcia told me this story. She said her friend thinks she even knows who did it. Anyway, this guy finds out he's got AIDS and he's mad and he wants to get back at the whole world, so he goes into a drug store. And he borrowed his grandmother's hat pin. So, when nobody is looking he takes the pin and he pokes it all the way through a condom box on the shelf. He does that four or five times. Then he puts the box back and he leaves. The next night he does the same thing with a different box. Anyway, he kept it up—night after night, box after box, until, you know, he got them all. All the condoms in the whole city and not one fit to be used. So now, people are getting pregnant, getting AIDS, getting VD. They think they're protected and they're not.

The "Pinpricks in the Condom" story is a typical contemporary legend. It is told as true or, at least, as plausible. It contains a mentioned pedigree or source that is a few links removed from the teller but nevertheless appears to be close enough to be reasonably accurate (generally, this is constructed as a friend of a friend). It narrates a series of events of contemporary concern and opens up debate about those issues. Like the well-known classic contemporary legends of dogs in microwaves, Kentucky-fried rats, and insects in hairdos, the condom story appeared on the local scene in a variety of versions, each supplying sufficient detail to concern, if not convince, the listener.

The term *contemporary legend* is used to describe "unsubstantiated narratives with traditional themes and modern motifs that circulate in multiple versions and are told as if they are true or at least plausible" (Turner 1993:5). Sometimes called "urban legends," "modern legends," or "modern myths,"[1] the contemporary legend has been described as a solidified rumor—a story that combines rumor with formal narrative devices (Kapferer 1989; Turner 1993:5). The legend form is dialogic: told to remark upon or debate issues related to contemporary concerns such as crime, technology, big business, government power, or sexuality. Health legends form a huge part of the genre, with hundreds circulating in most locales at any given time. These narratives cover a wide expanse of health issues—organ theft and transplantation black markets; medical consequences of sexual exploration; unusual animal, insect, and parasite infestations; medical experimentation and conspiracy; undisclosed forms of contagion; and numerous others. Of this massive and varied body of health legends, AIDS narratives currently comprise the largest corpus,[2] at least in North America. The vitality of legends

---

1.   This group of terms reflects both popular nomenclature for the type of narratives discussed here and paradigm changes based on philosophical debates within the discipline of folklore. Popular usage appears to prefer the terms "modern myth" or "urban legend." The phrase "modern myth" is one that folklorists abhor. While popular usage understands myth to be simply a story that has no basis in fact, it is used within the disciplines of folklore and anthropology to refer to sacred narratives involving strongly held beliefs. References to myth as synonymous with untruth appear to be based on the ethnocentric belief stance of someone outside of the teller's tradition (it is a myth; I believe it to be untrue; therefore it is untrue; therefore all untrue stories are myths). "Urban legend" and "modern legend" were terms used by folklorists intent on contrasting these narratives with older notions of legend as a genre that found its primary vitality in the rural past. Today, most legend scholars agree that contemporary legends are neither urban nor modern, in the sense that they do not exist to the exclusion of rural communities, nor are they "new" stories. In fact, many narratives of this type (see the discussions of precursors to AIDS legends throughout this volume) have extremely long histories with variation appropriate for commentary on current concerns. For this reason, the term "contemporary" legend has gained in popularity over the last twenty years, suggesting that while the narratives may borrow older types and motifs, they focus on contemporary contexts and concerns and the narratives are presented as contemporary with those issues. For further discussion of debates about terminology, see the introduction to Bennett and Smith (1996) or Bennett (1985).

2.   This assertion is based on my own survey of the genre.

about AIDS should not surprise us. Twenty-two million people have died from AIDS around the world over the past twenty years. Nearly twice that many, over thirty-six million worldwide, are now living with HIV. UNAIDS/WHO estimates indicate that in the year 2000, 5.3 million people were newly infected with HIV.[3] Legend follows worry and fear, not simply as a means of expressing anxiety, but also as a means to test information and sources, explore relevancies, and investigate the shape and nature of related issues. AIDS is a part of daily. reality, but its magnitude is terrifying, information about it is inconsistent, and the epidemic continually takes on new bizarre twists and turns. In other words, AIDS is the very stuff of contemporary legend.

Contemporary legends have fallen prey in recent years to the ravages of popularization, becoming fodder for numerous horror movies, situation comedies, and novels. The popularity of the narrative form in film, television, and literature is largely due to its vitality as a natural discursive form (Danielson 1979). Nevertheless, popularization of the genre has shifted attention away from its ethnographic context to the sensationalistic content of many of the stories. Counter to the image of contemporary legends in popular culture, legend scholars cite *mundaneness* as a central characteristic of the genre (Smith 1998:493). Contemporary legends make the extraordinary ordinary and the ordinary extraordinary by combining common situations and events with unusual complications or results. The combination gives the narratives their powerful characteristic of plausibility. As Jean-Noel Kapferer (1996:246) notes, the narratives are characterized by "persistence, pervasiveness and persuasiveness." These characteristics create a powerful threesome—prompting a number of public panics related to the kidnapping of children (Best 1990; Campion-Vincent 1990; Victor 1993), mass poisonings (Best and Horiuchi 1985; Grider 1984; and Kapferer 1989), forced medical experimentation (Turner 1991), and numerous others.

Because contemporary legends exist primarily as a conversational form, they don't tend to feature single definitive texts or formulaic openings and closings (Smith 1998:493). They are often embedded in other types of discourse such as jokes or personal experience narratives and appear sometimes more as a reference to

---

3.   Statistics used here have been taken from the "AIDS around the World" surveillance Web site http://www.avert.org/aroundworld.htm (accessed January 11, 2002).

a story than as a full narrative. Due in part to the fluid shape of these narratives, scholarly literature has focused intently on generic classification and definition, particularly in reference to the subtle distinctions between rumor and contemporary legend. While rumor tends to be defined as a "brief, oral, non-narrative statement based on hearsay" (Turner 1993:4), the legend is often seen as having a stronger narrative component, presented most often with fuller elaboration. Nevertheless, the tendency to shorten legend forms and embed them in other types of expression complicates the definitional problem. For the purposes of this study I will follow Patricia Turner's lead (1993), emphasizing the complementary nature of the two forms rather than continuing the debate about their exclusivity. Like Turner, I find that the material under discussion in this volume moves back and forth between rumor and legend but is nevertheless part of a clearly related narrative complex. For this reason, I have adopted Turner's usage—preferring "the term *rumor* to refer to short, non-narrative expressions of belief, *legend* to refer to the more traditionally grounded narratives of belief, and *contemporary legend* to refer to items containing particularly modern motifs" (Turner 1993:5).

Also part of the legend complex are numerous non-oral and mass-mediated versions of the narratives. As with many contemporary folklore genres, the legend has adapted to modern forms of communications technology and is now disseminated, at least in part, through television, radio, literature, film, sound recordings, e-mail, fax, and photocopy. This inclusion of new forms of technology in circulation should not surprise us, for as Smith notes, "in the real world, not just a single *oral* medium of transmission is utilized to communicate folklore, *but any available and relevant media* is employed" (Smith 1992:41). Because of the popular appeal of contemporary legends combined with widespread concerns about AIDS, the narratives discussed in this volume have been frequent topics of news accounts, editorials, advice columns, and other journalistic endeavors. As can be seen in some of the case studies developed here, journalistic dissemination often becomes a significant part of the narrative-transmission process, acting as tradition bearer in much the same way as do individual storytellers but reaching much larger numbers with a single performance.

Similarly, AIDS legends have extremely wide international circulation on the Internet. They are commonly sent between friends

and acquaintances by e-mail, much as narratives are exchanged face
to face between individuals. Legend telling has also become part of
mass-posting traditions that have developed over the last decade.
Part of a larger tradition of health warnings posted on e-mail, AIDS
legends circulate often as a form of activism, in which narratives
are sent out to warn the public of some new health menace. Such
warnings often report on links between widely used products and
health conspiracies (such as asbestos in tampons to make women
bleed more or hidden links between breast cancer and antiperspi-
rant). Many of these health warnings have their origins in fuller
contemporary-legend texts. Several of the most widely circulated
AIDS legends in the past two or three years (see, for example, chapter 6 on needle legends) have been forwarded as part of this larger
movement of Internet health activism.

Enacting Legends, Ostension, and Health Behaviors

Whether circulated by mass Internet postings, reported in the
newspaper, or discussed face to face in more traditional storytelling
contexts, contemporary legends retain certain important features:
as noted, they are told as true, factual, or plausible and therefore assume a level of authority; they provoke dialogue about the narrative
events, their interpretation, and their plausibility; they both articulate and influence beliefs and attitudes toward the subject matter;
and they have the capability of affecting the actions and behavior
of the listening audience. These features, combined with the intense mass circulation made possible by popular culture, the media,
and the Internet, provide contemporary legend with the potential
of widespread cultural impact. As a genre that advises, warns, and
informs with incredible speed and authority (Shibutani 1966), the
contemporary legend can become a formative motivating factor in
personal decision making, including decisions related to individual
health-seeking and health-care provision.

This impact of the legends can have a wide reach. The narratives provoke response from "official" as well as "lay" members of
the community—potentially affecting judicial and legislative action, public policy, the provision of social services, and health care.
Many contemporary legends have made it into the pages of medical
journals, either represented as assumed truths or deconstructed in

terms of their physiological or institutional probability.[4] An article by F. K. Taylor, for example, published in the *British Medical Journal* (1979), explores the medical implications of penis captivus symptoms described in contemporary legends concerning couples who lock during sexual intercourse. Fasting, Christensen, and Glending explore the potential realities of organ-theft legends in the *Journal of Nursing Ethics* (1998). Both of these articles, along with others that explore medical legends from the perspective of medical researchers and health-care providers, attest to the significance of health-legend complexes beyond trivializing functions of entertainment. Further, the attention these legends receive in the medical literature is characteristic of the legends' ability to create questions even in the minds of authorities on the various content areas discussed by the narrative.

Beyond medical exploration of questions such as "is there a real symptomatology connected to the narrative events?" or "does this narrative have a physiological basis?" or "can such failures of the medical system happen?" health legends continually affect the provision and use of medical services. Contemporary legends concerning AIDS have, in specific cases, had direct impacts on such crucial activities as blood-donation choices and blood-collection procedures (see chapter 6), contact tracing and partner reporting (see chapter 6), observance of universal precautions (see chapter 3), use of health facilities (see Farmer 1992), health related isolation of individuals and communities (Goldstein, Patton, and Worth forthcoming), and numerous other significant medical practices. The narrative informs the listener in ways that not only affect thinking but that also become enacted as the listener expresses belief or concern.

This relationship between narrative and action is referred to by contemporary-legend scholars as "ostension." In 1983 Linda Dégh and Andrew Vázsonyi introduced the notion of "ostension" to narrative research, borrowing the concept from semiotics (where it was defined as "a type of communication where the reality, the thing, the situation or event itself functions in the role of message") to account for actions that gain their primary meaning by being part

---

4. In addition to articles that explicitly deal with the legends, numerous others contain small assumptions or questions that betray narrative influence. Articles on AIDS origins in medical journals, for example, frequently betray exposure to the legend tradition (see Goldstein 2001).

of a recognized narrative (Dégh and Vázsonyi 1983). Ostensive action, in its narrowest sense, is similar to what is known popularly as a "copycat crime," in which an individual places him- or herself in the role of an antagonist in a crime narrative and performs an act previously known from narrative reports (Ellis 1989a). In 1993, for example, one individual, upon hearing narratives of intravenous needles found in food items, placed several needles and syringes in a soda can, which ultimately made its way to an unsuspecting consumer (de Vos 1996:154). Narrative ostension also affects behaviors in subtler ways that don't necessarily enact the entire narrative or suggest identification with the antagonist but that nevertheless indicate behavioral choices based on knowledge of the story. Contemporary legend and business rumor specialist, Fredrick Koenig, for example, was hired by Burger King Corporation in the late 1980s to help squelch the rumor that an HIV-positive employee had been ejaculating into the mayonnaise served to customers (Langlois 1991). Koenig's consultancy for Burger King was prompted by the company's recognition that rumors and narratives provoke choices by consumers, choices that took a significant toll on Wendy's and McDonald's when similar rumors suggested that the businesses incorporated ground earthworms into the hamburger meat (Koenig 1985). While consumers who act on narrative by withholding patronage are not *enacting* the narrative, they are making choices on the basis of narrative events and thereby transmitting the narrative through their actions. For this reason, the paradigmatic impact of ostension theory in contemporary legend studies includes a wider interest in the relationship between legend and action (Ellis 1989a; Fine 1991).

Legend and Vernacular Concerns about Health

The ostension focus in contemporary legend scholarship parallels similar theoretical interests in illness-narrativity research that have recently begun to explore the function of health narratives as culturally intelligible scripts or models for health and illness action (Good 1994; Mattingly 1998). As Mattingly suggests, "Since the stuff of narratives is the abnormal, the improper, and other departures from the norm, stories offer rich vehicles for passing along cultural knowledge about such matters as how to identify the appropriate social role as care giver for an ill family member . . . or how to adopt the proper cultural identity associated with a particular diagnostic condition" (1998:13). On some level, contemporary legends, while not always tied in obvious ways to specific actions, become embroiled in the complex relationship between experience, health worldview, explanatory models (Kleinman 1975), choice, and behavior. While such stories may not directly lead us to action with the transparent ostensive relationship of modeling our activities on those of protagonist or antagonist or even of prompting directly related panic reactions, they nevertheless influence and express an understanding of health and illness patterns that motivate our choices and concerns. Health-related contemporary legends betray numerous cultural associations with disease and medicine: an association of "otherness" with contamination (Bird 1996; Goldstein 1991); a distrust of medical bureaucracy (Farmer 1992; Turner 1993); a resistance to both public-health constructions of risk and the increasing medicalization of daily life (Sobo 1995); a fear of bodily intrusion and violation (Bennett 1997; Schechter 1988); and others. The narratives simultaneously shape and are shaped by vernacular ideas of health and illness, ideas that form the basis of health decisions and actions.

This link between attitudes toward health and illness and legend is beautifully illustrated in Laurie Stanley-Blackwell's analysis of the mysterious stranger and Acadian good-Samaritan legends, which became an inseparable part of the understanding and explanation of the leprosy epidemic in nineteenth-century New Brunswick. New Brunswick communities were hit hard by leprosy in the 1840s, particularly in the Acadian communities of Tracadie, Pokemouche, and Neguac. The disease quickly became linked, both in local belief and in official medical and government responses, to the Acadian way of life, emphasizing preexisting Anglophone attitudes toward Acadians as poverty stricken, backward, and morally depraved. Within Tracadie and its sister communities, the disease spawned a series of contemporary legends concerning the origin of leprosy in the area. These legends differed slightly in their plot but had some characteristic features; the disease was brought to the community by an outsider—a sailor or fugitive or a stranger from Europe—who accidentally left his host infected with the disease. This narrative made two issues clear: the disease was brought by an intruder, and the local community had no "sinful" part in the infection. A later version of the narrative underscored these issues. In this variant, the Acadian host invited the sickly visitor to her table, offered to launder his clothes, and provided a bed for the night. According to the story, local infection with leprosy resulted from the contaminated bed linens. The narrative not only denied the imputation of sin and personal culpability for the disease but also asserted the neighborly goodness and irreproachable hospitality of the Acadian people; the disease was a result of simple local kindness. The good-Samaritan version of the narrative became so entrenched in nineteenth-century New Brunswick culture that special treatment of bed linens used with leprosy patients was legislated by government and medical officials (Stanley-Blackwell 1993). Stanley-Blackwell argued,

> Somehow, when a distinct pattern of sequence and events was imposed on the progress of the enigmatic disease, it seemed less cryptic and more real. Moreover, details about time and place gave the stories an air of authenticity and authority. They helped reduce the crisis to manageable proportions, fending off leprosy's stigma and validating the contemporary contention that the 'poisonous virus was not the growth of this spot, but was brought here by some traveler.' With these narratives the Acadian inhabitants in northeastern New Brunswick created a humanized and indigenous aetiology for leprosy. (1993:39)

While Stanley-Blackwell's study of the Acadian leprosy narratives traces the impact of legend on the construction of disease and illness in the community, its conclusions focus largely on the functional aspects of the narratives:

> They [the stories] became the medium by which the inhabitants could explain leprosy's foothold in their midst. Essentially the narratives served a therapeutic function. They demystified the disease, mitigated its harshness and combated the pervasive notion that the disease was an hereditary scourge among the Acadian population. In other words, the residents of Gloucester County took recourse to the format of 'once upon a time' in order to create some useable context in which to understand the enigmatic disease and to diminish its terrors. (1993:33)

Beyond such functional arguments, however, which try to interpret *why* the narratives came to exist, the narrative corpus reveals the role of legend as a forum for the expression of (and creation of) deeply rooted attitudes and beliefs about disease and health. It is not simply the *need* for legend that is important or the legend's role in making individuals *feel* better but the nature and shape of the ideas themselves and the effect of those ideas on evolving lay understandings of physiology, contagion, and epidemiology.

Gillian Bennett, for example, in her article "Bosom Serpents and Alimentary Amphibians: A Language for Sickness" (1997), illustrates how legends serve as a language to describe symptoms and as an explanatory system allowing individuals to understand how they came to be ill and what they must do to restore health. Bennett traces geographically, historically, and thematically a corpus of legends concerning animals that invade the human body, arguing that such narratives constitute a form of medical discourse that emphasizes the prevalent lay notion that disease is an entity that takes up residence in the body and needs to be removed. The narratives are literal graphic renderings that reflect lay means of visualizing diseases, such as cancer, as "an animal creeping through the body and devouring flesh along the way" (226). Bennett argues,

> Stories of bosom serpents and alimentary amphibians are thus a complete language for talking about sickness. They are a metaphor-come-true which allows a rational aetiology to be deduced from the central image and a logical cure devised. But they are also a means whereby lay persons may talk informedly to each other and to their therapists about the nature and course of their sufferings. Best of all, they are a means through which the efficacy of the various medical alternatives may be debated. The doctor need never have the last word (though he often does even here). The stories are there to be told, to demonstrate that no matter how many times patients are told that their sufferings are imaginary, in the end the scoffers will be confounded and the patient will be dramatically vindicated. (1997:239)

Bennett's and Stanley-Blackwell's studies represent a portion of the still-small body of literature on medical contemporary legends that explores the connection between narratives and vernacular concerns about health or that focuses on applications of legend study to health care. In addition to Stanley-Blackwell's work on leprosy, Adrienne Mayor (1995) and Marcia Gaudet (1990) focus on legends concerning historical epidemics, demonstrating narrative associations of disease with moral regulation. Farmer (1992) and Turner (1993) explore issues related to distrust of medical bureaucracy through their ethnographic analysis of conspiracy legends. Véronique Campion-Vincent (1990, 1997) and Nancy Scheper-Hughes (1996) have written on narratives concerning abductions of children and adults for body-part theft, providing application of legend analysis to organ donorship and transplantation concerns. Most recently, Marianne Whatley and Elissa Henken (2000) have demonstrated what a biologist and a folklorist can accomplish when engaged in the collaborative analysis of health and sexuality legends.

Because of the multitheme nature of contemporary legend, others have discussed health legends but not as a primary focus, highlighting crime or sexuality aspects of the narratives or other issues, instead of the implications of legendary material for insight into vernacular health systems. Numerous folklorists and anthropologists have written on AIDS legends, focusing on historical precursors and variants (Smith 1990; Brunvand 1989; Ellis 1989b), gender issues (Fine 1992), oral tradition and the media (Bird 1996), transmission (Langlois 1991), moral regulation (Goodwin 1989), and community narratives (Czubala 1991; Farmer 1992; Kane 1998; Krawczyk-Wasilewska 2000; Turner 1993; Sobo 1995). These studies (and others) provide a wealth of comparative information and significant insight into the multifaceted corpus of AIDS legends but with a somewhat wider net—either exploring the legend as a small part of studies of the larger health picture in a specific location or focusing on the narratives with minimal consideration of health implications. All of these works, and the narratives themselves, point to the potential for a somewhat narrower study of patterns of lay articulation of health and illness concerns expressed in the form of AIDS legends.

Situated Legends and Emergent Meaning

Understanding narratives requires insight into their context. This is particularly true of contemporary legends, which tend to be highly interactional due to their conversational form and highly situated to address local concerns and provide the details necessary for convincing others of their plausibility. Legends circulate around the world, sometimes seemingly at the speed of light—here one moment, there the next. Globalized technologies increase both the speed and the geographical reach of narrative transmission, but ultimately the legends settle somewhere; they are told by individuals (or forwarded by individuals) situated in place and time. All folklore is context dependent, finding new words, new meanings, and performance styles in each telling. One of the first things folklorists learn as they begin to work with performed materials is that texts provide only a blueprint to what ultimately happens in a performance context. Meaning is situated and emergent. The setting, participants, goals, and numerous other factors affect what is said and how it is said, with each telling (or writing). Even the more inflexible forms of expression, such as Internet health warnings, which are generally forwarded relatively intact, have the addition of a whole new set of information added with each new forwarding address and perhaps an added comment or deleted bit of text—all small variations that might indeed make a big difference in how the narrative is interpreted and repeated.

Apart from, but intertwined with, the performance context of telling is the larger cultural and ethnographic context that informs the legends, providing a basis of meaning for their themes and issues. As Bennett and Smith note, "the events related in contemporary legends resonate with the life circumstances of the people who hear or tell them" (1996:xxii). We tend not to repeat stories that are lacking in personal and cultural meaning. Further, as legends move from place to place, time to time, and individual to individual, variation occurs that continually elaborates the narrative in culturally viable ways. The told narratives are culturally salient, expressing concerns and ideas that are recognized as "tellable" (Labov and Waletsky 1967) or as significant within the cultural context. Elizabeth Bird (1996) has in fact suggested that the focus of AIDS legends has followed stages in the developing cultural awareness of the disease as outlined by Paula Treichler (1988). Treichler suggests that AIDS awareness had evolved in three stages, focusing initially on AIDS as a gay disease that would not threaten the "general public," then with the death of Rock Hudson suggesting the possibility that it might be hard to tell who was a "carrier," and during the third phase perceiving of AIDS as a pandemic to which heterosexuals are vulnerable. Bird suggests that narratives of the "contaminated other" follow the gradual awakening suggested in Treichler's phases, beginning with stories of gay individuals infecting each other, moving to narratives of "sexually active males and promiscuous females," and eventually by the late 1980s including all sexually active women (1996:51).

Of course, Treichler's observations and Bird's are not only time dependent but also location dependent. Information about AIDS and reactions to that information are not globally uniform. As Treichler would be the first to admit, the phases noted above are tied to Western responses to AIDS and are not those found throughout the world. It is not just the availability of information, however, that creates the cultural attitudes that shape narratives. AIDS did not arrive on a scene void of other experiences and concerns. Cultural attitudes are shaped by past experiences—with health, with disease, with politics and economics, with isolation or overcrowding, with bias and prejudice, with power and oppression, and with a host of other potentially relevant factors. It is not surprising, nor is it accidental, that AIDS legends in some countries and within some groups favor government-conspiracy issues. History has laid the groundwork for medical distrust. As Paul Farmer notes, "Those who would dismiss persistent rumors of medical experimentation on disempowered black people should read accounts of the Tuskegee Experiment in which treatment for syphilis was withheld from some 400 black sharecroppers in Alabama in order to chart the 'natural history of the disease'" (Farmer 1992:297). The reality and the historical narratives of the Tuskegee Experiment and other incidents of maltreatment and deception feed conspiratorial thought and become prototypical, a "symbol of . . . mistreatment by the medical establishment, a metaphor for deceit, conspiracy, malpractice and neglect, if not outright genocide" (Sobo 1995:44). Contemporary legends articulate attitudes that are already there, below the surface and sometimes inaccessible, in response to more formal means of assessing cultural concerns. The narratives have to be contextualized in ways that trace relevance structures: personal, social, cultural, and comparative.

Comparative analysis is one of the most fruitful ways of analyzing contemporary legends. As the narratives move from location to location, they take on new motifs, new elaborations, new concerns, and sometimes develop into entirely different narratives. Identifying recurrent patterns in the narratives and locating differences helps to establish cross-culturally tenacious narrative associations and other associations that are more locally significant. Even minor variations can reveal culture specific concerns. The "Welcome to the World of AIDS" narrative described below is reported in some Muslim countries featuring two women and two men. A woman

alone would represent a cultural transgression countering the innocence required to project the narrative's message. Stories of food
contaminated with HIV-positive body fluids express considerably
different sentiments when told about Burger King than when told
about Mr. Hong's Chinese restaurant. The former narrative is likely
to be commenting, at least in part, on concerns about the nature of
fast-food establishments and big business. The latter variant turns
the narrative into commentary on ethnicity and "otherness." Both
variations express an association of a place or a people with HIV, an
association that may have significant health-belief implications. Patterns of variation can reveal deep-seated health ideas shared within
a group or culture. The caution, however, with this type of analysis is that it is easily misinterpreted within essentialist paradigms
that generalize statements about thought processes. Essentialist
constructions, such as "Newfoundlanders think . . ." or "Canadians
agree . . . ," skew the philosophical basis of the effort, which wishes
to use ethnography and narrative analysis to demonstrate patterns
of shared concerns and cultural differences in conceptualization.
The intent is to use a variety of articulations to explore cultural issues, opposing a priori stereotypical constructions.

While cultural variation in the narratives is instructive, so too is
their constancy. Although contemporary-legend analysis demands
that we recognize changes in the narratives over time and space,
legend scholars have also been fascinated with historical consis-
tencies in narrative plots and motifs, sometimes tracing them back
hundreds of years. The repetition of narratives that have remained
culturally viable and that resurface—albeit in new clothing—centuries later underscores the cyclical nature of cultural attitudes and
the centrality of narrative articulations of pervasive concerns. Although AIDS is a new disease, its legends are often reformulations
of narratives that circulated in response to smallpox, leprosy, bubonic plague, syphilis, and numerous other historical epidemics.
The precursors of current popular health legends are bone chilling
in their suggestion that hundreds of years of modern medical ad-
vancements make little difference in our gut reactions to illness and
disease.

One of the most widely disseminated and frequently told AIDS
legends involves a man who meets a woman in a bar, takes her to a
hotel or back to his apartment, and sleeps with her. In the morning
when he wakes up, the woman is gone. He gets out of the bed and

walks into the bathroom, where he finds a message written on the mirror in lipstick. The message reads, "Welcome to the World of AIDS." Paul Smith notes that Daniel Defoe's *Journal of the Plague Year* (1665) provides an early analogue to the "Welcome to the World of AIDS" narrative (Smith 1990). He quotes:

> A poor unhappy gentlewoman, a substantial citizen's wife, was (if the story be true) murdered by one of these creatures in Aldersgate Street, or that way. He was going along the street, raving mad, to be sure, and singing; the people only said he was drunk, but he himself said he had the plague upon him, which, it seems, was true; and meeting this gentlewoman, he would kiss her. She was terribly frightened, as he was only a rude fellow, and she ran from him, but the street being very thin of people, there was nobody near enough to help her. When she saw he would overtake her, she turned and gave him a thrust so forcibly, he being but weak, and pushed him backward. But very unhappily, she being so near, he caught hold of her, and pulled her down also, and getting up first, mastered her, and kissed her; and which was worst of all, when he had done, told her he had the plague, and why should not she have it as well as he?

Smith (1990) and others (Bird 1996; Brunvand 1989) note numerous antecedents to "Welcome to the World of AIDS," told about herpes, gonorrhea, and syphilis, as well as about incurable mystery diseases. The narratives share in common the notion of a deliberate infector who, upon finding out about his own condition, seeks revenge by transmitting his disease through sexual liaisons. The longevity of this narrative, continually resurfacing with new diseases and new health concerns, suggests the diachronic persistence of concepts such as the infected body as weapon, the personification of disease, and the evil, contaminated "other" seeking revenge. Over the last decade and a half, folklorists have come to refer to the "Welcome to the World of AIDS" story as "AIDS Mary" (or "AIDS Harry" when the antagonist is male). The reference came from writer Dan Sheridan of the *Chicago Times*, who recognized similarities between the narrative and the story of "Typhoid Mary," an Irish American cook (actually named Mary Mallon) who spread typhoid to some fifty people in the early 1900s (Brunvand 1989:197). Typhoid Mary supposedly knew of her "carrier" status and yet continued to spread the disease for eight years after her discovery of the risk. Sheridan's name for the story demonstrates his immediate recognition of the antagonist in the AIDS story as recognizable from the typhoid narrative tradition.

The motifs in these narratives persist because the vernacular health concerns they describe remain problematic. Stigmatizing the diseased individual, feeling vulnerable in the face of illness, distrusting particular societal subgroups, blaming the victim—all bridge the time span between the plague and AIDS because they still reflect our attitudes toward illness and disease. The case studies explored in the chapters that follow look at these concerns as they emerge in new forms adjusted to a new disease, in a specific social and cultural context. In what remains of this chapter, however, I will more generally explore the AIDS-legend complex as it relates to persistent, recurrent health themes.

Tainted Food and Contaminated Spaces

Contamination narratives are one of the most common forms of contemporary legend, circulating widely and creating panics about commercial products, general household items, or common food items that contain harmful ingredients, insects, parasites, deadly bacteria and viruses, poisons, or substances that consumers would find repulsive. Numerous contemporary legends about HIV/AIDS focus on the contamination of food, objects, or spaces, most often with HIV-positive body fluids, but not infrequently concerning a more amorphous general contamination achieved through close contact or through a kind of "contagious magic." Like all contemporary legends, the AIDS contamination stories combine themes, providing commentary on the disease but also on discomfort with fast food, specific ethnic groups and cultural differences, concerns about government conspiracies, and so forth. While the narratives might suggest, on the surface, a lack of knowledge about the "facts" of HIV transmission, surveys conducted in North America and internationally suggest that knowledge levels are much higher than the continued spread of the disease and reports of practice would lead us to believe (see chapter 3 on risk perception). Nevertheless, contamination narratives suggest difficulties with such issues as casual contact, low-risk body fluids,[5] and shelf life[6] of the live virus. These apparent incongruities between beliefs expressed in the narratives and reported knowledge concerning the disease could easily be interpreted as the result of lay misunderstanding or ignorance. Such an interpretation, however, treats narrative as a simple conveyor of information and neglects its role as a *social force*. The persistence of narratives that counter belief and knowledge surveys could alternatively be understood as an articulation of distrust of information authorities, resistance, logical reconsideration of issues through independent thinking, or suppression of "facts" in favor of other kinds of cultural truths. The narratives may actually be more about moral discourse than about mechanisms of contracting the virus, but as such they nevertheless reinterpret the disease and have the potential to create a master narrative that can fill interstitial gaps.

Contamination involves contact with something that is too distant from the self, either biologically or socially (Nemeroff and Rozin 1994). It focuses on things that are *outside* getting *inside*. "Dirt," as Mary Douglas argues, is a metaphor concerning things that are out of place. She notes:

> Shoes are not dirty in themselves, but it is dirty to place them on the dining table; food is not dirty in itself, but it is dirty to leave cooking utensils in the bedroom, or food bespattered on clothing; similarly, bedroom equipment in the drawing room, clothing lying on chairs; outdoor things indoors, upstairs things downstairs, under-clothing appearing where over-clothing should be, and so on. (1966:36)

Many contemporary legends involve private acts that are engaged in in public places (the "Castrated Boy," the "Hook," the "Surpriser Surprised"—all acts that are "out of place"). AIDS contamination legends, because of their focus on body fluids, depict both *activities* and *matter* out of place. Tim Cresswell, following on Douglas, notes that bodily secretions have a heightened "out of place" metaphoric connotation. He argues, "The orifices of the body connect the

5. Low-risk body fluids include saliva, sweat, tears, and urine. There is also no evidence that HIV can be transmitted through feces.

6. The shelf life of the virus is how long it lives outside the human body. The viability of the virus will be variable according to the kind of container or surface on which it is found. In general, the virus is extremely fragile outside the body, lasting only minutes to a few hours.

inside to the outside and the stuff that goes into them or comes out of them is subject to the strictest taboos as such substances transgress the inside/outside ordering of the world" (1997:341).

Food contamination legends concerning AIDS are generally not depicted as accidental but rather as occasions of premeditated substitution. In contrast, other food-contamination legends tend to be accidental; the mouse happens to get into the Coke bottle, the severed fingertip falls into the ice cream vat. In the AIDS legends, the contamination is most often constructed as random revenge for infection with the virus. Typically, a male employee of a large fast-food franchise (most often Burger King or Domino Pizza) learns that he is HIV positive. Out of anger and "unwilling to die alone," he ejaculates into the mayonnaise used on the hamburgers and then serves the burgers to unwitting customers. Janet Langlois, who has explored this legend in depth, has dubbed the story "Hold the Mayo."[7] In the coda to the story, the unsuspecting customer gets sick and must have his or her stomach pumped, or the manager acts on complaints of a foul taste by sending the food items to a laboratory, which ultimately discovers the semen after microscopic examination. While the legend is often constructed as a revenge narrative in which the person with AIDS intends to infect others, the story seems to stop short of actually asserting that the consumer contracted the virus from the food item. The report sometimes suggests the belief that you can get AIDS from eating the contaminated food but does not generally go so far as to offer narrative evidence of resulting infection. The following account is typical in this respect:

> You know why Burger King is putting out all those free Whopper coupons? The company is going bankrupt. There is a big lawsuit filed against the company in New England. Some employee had AIDS and decided to get back at people by jacking off in the mayonnaise. You can get AIDS by eating Whoppers. That's why they're giving them away. (Langlois 1991:155)

Like other contamination narratives, the "Hold the Mayo" story focuses on the contaminant itself, more than on the harmful effects.

---

7. Langlois notes that she borrowed the title from a student's field journal entry, "Hold the Pickle, Hold the Lettuce, Hold the Mayonnaise." She says, however, that this was also the title informally given the rumor by staff at Burger King (1991:168).

Gary Alan Fine notes in his study of the "Kentucky Fried Rat"[8] legend that only 13 percent of the collected narratives discuss resulting illness (Fine 1992:130). Interestingly, while other body fluids
are used in the HIV food contamination narratives, blood, despite
its association with AIDS, is rarely the fluid of choice. Langlois
notes,

> Although blood is one of the most potent ritual symbols . . . and
> is recognized as a major transmitter of the AIDS virus, rumor and
> legend literature has noted few instances of blood contaminated
> commercial food. One exception is Paul Smith's reference to my
> Palestinian student Dalal Aswad's account of her ten-year-old
> sister's story of an AIDS-infected McDonald's employee in their
> Dearborn, Michigan neighborhood cutting his finger and sprin-
> kling blood on the grill. (Langlois 1991:168)

In a similar story, the *Phoenix Gazette* reported that guards in local
county jails had requested that they be supplied with alternatives to
meals cooked by inmates. One of the training officers interviewed
on the issue indicated that inmates sometimes urinate or spit on the
food (Sanchez 1995:A1).

The focus in these narratives on semen, urine, and spit, rather
than blood, combined with the concentration on the contaminant
in the narrative but not the consequences, suggests that the story is
more about the repulsive imagery of the body fluids involved than
it is about beliefs about the efficient transmission of HIV. This is
not to say, however, that the story is not about AIDS. Like the
"blood libel" narratives about Jews in the fourteenth century contaminating local wells, the story depicts the HIV-positive person as
a danger and a threat to society, a contaminating force by virtue of
his or her implied lack of control. That lack of control is depicted
in the story not just through the revenge motif but also through
the imagery of the potent, diseased, ejaculating male. One version
of the narrative collected in Newfoundland indicated, "This guy
liked to ejaculate, always, everywhere—he'd cum here or there and
in the food and everything." The person with AIDS in the narratives is often depicted as hypersexed, and that hypersexualization

---

8.   This story chronicles a customer who is served a breaded and fried rat in a Kentucky
      Fried Chicken restaurant.

spills (pun intended) over into the lives of ordinary fast-food-eating individuals.

Most contemporary legend scholars would argue that "Hold the Mayo" is mainly a corporate or mercantile legend, providing commentary on our distrust of fast-food establishments or, alternately, small ethnic businesses. Certainly, the narrative fits into a large category of similar stories about fast-food companies. The choice of contaminator and contaminant, however, is not insignificant. As Langlois notes, "misplaced semen becomes a particularly potent symbol configuring the gendered body, the body politic and social crisis" (1991:160).

Non-food contamination narratives appear to work in a different way. Objects and spaces contaminated by AIDS in legend appear to be impacted *by contact or association*. Contamination by association is clearly illustrated in AIDS versions of the popular contemporary legend known as the "Death Car." In its non-AIDS version, "Death Car" details the story of a very fancy, normally expensive car selling at an incredibly low price. The reason for the low price is that the previous owner had died in the car and had remained undiscovered for a long time, leaving a lingering smell of death in the vehicle. In some versions the car retained a blood stain that was ineradicable, rather than the smell (Sanderson 1969). In the "AIDS car" version, both the smell and the stain are gone; what remains is the disease association. One story in Newfoundland reported,

> In the summer of 1988 an advertisement in a newspaper read '1987 Firebird for sale $1000.' My brother, who was looking for a car at the time, told me about it. Apparently, the owner of this car had AIDS and he had died. The owner's wife was having a great deal of trouble trying to sell the car and thought that reducing the price of the car would make it easier to sell. The story was told to me by my brother and it was told as truth, but I found it very hard to believe considering the facts about how AIDS is spread. (Goldstein 1991:128)

While this telling of the narrative leaves it unclear as to whether or not the car is seen as contagious through some kind of airborne misunderstanding of HIV, other versions suggest that the car had simply taken on negative connotations. In one story, a Newfoundland teacher had died of AIDS, and his family could not sell his expensive car at all, eventually being forced to dispose of the car by pushing it over a cliff.[9]

The "AIDS Death Car" motifs suggest a kind of contagious magic in reasoning, the belief that physical and moral properties are transferred through contact. Frazer's (1890) magical law of contagion, introduced over a hundred years ago as one of the principles of sympathetic magic (Frazer 1959), detailed thought processes that held that people and objects influence each other through the transfer of essential properties and that that influence continues after the physical contact has ended. From time to time social scientists have suggested that the principle of magical contagion is universally operative in the everyday thinking of adults and can be seen in numerous contemporary daily rituals. Despite the extension of such notions of contagion to quotidian reality, the principle still carries with it an unfortunate connotation of "primitive thought." Further, the notion of "magical" may suggest a conscious metaphysical understanding that is clearly not present in the material referred to here. Nevertheless, associative contamination does appear to address the "AIDS Car" motifs. The car is unsellable because it somehow retains something of the prior owner.

Similar notions are evident in numerous public and even legislative actions taken since the discovery of the virus. Pakistan initiated a ban on importing used clothing after the first HIV-positive case appeared within their borders (Rozin, Markwith, and Nemeroff 1992). Several states in the United States have debated adding AIDS to real-estate disclosure laws, which require that homeowners intending to sell must disclose to prospective buyers any issues that "psychologically impact" a property[10] (Hines 1991). Psychologists Carol Nemeroff and Paul Rozin have explored concerns about HIV contamination beyond microbial risk through a series of experiments involving attitudes toward objects previously owned or held by HIV-positive individuals. Nemeroff and Rozin found that contagion concerns operated both materially and symbolically, often in the same person; prior AIDS contact was seen as both a physical and a moral threat.

---

9.   It should be noted that disposing of a "perfectly good" car in this manner in a culture that has experienced such poverty is quite a significant statement.

10.   Disclosure laws are already pretty interesting. In several states, sellers are required to disclose anything that might have an effect on home purchase, including the reputed presence of a ghost.

The association contagion demonstrated in the "Death Car" narrative and in the activities and experiments discussed above dovetail with a body of legends associated with smallpox and other epidemics that Adrienne Mayor refers to as the "Nessus Shirt" legend. Mayor takes the name for the corpus from Shakespeare's Mark Antony, who cried out, "The shirt of Nessus is upon me!" (1995:54). Death by poisoned apparel, Mayor argues, has been a compelling image in folklore and literature since classical antiquity, but the motif enjoyed incredible revival in variations of "Smallpox Blanket" narratives that depicted infected blankets given by white men to native peoples to wipe the population out (1995:54). The narratives link disease to gifts of personal attire. While smallpox is highly contagious and transmittable through cloth and AIDS is not, the theme of the fatal gift nevertheless pervades AIDS folklore and concerns about contamination. Interestingly, Jan Brunvand suggests that the non-AIDS versions of the "Death Car" legend carry with them the message that you can't get something for nothing (1981:21). The "AIDS Death Car," in that context, like the blanket, suggests a contaminated fatal "gift" from a stranger (in other words, you "get more than you bargained for").[11]

The Deliberate Infecting "Other"

The construction of the infected individual as morally deficient, discussed above in terms of the original legends about New Brunswick Acadians and leprosy, occurs with regularity in relation to epidemic diseases. The more virulent diseases become, the more likely it is that certain groups and individuals will be seen as responsible for the threat on community welfare. In the case of HIV/AIDS, epidemiology's early concerns about homosexuals, Haitians, and drug users provided a series of already marginalized communities ripe for scapegoating. The later educational effort emphasizing risk activities instead of risk groups came too late; the scene had already been set for the association of specific communities with the evils of disease and devastation. Public policy and legal efforts continue to underscore connections between cultural "otherness" and HIV. Immigration laws that exclude HIV-positive individuals from entering

---

11.   This would fall under what George Foster has called "the image of limited good" (1965:309).

countries such as the United States; discussions worldwide about the internment of infected individuals; loss of jobs, homes, and insurance for those who test seropositive or for those who refuse to take an antibody test; and the creation of new HIV-related criminal legislation in numerous countries and jurisdictions—all add to the growing sentiment that the world is divided into "them" and "us," the "positives" and the "negatives." In this context (which is already poised by human nature to scapegoat), the *infected* other becomes the *infecting* other. As Elizabeth Bird notes, "The AIDS sufferer is a victim-turned villain[12] in the popular mind, recalling the lepers, and maimed, crippled evil-doers of popular culture" (1996:50).

While contemporary legends about AIDS are numerous and varied, by far the most popular and consistent theme is deliberate infection. Such stories range from "Lipstick on the Mirror," "Pins Used to Deliberately Destroy Condoms," and "Hold the Mayo," all noted above, to narratives concerning AIDS-infected stick-on tattoos (containing millions of small infected needles) sold to children, prisoners who slit their wrists and attempt to infect their guards, HIV-positive hotel robbers who are caught on security cameras contaminating toothbrushes of hotel guests before leaving with their valuables, and dozens of others. While different in structure,

---

12.   Moral-panic theorists refer to the creation of "folk devils"—individuals or groups seen as perpetrators of a major threat to the social order (Cohen 1973). Moral-panic theory shares many issues of interest with contemporary-legend scholarship. Stanley Cohen, who is credited with systematically introducing the concept, defined it by writing the following:

> Societies appear to be subject, every now and then, to periods of moral panic. A condition, episode, person or group of persons emerges to become defined as a threat to societal values and interests; its nature is presented in a stylized and stereotypical fashion by the mass media; the moral barricades are manned by editors, bishops, politicians and other right-thinking people; socially accredited experts pronounce their diagnoses and solutions; ways of coping are evolved or (more often) resorted to; the condition then disappears, submerges or deteriorates and becomes more visible. Sometimes the subject of the panic is quite novel and at other times it is something which has been in existence long enough, but suddenly appears in the limelight. Sometimes the panic passes over and is forgotten, except in folklore and collective memory; at other times it has serious and long lasting repercussions and might produce such changes as those in legal and social policy or even in the way society conceives itself. (Cohen 1973:9)

One of the major criticisms of moral-panic theory concerns its insistence on disproportionality as a primary characteristic, focusing on the irrationality of the societal response to the issue (Thompson 1998:10). While this characteristic fits well with trends in contemporary-legend research focused on debunking narratives, it moves us away from the "hermeneutic of generosity" discussed later in this chapter.

the stories share two striking motifs, often nearly identical in their articulation: the infected individuals find out about their HIV status and reason, "If I am going to die, I am taking other people with me"; and, despite variation in plot, the tagline ("Welcome to the World of AIDS" or "Welcome to the AIDS club") is incredibly consistent. As is seen with the Defoe excerpt, the motive and even the tagline have historical precursors. The infector in these narratives has murderous intent, portrayed as a desire for random revenge. Generally, the attack is not directed at specific individuals, which makes the revenge motif even more frightening as it suggests that everyone is equally at risk (Best 1991:113). The "Welcome" tagline makes the interaction all that much more sinister in its seeming self-satisfaction with communicating the virus.

Parallel to the "Welcome to the World of AIDS" narratives is a series of localized panics related to specific, sometimes even named, individuals constructed as AIDS villains. In 1991 a letter published in *Ebony* magazine by a writer signed C. J. AIDS, Dallas, Texas, began a huge local and even national scare. The letter said,

> I have AIDS. No one knows it. I go to clubs more now so I can meet new men. I feel that I am a beautiful person and I couldn't believe I got it. I sleep with four different men a week, sometimes more. I've slept with 48 men so far, some of them married. I feel if I have to die a horrible death I won't go alone. I know I'm not right in what I'm doing. Can you tell me what's wrong with me? Why don't I feel guilty? (*Ebony* 1991:90)

C.J.'s letter was eventually exposed as a hoax but not before creating terror in the Dallas community (Bird 1996).

The C.J. story is similar to a panic created in Dungarvan, Ireland, in 1995, when Father Michael Kennedy, a parish priest, told his congregation that a twenty-five-year-old woman with AIDS had confessed to sleeping with between sixty and eighty men in the area. According to *The Guardian*,

> Father Kennedy said the woman had emigrated to London 10 years ago. She returned last November, picking up her victims in pubs and nightclubs across four counties. "Out of her anger and desperation she wanted to get her own back on as many as she possibly could," said the priest, who is a cousin of Senator Edward

Kennedy and officiated at the wedding of a daughter to the American ambassador to Dublin, Jean Kennedy Smith. (1995:2)

The Dungarvan "Angel of Death," as she was called, was never arrested; and area health officials found no evidence of truth to the
story, nor was there any resulting increase in local HIV statistics.

Rumors of localized "Angels of Death" and "Black Widows"[13]
are supported by the many legal cases of nondisclosure of HIV status that have been prosecuted in the last decade and a half. These
cases help to construct an image of uncontrollable hypersexed
AIDS criminals or outlaws intent on infecting their innocent victims. While legal cases of "deliberate" infection generally involve
one or two counts of the crime, narrative tradition often wraps itself around the local and media accounts inflating the numbers of
individuals infected by the defendant (see chapter 6) and portraying
sensational murderous intent. Unfortunately, both the narrative
tradition and its effect on the media and public opinion do significant damage to the notion of safe sex as the equal responsibility of
all partners.

In many of the deliberate-infection narratives, the aggressor is
portrayed as a member of a threatening ethnicity or social group—a
group already thought to have eroded morals. The infecting other
is often a person who was already thought to be a predator: a prostitute, a foreigner, a homosexual, a criminal, or some other *known*
individual. Gilmore and Somerville refer to this as "double scapegoating"—people who are scapegoated on the basis that they are
HIV positive are people who were already scapegoated on some
other basis (1994:1346). Beyond associations with crime, Islanders
blame Mainlanders, Anglophones blame Francophones, one community blames another—but often with a certain closeness between
the blaming and blamed groups, reflecting localized rivalries. Gilmore and Somerville suggest further dualities that are intrinsic to the
localized assignment of blame:

---

13.   Early deliberate-infection narratives featured women as antagonists, inspiring
      Gary Alan Fine to explore the narratives as functioning more as discussions about
      relationships between women and men—articulating revenge fantasies toward men
      for rape and expressing male collective paranoia toward women (Fine 1987). In the
      1990s deliberate-infection narratives featured male antagonists as often as female,
      but localized rumors such as C.J. or the Dungarvan "Angel of Death" still seemed
      to focus on women. Interestingly, legal cases attempting to prosecute AIDS crimes
      focus nearly always on males.

Duality is . . . intrinsic to scapegoating, namely that the the the scape-goated person is at once seen as innocent and guilty; human and dehumanized; identified with the persons undertaking the scape-goating and disidentified from them. People who are scapegoated must be sufficiently similar to the people who scapegoat them to allow the scapegoater's problem which triggered the scapegoating to apply to them. At the same time, however, they must be suffi-ciently different that it is possible to blame them or find them guilty, without finding oneself likewise blameworthy or guilty and, con-sequently, to justify expelling them as a scapegoat. (1994:1346)

The Number and Names Game

The fear of randomness expressed in the deliberate infection narratives is ironically accompanied in tradition by a fear of speci-ficity, expressed through a series of narratives that place the virus in hugely inflated proportion in one's own backyard. One of the narra-tives that has circulated extensively or that may indicate polygenesis (multiple origins) indicates that a high-school blood drive rejected a high percentage of locally collected blood due to HIV found in test-ing. The venue of this narrative varies, but the result is HIV found locally in epidemic numbers. Mike Royko, a Chicago newspaper columnist, reported a phone conversation that he had received from an elderly man. The man said:

> "I'm calling to give you a story about a very shocking and danger-ous situation that is being covered up by school officials in Hoff-man Estates. A volunteer blood drive was held at the Conant High School," the man continued. "It was for senior students only. Blood was given by 317 seniors. The blood has since been tested, and 61 tested positive for the HIV virus." (Royko 1992:C3)

Royko interviewed the principal of the school, who reported that 125 students and 37 teachers donated blood and none of the dona-tions had tested positive for HIV. The blood-drive rumor, however, continues to appear periodically in new locations. Barbara and Da-vid Mikkelson have reported the following:

> The rumor has raced through Chicago (1992, 20% of the stu-dents in one particular high school), Los Angeles (1992, 12%),

Dubuque (1996, "dozens of students"), Kansas City (1996, 15%), Orlando (1992, "dozens"), Seattle (1992, 15%), St. Petersburg (1991, 20%), Orange County, CA (1987, 14%), Sonoma County, CA (2001, 82%). (2001)

While most versions of the story show a fascination with numbers, similar narratives simply characterize the suggestion that the local community is the "AIDS capital of the World" or suggest that the "bloodmobile" was immediately removed from the neighborhood following testing (see chapter 6). Whatley and Henken reported that the numbers story circulated in Athens, Georgia, in 1996, claiming that 35 percent of donors at the student blood drive tested positive for HIV (2000:76).

While Whatley and Henken discuss the negative impact of the narrative and the resulting drop in blood donations, they also note that the narrative indicates positive recognition of the possibility of HIV in one's own group (2000:76). As Sobo and others have argued, the emphasis in early public-health messages on knowing your partner has helped to create the perception that it is safe to have sex with people you know because they are less likely to be infected (1995:30). Whatley and Henken suggest that the blood-drive narrative indicates a move away from the "stranger danger" notion that exposure is more likely outside the safety of your own community (2000:75–76).

In Newfoundland, the epidemic numbers story circulated with the added motif that initial samples from the school blood drive suggested so many positive donors that public-health officials were going to conduct house-to-house mandatory testing. The blood-drive and mandatory-testing narrative suggests links to another story found extensively in Newfoundland, either as a relatively undeveloped rumor or attached to other AIDS legends. Current AIDS narratives frequently feature mention of a list, either developed as a "hit list" in deliberate infection narratives or as a long list of sexual contacts given to public health by someone who tests positive. One of my colleagues wrote to me in 1989, for example,

[A]nother student had heard that there are "four girls down at the Sundance [a local popular bar] who have AIDS and that the police have compiled a list of contacts. . . . [She] made a gesture as if to say "long as your arm," as if she were rolling out a scroll.

The "List" narratives comment on excessive numbers of infected local individuals (similar to the blood drive) but also suggest fear that contact tracing might lead authorities to individuals too close to home for comfort. One narrator from a community near St. John's indicated,

> I know there was a girl from my community who was going to the doctor for an entire year and he was treating her for flu when finally he sent her for a blood test. The test showed that she had full blown AIDS. She was admitted to the hospital and two weeks later she died. It was going around that she gave fifty-four names of the men she slept with. There are also a few from my home town who people believe have the virus and are maybe even passing it on to their wives.

The "List" narratives carry with them not just the implication of large local numbers of infected individuals but also the added theme of those individuals being specifically named. The identification motif posits the frightening possibility that, correctly or not, one could find one's own name present on the list of infected individuals. Fear of identification on such a list mirrors larger anxieties about methods of medical epidemiological contact tracing, providing a vernacular critique of a practice that is seen to have the potential to "implicate" individuals on the basis of hearsay. Debates about epidemiological contact tracing have focused on this very concern—exploring how one should learn of one's serostatus and who has the right to discover someone else's. It is possible that list and naming anxieties, popular also in contemporary legends of crime "hit lists,"[14] suggest concerns parallel to classical notions of the possession of someone's name as having power over the individual. Being named on the list is life changing even if the identification is incorrect; one "becomes" HIV positive by implication whether or not one's serostatus or contact with the original individual

14.   These hit-list narratives are currently popular in the context of stories about school shootings. Following the Columbine shooting, numerous hit-list stories appeared in North American papers.

is confirmed. In this sense, in a small community, being named is nearly as frightening as being infected.

Conspiracy Theory

Conspiracy beliefs are widespread in medical folklore and are rife throughout the subgenre of AIDS legends. The traditions articulate the distrust of government and medical officials that underlie lay responses to the AIDS crisis. The narratives implicate the government, the CIA, scientists, and medical researchers in a variety of AIDS cover-ups largely linked to targeted genocide. Conspiracy narratives suggest that government created or nurtured the AIDS virus to control "undesirable" populations: the poor, people of color, homosexuals, drug users, prisoners, and other marginalized communities. Conspiracy theories suggest that government was responsible for the origin of AIDS (that it was man-made in laboratories, accidently created through government mishandling of vaccines, or created in a government experiment in biological warfare), that transmission vectors are hidden in the daily life of targeted populations (contaminating particular ethnic foods or certain neighborhood food establishments or sprinkled contaminants on the floor of gay bathhouses), and that there are known cures that government refuses to release (because the virus is so efficiently wiping out minority and undesirable populations).

Patricia Turner quotes a typical articulation of AIDS conspiracy belief from an African American/Seminole woman, who reported,

> The story was told to me by an aunt. Apparently the CIA was testing to find a disease which would resist any cures known to man. They did this testing somewhere in [South] Africa. The purpose of finding this incurable disease was to bring America back to the old days of the moral majority. Therefore this disease was to be transmitted sexually among the outcasts of society, namely people of color and gay men. (Turner 1993:159)

The conspiracy theory of AIDS origins is particularly popular in Africa and Haiti, forming a cultural critique of the industrialized West and, as Paul Farmer (1992) argues, a counterprotest of those who themselves have been accused of introducing AIDS to the United States. As Paula Treichler notes,

The notion that AIDS is an American invention is a recurrent element in the international AIDS story, yet one not easily incorporated within a Western positivist frame, in part, perhaps, because it is political, with discursive roots in the resistance to colonialism; the Western response, accordingly, attributes it to ignorance, state propaganda, or psychological denial. (Treichler 1989:43)

Treichler's comments reflect the Western political discursive tradition but not the extent of conspiracy belief in North American *vernacular* tradition. In North America, like in Africa and Haiti, conspiracy theory appears to also be most often reported among those communities regularly "blamed" for the disease. Ethnographies, particularly of African American AIDS traditions, suggest that notions of government and medical origins or cover-ups have a significant hold in popular belief. Less work has been done exploring the extent to which AIDS conspiracy beliefs are held within the general North American population. Recent surveys, discussed in the next chapter, suggest a more widespread sense of distrust along with the perception that AIDS conspiracies are at least possible in the current medical and political climate.

Because blame is ever present in epidemic and health crisis situations, it is not surprising that conspiracy beliefs arise as a counterattack from those who feel disempowered in general, but even more significantly in the face of such blame. It is important, however, that counterattack theory not lead analysts to be dismissive of conspiratorial thinking as simply a mechanism of defense. Conspiracy theories point to areas of vernacular concern and highlight basic notions of distrust, the identification of inequalities in the system, and areas of clash in medical worldviews. Paul Farmer suggests reading conspiracy theories with what he calls "a hermeneutic of generosity":

What might happen if we were to insist that such commentary is worthy of investigation? What might happen if we were to proceed as if our informants were themselves experts in a moral reading of the ills that afflict them? What follows is an attempt to extend a "hermeneutic of generosity" to the very notions dismissed as paranoid rubbish by the experts. Such an exercise leads us once again to an interpretive analysis accountable to history and political economy, the force field from which the conspiracy theories initially rose. (Farmer 1992:235)

Farmer's hermeneutic of generosity captures the spirit in which the following chapters were written. Each case study attempts to address the concerns and ideology behind the narrative, focusing on the AIDS legend as an articulation of vernacular perceptions of risk. First, however, it is important to explore risk and notions of vernacular perception as they are understood by health educators, public health researchers, and social scientists. It is to that task that we turn next.

3

Making Sense

Narrative and the Development of Culturally Appropriate Health Education

Lazzaro Timmo, a Tanzanian journalist, reported one day observing a thirty-five-year-old Waarusha man reading a poster explaining that to avoid infection with HIV one should "have sex with only one faithful partner." The man burst into laughter. "What am I going to do with my other wives?" he asked. Timmo noted that the man had three wives and was thinking about marrying a fourth if the harvest was good the following season. He commented, "To tell . . . [him] to relate to only one faithful partner is like telling him to get rid of his other wives, who are his source of wealth and prestige" (Timmo 1988:125–126).

Timmo's story is an example of a health education campaign gone terribly wrong. The one faithful partner recommendation makes no sense as a campaign theme in parts of Africa where polygamy is an accepted and perhaps even an expected part of traditional culture.[1] The campaign that Timmo commented on was an artifact of the mid-1980s. Since that time health educators have learned a great deal about the need for developing culturally appropriate and culturally sensitive health education. Today, most health educators would agree that educational campaigns must include unambiguous information that addresses local issues and is presented in a culturally sensitive fashion. There is general agreement that we must

---

1. Other African campaigns took polygamous culture into account through themes such as "graze at home" in Kenya and "love carefully" in Uganda.

recognize cultural, political, geographic, and economic barriers to behavior change (whether generally understood or perceived) and be aware of norms and values that sanction high-risk activities and that present real risks[2] to individuals and to the community. Ultimately, most health educators would agree that health education campaigns must suggest real alternatives to high-risk behaviors, alternatives that make good cultural sense as well as good public-health sense.

Culturally sensitive health education must adapt itself to the existing beliefs, attitudes, and practices within a community rather than expect that the community will change to fit the educational program. The issue is not one of style or pedagogical philosophy but rather basic pragmatism. As Ronald Bayer notes,

> In short, AIDS prevention efforts that are not culturally sensitive will be ineffective. They will fail to promote, support and sustain the behavioral modifications that are the *sine qua non* of AIDS prevention. They will fail because they will not reach their intended audience, will not be understood by those who are reached, and will not be accepted by those who understand. They may indeed provoke outright opposition. (1995:20)

The nod toward cultural sensitivity in health education, while being emphasized with the best of intentions, has not been unproblematic. Critics of these programs note that they are often based on stereotypes of the communities in question or are dependent on overgeneralized and badly contextualized cultural information (Goldstein 2001). Critics have also been concerned about the reinforcement of heterosexism as normative in programs designed to be culturally sensitive (Patton 1996:114) and about the absence of subgroup-specific cultural materials (Stevenson, Gay, and Josar 1995). Many of the concerns about the cultural movement in health education refer to the search for linguistic equivalencies, where intimate language comes under scrutiny and sexual vernaculars are coopted and turned back on the community in the form of "folksy"

---

2.   What is meant by "real risks" here is risks that actually provide a health threat for the individual or community rather than risks that are merely assumed by virtue of cultural bias or a lack of cultural knowledge. As Timmo notes, "Where no one in a polygamous sexual unit is already infected with HIV, grazing at home is every bit as safe with two or three wives (or husbands) as with one. . . . And if one or more individuals within the unit are already infected, grazing at home will at least confine the infection to that unit" (Timmo 1988:127).

explicit campaigns that have only negative impacts, both internally and externally (Patton 1996:142–147).[3] Other critics have argued that guidelines for evaluating materials designed for cultural responsiveness have been lacking (Walters, Canady, and Stein 1994).

Ultimately though, health educators and AIDS activists know that cultural concerns must form the center of any educational or intervention effort if it is to be successful. Ideally, health education programs should be community based, involving collaborative partnerships between communities, researchers, and service providers. Projects that involve such collaborations are able to redirect outsider misinterpretations, identify community subgroups and hidden or hard-to-reach populations, recognize significant issues and behavioral patterns, strategize culture-appropriate mobilization, and localize support infrastructures. Even within collaborative projects, however, the need is increasingly clear for the skills of trained ethnographers. Since community members themselves are only ever partial members of the dynamic group—never fully representing all its knowledges and concerns—the need remains for qualitative research methodologies that can be more fully representative and provide a degree of critical distance. As Joseph Kotarba, editor of a special issue of the *Journal of Contemporary Ethnography* on "Ethnography and AIDS," wrote,

> Of the major social and medical problems to appear in the past 10 years, including abortion rights, homelessness, the environment and crime, AIDS more than any other issue occasioned the application of ethnographic strategies to both policy and basic research. The study of AIDS not only demonstrates ethnography's particular ability to describe in elegant detail the ways by which people make sense of and cope with everyday life and its problems, but provides the occasion for refining ethnographic techniques and technologies. (1990:260)

From the outset of the AIDS epidemic, ethnographers have worked actively at applying their research skills to exploring settings and activities believed to be significant to the transmission of HIV

3. In earlier publications I myself have argued for the cooptation of sexual vernaculars (Goldstein 1991, 1993). I since regret taking this stand. As Patton notes, "mere imitation or reproduction of a vernacular will not suffice; it may even be a dangerously subtle cultural imperialism. . . . If comprehended at all, most sexual vernaculars are offensive or embarrassing to those for whom it is not a native tongue" (Patton 1996:146).

but about which little was known. Ethnographers explored every-thing from the culture of intravenous drug use and "shooting gal-leries," where knowledge of the culture could illuminate possible solutions to the development of safer injection practices (see, for ex-ample, Des Jarlais, Friedman and Strug 1986; Fox 1991; Broadhead, Heckathorn, Grund, Stern, and Anthony 1995), to ethnographies of sexual choices and motivations used to explore unsafe sexual prac-tices (see, for example, Sobo, Zimet, Zimmerman, and Cecil 1997; Lear 1995; Sobo 1993; Parker and Carballo 1990; Tarr and Aggle-ton 1999; Adam, Sears, and Schellenberg 2000).

Ethnography clearly went beyond more typical knowledge, atti-tude, belief, and behavior studies (KABB[4] studies), which were largely quantitative in nature and which, while supplying useful statistical data, left great gaps in our understandings of deeper symbolic mean-ings and the reasons behind practices related to HIV/AIDS. KABB studies were aimed at producing scientifically valid data that would explore social determinants and variables serving as predictors of con-dom use, needle sharing, sex with multiple partners, and such, or that would illuminate target areas for AIDS education. Most of these stud-ies were heavily dependent on questionnaires, continually refined and modified according to the results of complex pilot studies and presur-vey focus groups. The studies would survey, for example, sources of HIV information, accurate and inaccurate belief in forms of transmis-sion, beliefs about condom use, awareness of personal risks, and so forth. Many KABB studies were refined to be context and culture spe-cific, creating regional and subgroup versions of international ques-tionnaires and resulting in statistical data on knowledge, beliefs, and behaviors among, for example, Chinese adolescents in Hong Kong (Davis, Noel, Chan, and Wing 1998), female Mexican migrant farm-workers (Organista, Organista, and Soloff 1998), university students in Delhi, India (Sachdev 1998), and medical school students in the urban midwestern United States (Chavis and Norman 1995).

Fact vs. Behavior

Quantitative studies told us repeatedly that AIDS education, per se, was working–at least in the sense of developing widespread high

---

4.   Also known as KAB (without behaviors) and KAP (using practices instead of behaviors).

levels of AIDS knowledge. Questionnaire data and public information polls administered in a variety of countries and among a variety of subgroups appeared to reveal relatively consistently that surprisingly high numbers of respondents were knowledgeable about the major modes of human immunodeficiency virus transmission (see, for example, Organista, Organista, and Soloff 1998; Sachdev 1998; Davis, Noel, Chan, and Wing 1998).[5] But knowledge, attitude, belief, and behavior surveys also indicated that, as the AIDS epidemic entered its second decade, AIDS-related behaviors continued much as they had before the epidemic.

The Bureau of HIV/AIDS Health Canada (1999) and the 1992 American National Health Interview Survey (Schoenborn, Marsh, and Hardy 1994) found that 94 percent to 96 percent of Canadian and American adults know that HIV can be transmitted through sexual intercourse with an infected partner, from pregnant women to their babies perinatally, and by needle sharing with an infected individual. Similar statistics indicate that a vast majority of Canadians and Americans possess reasonably accurate information on risk reduction, particularly in relation to the practice of safe sex and blood precautions. Nevertheless, only 13 percent of Canadians report that they have changed their behavior because of AIDS, and Bureau of HIV statistics indicate that among Canadian sexually active fifteen- to nineteen-year-olds, 51 percent of females and 29 percent of males reported never using a condom in the past year (Bureau 1999). And as Sobo notes concerning the American situation,

> most studies conclude that no significant relationship exists between safer sex and the degree of AIDS or HIV knowledge people have . . . ; behavioral changes made by homosexual men . . . living in areas with firmly established gay social and political structures

5.   Demographic and Health Survey reports from UNICEF for 1994 through 1999 show an enormous information gap in parts of Africa, Asia, and Central America. Their data indicate, for example, that 96 percent of females and 88 percent of males in the fifteen to nineteen age group in Bangladesh reported that they did *not* know any way to protect themselves against HIV/AIDS. In Mozambique, 74 percent of females and 62 percent of males reported the same lack of information. Several of the countries reported in the UNICEF data have been surveyed with very different results than those found in the KABB studies. Proper analysis of these differences would require a close look at the type of questions posed, how those questions were articulated, how they might have been interpreted, and so forth. Nevertheless, the UNICEF study should serve to remind us that availability of information and rights to information do differ significantly from group to group and country to country.

are the exception. But even among this group patterns of relapse
have been documented. Factual information is necessary, but it
is certainly not sufficient to drive and sustain behavioral change.
(Sobo 1995:25)

AIDS facts appear to be well known in North America and easily
repeated in response to survey questions but not so easily acted upon.
A number of explanations have been suggested for this apparent in-
consistency, but none is intended to represent the entire spectrum
of behavioral motivations. Numerous studies have demonstrated
that while respondents are able to accurately repeat facts related
to transmission risk factors and protective actions, they simultaneously report inaccurate lay beliefs, sometimes referred to as "older"
health beliefs (Kimmel and Keefer 1991; Sobo 1993; Sobo, Zimet,
Zimmerman, and Cecil 1997; Herek and Capitanio 1994). Fear of
public toilets, shared drinking glasses, giving blood, mosquitoes,
and door handles appear to coexist comfortably with more accurate
knowledge of transmission factors. Social scientists tend to favor a
survivalist notion of why these beliefs continue to be held, arguing
that they involve "primitive" thinking involving ideas of "magical
contagion" and that individuals will hold beliefs concerning magical
contagion despite the fact that these beliefs make no logical sense
even to the individual in question (Nemeroff, Brinkman, and Woodward 1994).[6] Some authors have suggested that these "older beliefs"
support risky action, even when they are held simultaneously with
accurate information about AIDS (Sobo, Zimet, Zimmerman, and
Cecil 1997; Nicoll et al. 1993). Without further support, however,
this argument is untenable. Fears of public toilets, shared drinking
glasses, giving blood, mosquitoes, and door handles, while incorrect and problematic in terms of understanding the virus and treatment of people with AIDS, are not in and of themselves beliefs that
contradict the need for safer sex or blood precautions.[7] It is hard

---

6.   The assumption that beliefs that are illogical to AIDS educators are therefore also
      illogical to those who hold those beliefs is ethnocentric at best. Analysts should
      always begin with the assumption that such beliefs are logical and rational in terms
      of the larger belief system of the individual involved. While it is possible that
      individuals will hold illogical beliefs, it is more likely that the investigator simply
      does not understand the believer's context and system of reasoning. See O'Connor
      (1995) and Hufford (1982; 1984; 1991) for discussions of this issue.
7.   This is not to say that beliefs that threaten protective practices don't exist. The
      belief, for example, that condoms are deliberately impregnated with HIV during

to see, without further ethnographic information, how any of these beliefs support risky action if they truly are accompanied by accurate knowledge of the main transmission factors and protective practices. It is important, if we are to understand lay health belief, that it not be interpreted a priori as a threat to health safety, unless it presents a real obstacle. Of course, the problem is that clearly *something* is presenting that obstacle, and that *something* seems to elude the grasp of AIDS educators. The real concern about the coexistence of inaccurate lay health beliefs with high levels of reportable correct knowledge should be that it suggests a larger health worldview that educators are not understanding.

Many AIDS educators suspect that the resilience of certain inaccurate lay beliefs about transmission vectors is a result of early epidemiological confusion that associated risk factors with risky populations (Patton 1996); that publically identified mistaken sources for the disease, which then had to be recanted (such as the use of "poppers"); and that failed to clarify why some modes of body fluid exchange were riskier than other modes (Sobo 1995:27).[8] Many of the erroneous beliefs retained together with accurate knowledge of transmission factors would appear nearly counterintuitive to discount. Anyone, for example, who has crushed a mosquito and detected how much blood the small insect can contain would wonder about its potential as an effective transmitter (Nicoll et al. 1993:231). Common sense would argue that if small amounts of HIV are detectable in mosquito blood or saliva, the insect should also be able to transmit the virus. Similar commonsense arguments could be made for beliefs about the retention of saliva on drinking glasses and toothbrushes. Issues of quantity and magnitude of the detectable

---

manufacture would dissuade the believer from condom use and thus provide a real basis for concern. My point here is that some beliefs present more of a problem than others. Of course, beliefs that result in negative attitudes toward people with AIDS, blood donation, and so forth present a different problem but *not* one that (on the surface) explains nonprotective choices.

8. The absence of information from official sources creates a risk-information vacuum. As Powell and Leiss note, "Society as well as nature abhors a vacuum, and so it is filled from other sources. For example, events reported in the media (some of them alarming) become the substantial basis of the public framing of these risks; or an interest group takes up the challenge and fills the vacuum with its own information and perspectives; or the intuitively based fears and concerns of individuals simply grow and spread until they become a substantial consensus in the area of public opinion; or the vacuum is filled by the soothing expressions beloved of politicians: "There is no risk of . . . . [fill in the blank]." (1997:31)

virus needed for efficient transmission have presented continuous
problems with alternate vector beliefs.

A significant number of AIDS studies, particularly concerning
African American and Hispanic communities, suggest that the sur-
vival of "older" AIDS beliefs may be tied to mistrust of health experts (Thomas and Quinn 1991; Herek and Capitanio 1994; Smith
1996; and others). Conspiracy theories about government targeting
of specific communities for annihilation, holding back of existing
drugs and vaccines, dishonesty about the dangers of casual contact,
information kept from the public, and policing of sexuality and drug
practices appear to be common—particularly in communities that
are disenfranchised. Numerous superb ethnographies have demonstrated the centrality of conspiracy beliefs to understandings of
AIDS in subaltern communities (Farmer 1992; Turner 1993; Sobo
1995). Quantitative studies suggest that distrust of AIDS experts is
widespread, with one survey (conducted by the Southern Christian
Leadership Conference of 1,056 church members in five cities in the
United States) finding that 35 percent of the respondents believed
that AIDS is a form of genocide, 37 were unsure whether AIDS was
genocide or not, 44 percent believed the government is not telling the truth about AIDS, and 34 percent believed that AIDS is a
man-made virus (Thomas and Quinn 1991).[9] Other studies revealed
similar numbers with nearly all who surveyed this issue indicating
that their findings demonstrate considerable mistrust related to
HIV/AIDS, particularly among youth and minority communities.[10]

The preponderance of AIDS conspiracy theories and expressions of mistrust has a direct relationship to safe sex and safe injection practices. Where there is a lack of trust in experts linked to
the epidemic, there will be a lack of compliance. But the expressions of mistrust, the reporting of nonuse of protective measures
despite accurate knowledge of transmission vehicles, and on some
level, the continued signs of externalizing health beliefs point to

9.   The legacy of the Tuskegee syphilis study is evident here. From 1932 until 1972, 400
        southern African Americans infected with syphilis were deliberately left untreated
        to allow scientists to monitor the progression of the illness. This study stands out
        as a horrific example of inhumanity and racism for the sake of "research" (see also
        Stevenson 1994:72).

10.   Some studies have suggested that mistrust of experts related to AIDS exists at
        the same rate throughout the entire population. Herek and Capitanio found, for
        example, that 44.5 percent of the white population in their survey also expressed
        distrust.

problems in risk perception and an inability to internalize personal vulnerability.

Risk Perception

Over the last sixty years health educators and social psychologists have designed a number of different models in the hope of explaining or predicting how health choices are made by members of the lay community. Models designed to predict health-related behaviors, such as the Health Belief Model, the Theory of Reasoned Action, and the AIDS Risk Reduction Model, all emphasize that perceived susceptibility is a key variable in health decision making. Each of these models posits a process by which behavior change is thought to occur in the cognition and lives of "normal" individuals.

The Health Belief Model was developed in the 1950s by social psychologists involved in the U.S. Public Health Service to explain the lack of public participation in tuberculosis-screening projects. The model attempts to predict health behaviors by focusing on the beliefs of individuals faced with a series of health choices. The model suggests six[11] variables that come into play as health choices are contemplated: perceived susceptibility to health threats, perceived severity of the health condition, perceived benefits of strategies to reduce the threat, perceived barriers to taking action, cues that motivate individuals to take action, and demographic and structural variables that affect decision making. Application of the Health Belief Model in a number of studies identified perceived barriers to taking health action as the most significant variable, with perceived severity of the health condition identified as the least significant motivator in health-related behaviors (Janz and Becker 1984). The Health Belief Model—although rife with limitations—was, in many ways, quite forward thinking for its time, particularly in its recognition of the importance of individual beliefs and perceptions as crucial to health choices and actions. The model does not, however, provide guidance in identifying the reasons for variety in the ways that individuals evaluate the potential consequences of their behavior.

The Theory of Reasoned Action, developed by Ajzen and Fishbein in 1980 as a general theory of behavior, is predicated on the

11. Some assess the model as consisting of five variables by collapsing the final two into perceived ability to perform the task. (See, for example, Vanlandingham et al. 1995:196.)

notion that humans are rational and that their behaviors are under volitional control. According to the Theory of Reasoned Action, behaviors arise from intention, and intention is influenced by a set of attitudes along with a set of perceptions about group norms concerning the behavior. The theory links beliefs, attitudes, intentions, behaviors, and norms in a linear process that essentially argues that changes in an individual's behavioral beliefs (beliefs regarding outcomes) and normative beliefs (beliefs regarding other people's views of a behavior) will ultimately affect the individual's behavior change. The model is praised for its inclusion of peer influences on behavior, previously left out of the Health Belief Model (Vanlandingham et al. 1995:198). The Theory of Reasoned Action, however, is frequently criticized for its intentionality and for its linearity, which insists that changes in beliefs and attitudes must precede changes in behavior. Critics of the theory have pointed out, for example, that studies of seatbelt behaviors found that negative attitudes about seatbelts changed as individuals grew accustomed to using them (Kippax and Crawford 1993).

The AIDS Risk Reduction Model was first introduced in 1990 as a framework for predicting individual behavior change regarding sexual transmission of HIV/AIDS (Catina, Kegeles, and Coates 1990). The Risk Reduction Model incorporates variables from the other two behavior-change theories into a three-stage model. The three stages include (1) recognition of one's behavior as high risk; (2) making a commitment to reduce high-risk sexual contacts and to increase low-risk activities; and (3) taking action, including information seeking, obtaining remedies, and enacting solutions. In addition to the three stages, the model suggests influences that move the individual through each stage (for example, stage one includes knowledge of sexual activities associated with AIDS, belief that one is personally susceptible, belief that AIDS is undesirable, and social norms and networking). The AIDS Risk Reduction Model, while generally understood as a useful framework for designing interventions to reduce sexual behavior, is also criticized for not taking adequate account of the social influences that limit individual behavior choices (Denison 1999; McGrath et al. 1993).

Ramos, Shain, and Johnson (1995:499) argue, concerning the AIDS Risk Reduction Model, that "although this model makes intuitive sense, it does not provide an understanding of how to accomplish its goals." This comment is easily applicable to all three behavioral-change models and captures the commonly held feeling that all three are more appropriately described as conceptual frameworks for thinking about illness behaviors rather than as actual "models" (Fitzpatrick et al. 1984). While the models give us a means to begin to think about the variables involved in decision making and change, they serve only as templates for information that we know is elusive, and they do not give us any idea of how much weight to attach to each of the variables. The problem is, as Byron Good notes, that the health behavior models don't really reflect "real world decision processes" (1994). The models ultimately are too synthetic in their view of "the value maximizing individual, responding adaptively to disease, selecting among a stable set of choices, and motivated by a set of meanings external to the subject" (Good 1994:44). Behavior change models construct the individual as, in Good's terms, "a universal economic man, proceeding . . . toward the goal of positive health, a preference only slightly modified by health beliefs" (1994:42). The fundamental rationality of behavior depicted in the Health Belief Model has been attractive to folklorists, who have long argued that vernacular health choices are not ipso facto irrational (see Hufford 1984; O'Connor 1995). But the models appear to work better in this regard and not as they have been applied to behavioral change. In the behavioral-change application, all three models become mechanical descriptors of what are considered "normative" decision-making processes.[12] As normative, rather than descriptive, models, they depict us all as autonomous health seekers—free to make what are seen as the "right" choices and needing just a bit of a shove to be oriented like any "rational" person toward the obvious steps leading to the obvious goals. So what, then, of the woman who dares not suggest her partner use a condom because she knows that he will interpret her request as a comment on his (or her) sexual history and the discussion will end in physical violence? In the risk-benefit ratio that is so central to

---

12. Folklorists have read the Health Belief Model as an open model that "can be applied within any health belief framework and set into any cultural background, to assess how a given individual understands health or illness circumstances and how health behaviors follow from this understanding" (O'Connor 1995:31). The inclusion of perceived benefits and barriers and other aspects related to perception does suggest cultural openness. In behavioral-change psychology, however, the model is applied as a closed model, oriented toward moving the individual from one set of choices to another set of choices in as economic a means as possible. In this latter sense, the three models offer little guidance and continually frustrate health educators. In some sense, the models are both too open and too closed for this endeavor.

behavioral models, it is unlikely that protection against AIDS will ever weigh in as a benefit, when the perceived barrier is a black eye and a couple of broken bones. The problem with these models when used as behavior change models is that they are compliance models, oriented toward correcting wrongness—wrong beliefs and wrong behaviors—but they treat those "wrongnesses" as though they are singular and self-evident and as though they exist in isolation. Such an orientation destroys the notion of choice and yet simultaneously raises it to an unachievable stature.

In the behavior change calculation, risk is seen as having a consistent shape and a limited set of meanings, and "risk perception" is understood as concerned with a single "objective" form of risk. But, as the woman described above will tell us, the world is full of risks that have to be assessed, not only in relation to themselves, but also in relation to a multitude of other events and issues.[13] In part, the problem with risk-reduction models is a problem with the erosion of the term "risk" over time. As Mary Douglas notes,

> 'Risk' is the probability of an event combined with the magnitude of the losses and gains that it will entail. However, our political discourse debases the word. From a complex attempt to reduce uncertainty it has become a decorative flourish on the word 'danger.' (1992:40)

The sense of risk activities as associated with danger distances the notion from issues of cultural understanding involved in the weighing of gains and losses used in personal risk assessments. Risk activities (translated in Douglas's terms as "danger") tend to be seen in institutional terms as generalized, predetermined, and unquestionable. Richard Stoffle and his colleagues, in writing about environmental risks, discuss this institutional imposition of definition:

> Often, the specialists who conduct these assessments believe their estimates reflect the "real risks" of a technology or project because the estimates derive from scientific calculations. These "real risks" typically are presented through formal processes, such as public meetings, in which information flows one way, from risk

---

13.   Stephanie Kane argues that one of the four central characteristics of risk is that risks are link..d to each other and to non-health-related phenomena (1993:227).

communicator to the public with little or no exchange of information between the two groups. (1991:612)

The emphasis on "real risk activities" as predetermined areas of danger frames risk assessment in externally defined values and concerns, leaving locally defined concerns out of the picture. Risk assessments, on the other hand, that are based on local criteria focus on risk as it is perceived and evaluated by the lay public. The tendency to ignore perceived risk as a valid component in the assessment of risk is based on the notion that perceived risks are neither objective nor scientifically derived—a position that hardly matters if the party one is trying to motivate does not care about or trust either of those criteria. While it is clear that the Health Belief Model and other predictors of behavior change have tried to account for risk perception by focusing on perceived susceptibility, perceived severity, perceived benefits and barriers, they still assume that the object of those variables is a single constellation of factors that represents an objective thing (self-evident and devoid of ideological content) that we can call "risk." But understanding attitudes toward susceptibility is dependent on understanding the variety of cultural issues and influences that constitute risk *for the communities and individuals in question*. The following observation concerning sex-workers' risk behaviors should immediately tell us not only that generalized risk categories can themselves be culture bound, political, and moralistic but also that risk perception is multifaceted and complex.

> Evaluation of sex worker risk reduction projects suggest that women who sell sex are more likely to adopt prevention measures (especially condom use or avoidance of intercourse) than are women who simply have sex in the context of recreation, love, or other socially condoned sexual arrangements. But the strong separation between sex for hire and sex for 'love' also results in a bifurcation of sex workers' risk reduction strategies. Women who sell sex are more likely to engage in prevention behaviors while having sex in the context of 'work' than in their domestic relationships. Several studies also show that condom use tapers off as a sex worker establishes a regular relationship with a client. Sex has a range of symbolic meanings and use of preventative measures also has symbolic meanings: apparently, the better one knows a partner—paying or

not—the less appropriate it seems to enforce condom use. (Patton 1994:53)

The real problem is in trying to understand what risks look like to those who take them and in trying to understand the criteria that communities and individuals use to assess susceptibility. As Sobo notes, research on risk perception suggests that the meanings associated with a given risk affect how individuals "personalize, internalize and apply to themselves the information they receive about that risk" (1995:33).

In discussing risk management in relation to a series of case studies including E. coli, mad cow disease, silicone breast implants, and other high-profile risk-management controversies, Powell and Leiss note that good risk communication, focused on public perception of risk, seeks to

> 1. Understand the public's "framing" of the risk issue, especially in qualitative dimensions; 2. Acknowledge the specific questions that arise in this domain (which may be, and often are, quite different from those posed by experts); [and] 3. Analyze the conditions needed for allowing the public to acquire needed information, skills and participatory opportunities. (1997:30)

Management and marketing efforts focusing on purely persuasive techniques of risk reduction must be replaced with new ways of listening and responding to lay perceptions of the situation, if they are to be at all effective.[14]

Health Belief, Vernacular Theory, and Behavior Change

One of the issues that is most problematic in the behavior change paradigm of risk management is an underlying attitude that the concern with lay or public health belief and risk perception can

---

14.   The risk-perception model presumes a high degree of agency in the practice of AIDS risk reduction. Some AIDS scholars have favored a model closer to that of the universal precautions used in health care because that model was not dependent on identifying and persuading specific individuals or groups that they are at risk in specific situations. Compliance with universal precautions tends to be extremely high (80 percent is reported in surveys of nurses) regardless of perceived risk. At the beginning of the AIDS epidemic, however, health educators favored a risk-based strategy over a population-wide strategy, emphasizing risk groups and "choose carefully" campaigns (Patton 1996:160). The result is our current struggle with risk perception.

go only so far before it will be incumbent on health experts to *correct* public perception, assert the *real* dangers associated with specific activities, and *manage* behavior change. This assumption is linked to the equation of risk assessment with scientific and technological "truth" and risk perception with "false" understanding. As David Hufford notes in connection to academic treatment of folk belief, the implicit attitude is "what I know, I know; what you know, you only believe" (Hufford 1982:47). This "arrogance of technical expertise," as Powell and Leiss call it (1997:35), varies in its expression from open articulation of contempt for the lay public to the zealous and sincere defense of passionately felt concerns about public danger. While the latter is at least backed by an overwhelming concern for the public good, both perspectives demonstrate an impatience with a public seen as noncompliant and, by definition, unsophisticated in its evaluation of risk realities. Like other compliance models, attitudes of risk experts toward public risk perception and lay decision making arrange themselves along an authoritarian/democratic continuum with ideological concerns expressed as the need for, at one end, obedience and adherence and, at the other end, cooperation and collaboration. But, as Bonnie O'Connor comments concerning patient education,

> Patients to be educated are often assumed to be "empty vessels" who, in the absence of medically accepted knowledge about health and illness, are assumed to have *no* knowledge about them as a basis for making choices or taking action. . . . The conception of patient education thus frequently operates on the basis of an extremely simplistic view of its mission: "communicate successfully with people so they will understand their health problems (usually as we, not they, define them) and they will want to change their behavior. . . ." When the proposed changes do not occur, or when they come about very slowly, the cause is generally interpreted as "resistance to change" and defined as a "problem" which is located in the "target population." (1995:177)

O'Connor continues by noting that this model omits the "actualities of patients: their circumstances, experiences, worldview, knowledge, values, self-perceived needs, and their agency in responding to these" (177). Assumptions made by risk theorists have tended to mirror those noted by O'Connor in relation to patient education, treating the members of an educational target population as though past and present sexual, social, and health experiences, cultural associations, social contexts, influences, and knowledge have no significant bearing on health decision making. The notion that individuals have "expert knowledge" in their own cultural milieu is not a comfortable notion for health educators trained in a compliance, information-dissemination model. Nevertheless, most individuals, if asked, can provide clear, and sometimes quite sensible, "explanatory models" (Kleinman 1975) for how they arrived at health choices.

The task of risk-perception theorists is to uncover the cultural assumptions that dominate both within health education and within individual cultural contexts. For example, as Calnan (1987) and others have shown, lay health-belief systems tend to place high value on subjective experience and focus heavily on ability to function and social well-being as evidenced by physical fitness, energy, vitality, absence of pain, feeling healthy, and the ability to maintain social relationships. This contrasts with the biomedical valuing of objective experience over the subjective and the emphasis placed in Western biomedical paradigms on health as the absence of disease and the appropriate functioning of biological and psychophysiological process. These contrasting characteristics of health belief systems are reflected in risk perception in terms of the following: issues of immediate and ultimate causes of illness and the identification of risk; what counts as evidence of risk and standards of credibility for risk managers; what degree of risk is acceptable, normative, or even desirable; whether or not one combats risk once located and how; what type of information is needed and how information is appropriately obtained; and what are seen as acceptable alternatives to activities internally identified as risky.

While it is tempting to create a dichotomy in which all medical researchers, scientists, and health educators understand the world through biomedical paradigms and all nonmedical and nonacademic individuals become the "folk," understanding the world through lay health paradigms, the formula is misleading. Although lay models of health and illness tend to differ from biomedical models, this does not necessarily mean that physicians, medical researchers, or health educators hold strictly to medical models. As Lock (1982) has shown in an examination of gynecologists' approaches to menopause, practicing physicians' views are based on a melding of folk, as well as textbook, concepts. According to Lock, the combining of views assists physicians in dealing with the practical interactive aspects of their clinical work. A similar combination of lay and medical concepts can be found in explorations of risk assessment among physicians. Numerous studies have highlighted pervasive fears of HIV exposure and transmission among health-care workers, associated with stated intentions to leave the medical field. Heath, Acklin, and Wiley note that these fears are "often bordering on hysteria, exist[ing] despite the reportedly low percentage of patients who are seropositive (three percent . . .) and the even lower incidence of seroconversion following a single exposure (estimated by the Center for Disease Control at one percent upper confidence boundary following needle puncture exposure)" (1991:1860). Heath and her coauthors argue, based on these observations, that "although such fears are understandable given the horror of the disease, biases and distortions in the risk assessment process might be leading those at comparatively low risk to be excessively fearful" (1991:1860). It is likely that in most areas of health, both patients and physicians hold a variety of lay and conventional ideas, ideas that can play a significant role in risk assessment and response. For this reason, understanding lay risk models is crucial, not just to the ability of health educators to reduce risk-taking behavior in the general population, but also to understanding attitudes toward risk at the very core of health care.

The ability of analysts to gain access to lay risk models is dependent on their ability to sacrifice the mind-set that "theories" can be held only by a certain intellectual elite. Useful in this regard, both for social science perspectives and for changing paradigms in health education, is the notion of "vernacular theory," initially coined by Houston Baker in his book *Blues, Ideology, and African American Literature: A Vernacular Theory* and elaborated by Thomas McLaughlin in *Street Smarts and Critical Theory: Listening to the Vernacular*. The term "vernacular" has been used for some time to refer to community-based forms of cultural expression, such as vernacular architecture, vernacular design, and vernacular language. The sense in which vernacular is meant here, however, goes a little bit further than community-based expression, following on McLaughlin's contrast of "vernacular theory" with "critical theory." McLaughlin defines vernacular theory in this way:

> It refers to the practices of those who lack cultural power and who speak a critical language grounded in social concerns, not

the language spoken by academic knowledge elites. They do not make use of the language of analytical strategies of academic theory: they devise a language and strategy appropriate to their own concerns. And they arise out of intensely local issues that lead to fundamental theoretical questions. (McLaughlin 1996:5–6)

Vernacular theory can be seen as parallel to Michel Foucault's notion of "subjugated knowledges." Foucault notes, "A subjugated knowledge is an autonomous, non-centralized kind of theoretical production, one . . . whose validity is not dependent on the approval of established regimes of thought" (1980:81). These knowledges, according to Foucault, "have been disqualified as inadequate to their task or insufficiently elaborated: naive knowledges, located low down on the hierarchy, beneath the required level of cognition or scientificity" (1980:81). Foucault contrasts these knowledges with what he calls "the tyranny of globalizing discourses" (1980:83). Popular culture theorist John Fiske contrasts a similar notion, which he calls "localizing knowledges," to the "imperializing knowledges" of dominant culture (1993:19). He argues that localizing knowledges

> function not to extend a great vision over the world but to produce a localized social, ethnic, communal sense of identity. They create cultures of practice, ones that develop ways of living in the world and which seek to control only those ways of living rather than the world in which they live. (1993:19)

While Fiske's comments appear to sell short the potential for proactive vernacular response, he nevertheless stresses the immediate and quotidian nature of local knowledge in a way that mirrors McLaughlin's sense of vernacular theory.

Vernacular theory is useful to the understanding of risk perception in that, like ethnoscience, ethnomethodology,[15] standpoint feminism, and a number of other social-scientific frameworks, it accepts local voices and native expertise as the starting point of analysis. Vernacular theory as applied to risk perception reminds us that

---

15. Ramos, Shain, and Johnson apply ethnomethodology to risk perception in their study "Men I Mess With Don't Have Anything to Do with AIDS: Using Ethnotheory to Understand Sexual Risk Perception" (1995).

1. the authority of experience is frequently weighed as superior to "objective" information in individual and cultural analysis defining risk;
2. shared experience creates observable *patterns* identified by community members as a basis for risk theory (in a process clearly identifiable as a kind of folk surveillance or folk epidemiology);
3. vernacular theory provides an experientially based, alternative construction of risk, which, while subjugated in terms of medical authority, is likely to address the daily concerns, experiences, and worldviews of those coping with health, illness, sexuality, and other risk-related issues;
4. vernacular theory raises questions about dominant cultural assumptions, and like all theory, it begins in specific interpretive complexities, proceeds by local rules, uses local forms of discourse, and makes its fullest sense in the cultural context out of which it arises.

Illness and Narrativity

While research in the social sciences has increasingly stressed the cultural construction of health and illness and the critical importance of an adequate understanding of lay health decision making, researchers continually struggle with the means to access vernacular health belief. Attitudes toward health and illness are often out of awareness and are not easily articulated in response to standard survey methods (such as questionnaires, polls, or directed and semi-directed interviews). The struggle to access vernacular health belief has prompted, among both medical researchers and social scientists, an exploration of the use of illness narratives as a natural form for articulating the meanings and values associated with health, illness, and suffering, within specific individual and cultural contexts. The growing literature on narrative dimensions of illness, care-seeking, and therapeutic process asserts that experience is organized in narrative form and that cultural knowledge and scripts for health decisions are encoded in illness narratives. Cheryl Mattingly makes the case for the study of illness narratives:

> If narrative is based, as Jerome Bruner (1986, 1996) notices, on a "breach" of the commonplace, then profound physical and mental suffering constitutes one breach that seems to demand a narrative

shape. It is one liminal place within the human condition that calls for sense-making and this often takes narrative form.

Speaking of the need for narrative among the very sick, the literary critic Anatole Broyard, dying of cancer, writes: "my initial experience of illness was a series of disconnected shocks, and my first instinct was to try to bring it under control by turning it into a narrative. Always in emergencies we invent narratives." (1998:19)

Illness narrativity research focuses on narrative as a means of experiencing, representing, and negotiating illness, highlighting the interface of experience with cultural models of thought and action. The theory behind narrativity research is that attitudes toward illness and health are better apprehended through narrative than through abstract or formal discourse and that a wealth of vernacular health information is revealed in the telling of narratives and their interpretation by others within the same culture.

Illness narratives are most often culled through a process that expands on the clinical history model used by physicians by focusing on the interpretive significance of fuller illness-related life histories. Good, Brodwin, Good, and Kleinman (1992), Good (1994), Mattingly (1998), and others assert that experience has a fundamental narrative quality and that illness stories both represent the past and provide a frame for organizing and understanding the present and the future. In this sense, illness narratives serve as statements of cultural knowledge and understandings and also provide scripts for future care seeking and health decision making. Byron Good argues that much of what we do in daily life, and much of what happens to us, is not worth narrativizing (or, in William Labov's terms, is not "tellable" [Labov and Waletsky 1967]); therefore, what does become a narrative indicates some level of significance for the teller or the audience[16] (Good 1994:139). In this sense, illness-narrativity scholars see narrative as a means of marking the impact and importance of a narrated health event or incident on the individual, thereby articulating complex symbolic meanings and cultural values. As Farmer notes, "illness meanings emerge in situated discourse" (1994:806).

---

16.   This is not understood by illness-narrativity scholars in quite the situated and
       emergent way that performances are understood by folklorists. Nevertheless, the
       notion that the creation of a narrative indicates significance (at some point, in
       some way) for the teller or audience (or both) is not, all in all, a notion with which
       folklorists would disagree.

Evelyn Early's work on therapeutic narratives among women in Cairo was among the first studies to focus on illness narratives. Early focused on everyday stories of illness that, she argued, operated as a "middle level system between experience and theory," allowing the women to develop an interpretation of illness in relation to "local explanatory logic" and biographic context and to negotiate reasonable action (1982), thus, as Good notes, "embedding the illness and therapeutic efforts within local moral norms" (1994:143). Early's work demonstrates the use of illness narratives as a means of gaining access to health worldview. Later studies in illness and narrativity have experimented with the benefits of applying methods of literary analysis and structural analysis to stories of personal illness experiences. Scholars such as Garro (1992) and Mattingly (1998) have focused on the relationship between the chronological structure of illness narratives and the parallel structure of illness and have explored the usefulness of literary concepts such as temporality and enplotment in illness narratives. While these studies are interesting and potentially very useful for our understandings of illness experience, it is primarily the use of narrative as a tool for uncovering vernacular health belief and explanatory models that has potential implications for accessing risk perception.

The following study will not focus on the narratives of those currently experiencing illness through the eyes of a patient; nor will it focus on illness history narratives, although AIDS research would certainly benefit from both perspectives.[17] Because this volume is primarily concerned with risk prevention rather than the experience of those who are already ill, the focus will be on illness encounter narratives. While illness narrative theorists have generally recognized the existence and importance of nonpersonal, shared, or "prototypical" (Good 1994:133) narratives, they have tended toward the construction of such narration as rare and located primarily in the past, while casting contemporary North American health narratives solely as reports of personal experience.[18] Nearly all of the more extensive works on illness narratives discuss the search for meaning in older exotic "myths," "magical stories," and "ritual

---

17. And has benefitted from such studies. See, for example, Chandler (1991) on narratives from AIDS support groups and Dean (1995) on AIDS in autobiography.
18. A significant exception concerning the role of collective narratives in understanding cultural models of AIDS is Paul Farmer's article "AIDS-Talk and the Constitution of Cultural Models" (1994).

performances" (Mattingly 1998; Good 1994), but contemporary collective or fictional narratives are somehow not seen as relevant to the contemporary scene.[19] As Cheryl Mattingly notes, "current analysis of narratives, especially within medical anthropology, focuses increasingly on personal stories of individual experience rather than collective stories" (1998:9). Such a construction ignores the vast body of *shared* nonpersonal narratives about health that encode associative meanings linking illness and health to fundamental cultural values, explanatory models, and social relations. In the pages that follow, these stories—the ones that we use to explore AIDS, the ones that we share with others who share our cultural outlook, the stories we use to understand and discuss risk—will help us try to make sense in *and of* health education.

---

19.   This treatment of shared narrative as primitive betrays the lack of folklorists' writing in the field of illness narrativity. Generally, this literature cites only the work of Vladimir Propp and one or two other scholars in the field.

4

What Exactly Did They Do with That Monkey, Anyway?

Contemporary Legend, Scientific Speculation, and the Politics of Blame in the Search for AIDS Origins

Cross-culturally, traditional narratives have consistently displayed an interest in the issue of origins. Etiological (or origin) tales form a significant part of most folktale collections, providing narrative explanations for such issues as how the moon got in the sky or why the mouse has such a long tail.[1] In part, these narratives envisage a world that predates the one we know today; and perhaps our long time fascination with origins is, at least in part, about nostalgic or historical fantasy. But etiological tales also speculate about how we came to our current state of being, how the things that we take to be normative developed or appeared where once they were not. AIDS narratives are no different. A significant part of AIDS legendary tradition betrays our obsession with origins. Whether the narratives focus on government conspiracies, African or Haitian AIDS, "patient zero" type characters, superbugs transmitting the virus through bites, or hundred-year-old AIDS cases, the concern is the same: establishing a first—a source for this thing that made our world change so irreversibly. The search for disease origins illustrates the parallels between vernacular and scientific theory. As Waldby notes, one of the primary logics that informs HIV medicine

---

1. Etiological tales are also called explanatory tales in classical folklore generic classifications (see Bødker 1965).

is a drive to establish the origin of the disease, evidenced by concerns with the evolutionary origin of the virus, its epidemiological categories, and the effort to trace contacts for each new case of HIV (Waldby et al. forthcoming). "Knowing the origin of infection establishes some intellectual control over it," Waldby and coauthors argue, "allowing logical patterns of diffusion and transmission to be discerned, and prevention strategies to be formulated" (forthcoming:11).

While a great deal of scientific effort and speculation has been devoted in recent years to attempts to find the origins of the HIV virus that causes AIDS, the debate has, perhaps predictably, become intertwined with questions of *who* (which race, which country, which subgroup) is to blame for the epidemic. Similar epidemics of dangerous infections, such as the bubonic plague, smallpox, syphilis, and even influenza, have prompted parallel speculation throughout medical history, with members of one group or region blaming members of another. Debates in the fifteenth and sixteenth centuries over origins of syphilis, for example, raged furiously, with the Russians blaming the Polish, the English blaming the French, the French blaming the Italians, and the Italians calling it the Spanish disease (Pucey 1933). While we might think that the medical revolution and the development of germ theory would put an end to such debates, the recent history of AIDS demonstrates a continued concern with imputing blame intertwined with genuine medical concerns about origins. Discussions of AIDS origins by many Western scientists have advanced etiological arguments concerning Haitian and African voodoo traditions, prostitution, drugs, and promiscuity (see Stillwaggon 2003; Goldstein 2001; Watney 1989; Patton 1988), while some German and Russian scientists have speculated about the involvement of U.S. germ warfare and conspiracy theories in development of the virus (Greco 1983; Chirimuuta and Chirimuuta 1987; Chirimuuta, Harrison, and Gazi 1987). Despite the dangers of such blame, origin research and speculation continue since they are seen by some medical researchers to provide the greatest hope for teasing out the information necessary to the eventual development of more efficacious vaccines and treatments.

While medical theories about AIDS origins have been posed in terms open to experimental confirmation and rebuttal and have been presented for scrutiny in scientific journals and conference papers, they clearly make use of themes commonly found in contemporary legend. Despite the fact that contemporary legend scholars have focused primarily on the origin conspiracy legends, virtually all major medical AIDS-origin theories have been transmitted as rumor campaigns, with various versions relayed through the media and through popular tradition. And while the scientific, media, and popular debates concerning AIDS origins rarely exhibit the "friend of a friend" or similar pedigree consistent with many contemporary legends, they *all* exhibit the effort to make sense of events through narrative, and they all focus on themes we recognize immediately as the "stuff" of legend—contamination, food and sexual taboos, distrust of big business, and conspiracy. The disease-origins debate is a natural context for contemporary legend for two reasons:

1. Resolution of the issue requires accounting for mutation, creation, or transmission of viral agents, reconstructing that series of events, and carrying an audience through that reconstruction (whether the audience be medical-conference participants, a newspaper's readership, or a peer group). This process, conducted in any of those contexts, is one of story making and narration.

2. The question of origins is by definition a question of the transgression of alien substances (the virus) across categorical boundaries into the familiar; in other words, it is necessarily about contamination. The events are extraordinary, controversial, and they invite debate. They threaten cultural norms and encourage the expression of opinions, variants, and negotiated facts. Under these conditions, the contemporary legend is inevitable: the topic, the format for discussion, and the contexts of meaning lend themselves easily to the genre.

This chapter will look at the contemporary legend-making impulse in AIDS origins debates, both medical and popular, focusing on how narratives and narrative motifs serve to combine epidemiological ideas with notions of primitivism, exoticism, sanitation, contamination, political power, and good and evil. I intend to show the overlapping nature of popular culture and medical culture, demonstrating the narrative core of medical origin theories and the use of a kind of "folk epidemiology" in popular origin narratives. AIDS origin narratives form a complex discourse concerning identity and the construction of "otherness," a discourse that articulates perspectives on trust and blame, which form the basis of worldviews that ground risk perceptions. When taken as a group and set against the background of medical debates, the narratives from popular tradition provide a great deal of information on the location and constitution of cultural others, the designation of evil, and the identification of keepers and transgressors of cultural good. As such, if taken as a legend complex, the variety of origin theories provides information that casts light on attitudes toward disease, medicine, and perceived vulnerability.

Theories of AIDS Origins

Three main scientific theories have continually been put forward in different forms to account for origins of the disease:

1. that AIDS has developed from a natural disease previously existing only in some other species of animal, which has recently managed to infect humans thus triggering the epidemic (Noireau 1987);
2. that AIDS has developed from a much older human disease not previously noted by science, either because it has always been confined to a small group with an acquired immunity or because it has only recently become virulent (deCock 1984);
3. that AIDS is a man-made virus manufactured either accidentally or deliberately in a laboratory (Sabatier 1988).

While these theories have been proposed in a variety of forms with variation in detail, the three types nevertheless account for most of the arguments about AIDS origins found in medical, media, and popular tradition.[2] It is also worth noting that arguments related to all three theories can be found in each tradition. Theories of a man-made laboratory virus are not dependent strictly on popular tradition for transmission and maintenance; nor are the medically more complex theories of isolated case immunity strictly dependent on medical tradition. In fact, one of the more interesting parts of this debate is the facility with which each tradition has speculated about virology, evolution, cultural practice, geography, history, and a massive variety of topics normally requiring some degree of either medical or cultural expertise for even superficial discussion. While some of the narrative and belief material discussed here will not resemble contemporary legend as much as others, the entire complex

---

2.   Of course, a fourth argument suggests that the HIV virus does not cause AIDS, but this argument tends not to take a discursive form focusing on origin issues.

taken together provides a necessary context for understanding its parts. The theories are closely tied together, overlapping and dovetailing in intricate ways, all of which cast light on the legend-making impulse.

Animal Theories

The bubonic plague, malaria, and yellow fever epidemics were all traced, eventually, to infectious organisms carried by animals or insects. It has been known for some time that both domestic and wild animals can harbor organisms that can be contracted by and transmitted by human beings. This process is known as zoonosis. Occasionally with diseases contracted from animals, the disease is far more severe in the human host than it was in its original animal source. It is not surprising then that research scientists have looked to the animal world for origins of AIDS. In popular tradition, animal sources also appear to have made sense or at least have filtered down and are maintained in tradition, resulting in a list from the Newfoundland data that includes monkeys of various types, regional origins, and colors (African green monkeys, blue monkeys, red monkeys, green-eyed monkeys, chimpanzees, baboons, tree monkeys, and rhesus monkeys); insects of various types (fleas, flies, mosquitoes, and cockroaches); and finally sheep, lambs, and even the co-rectal gerbil.[3] While the specific types and varieties of each species mentioned in the data have gone through elaboration and variation in tradition, monkeys, insects, sheep, and rodents have all been posited at one time or another by scientists as possible sources for the disease.

The best-known medical argument for an animal source for the disease was the highly publicized "African green monkey theory," published in scientific journals in the mid-1980s and seized upon by the press as "the" original source of the HIV virus. The African green monkey theory was based on the notion that HIV arose in Africa in the 1950s when a virus crossed over from monkeys to humans. The evidence for the theory, most of which has since been retracted, is based on the genetic analysis of viruses isolated from green rhesus monkeys and humans in West Africa and from Asian

---

3.   The co-rectal gerbil refers to another contemporary legend (usually not reported concerning AIDS motifs) in which a gerbil, being used as a sex toy, is found stuck in the rectum of a man rushed to the emergency room.

macaque monkeys captive in U.S. laboratories in 1983 (Henrickson et al. 1983). Since the green monkey and African connections figure heavily in much of the contemporary legend material, it is necessary to explain at least a part of the story of the green monkey theory and its technical basis. In 1983 a California primate research center reported an AIDS-like disease in laboratory Asian macaque monkeys (Henrickson et al. 1983). An attempt was made to trace the virus back to macaque monkeys *in the wild*—with no luck; the virus did not seem to exist in the *wild* Asian monkeys. It was then reasoned that the macaque monkeys may have caught the virus from cage mates of a different species or place of origin. African green monkeys had shared laboratory cages with the Asian macaques and, thus, the search led to African green monkeys in the wild. In 1985 researchers announced that they had isolated a similar virus in African green monkeys, likely to be the source of the virus in the original captive macaques (Kanki et al. 1985). The next step was to look for evidence of a crossover infection in humans from the same geographical area. Blood samples taken from the people of Senegal, West Africa, contained the antibodies, though the people demonstrated no signs of illness (Barin et al. 1985). The fall of the African green monkey theory came, however, in 1988 when a second group of researchers decided to compare the three genetic samples (from the captive macaques, wild African green monkeys, and West African humans) and discovered that they were genetically identical despite the fact that they came from three different species. On rechecking the results, it was announced that contamination of laboratory samples was responsible for the earlier discovery of the virus in the African wild monkeys and the people of Senegal. The African green monkey theory was retracted (Sabatier 1988; Doolittle 1989). Green monkey theory, however, had been by this time so heavily discussed in the media that its retraction was largely missed in popular tradition, in part perhaps because of the technical nature of the contamination explanations. Later research did find that certain simian immunodeficiency viruses (SIVs) are closely related to HIV, particularly a virus found in the sooty mangabey monkey of western Africa, which closely resembles the HIV-2 strain of the virus. Nevertheless, a definite source for the HIV virus continues to elude scientists. Despite the continually compromised status of direct evidence for green monkey theory, it is clear from the Newfoundland data and continued media coverage that it is still by far the most popular theory for AIDS origins.

Animal-source theories require more than simply establishing one or more viruses in animals that are related to the human virus: they also require establishing modes of transmission of the virus to humans in ways that are biologically, culturally, and ecologically feasible. And, thus, we arrive at narrative. Medical, media, and popular tradition have gone to great lengths making up alternative chronologies of events that might explain the modes of transmission. Put more plainly, as one piece of graffiti did, "Just what exactly did they do with that monkey, anyway?" Here, the intensely emotive issues of food, violence, and sex come into play, calling up deep stereotypes and complex symbolic worlds and providing grist for the imagination. Uncooked meat, ingestion of internal organs, sexual contact, blood injection, bites, and experiments all are equally noted in scientific journals and over the dinner table as explanations for transmission. And here, thanks perhaps to Tarzan movies and romantic ideas of safaris through the jungle, we find a portrait of African culture and life assumed or made up and presented as scientific fact—a kind of native exoticism or what one might call "fake ethnography."

Two medical researchers offered one such explanation to provide evidence for the ingestion of contaminated monkey meat:

> Monkeys are often hunted for food in Africa. It may be that a hunting accident of some sort or an accident in preparation for cooking brought people in contact with infected blood. Once caught, monkeys are often kept in huts for sometime before they are eaten. Dead monkeys are sometimes used as toys by African children. (Green and Miller 1986:66)

Sources for this information on monkeys as folk toys are not given, and two African scientists responded to the comment by writing: "The authors do not tell us where they obtained this remarkable information, but the rapidity with which dead animals putrefy in the tropics alone makes nonsense of these assertions" (Chirimuuta and Chirimuuta 1987:72). In 1987, the British medical journal *The Lancet* published a letter citing exotic African sexual practices as a possible mechanism for transmission. The letter described the sexual practices of Africans, noting,

> To stimulate a man or a woman, and to induce in them intense sexual activity, they are inoculated in the thighs, pubic region and

back with blood taken from the male monkey (for a man) or the female monkey (for a woman). (Noireau 1987:1499)

The same kind of exoticism appears in popular tradition. From the Newfoundland data, I collected the following story involving transmission through the ingestion of monkey meat:

> I heard there was a tribe in Africa which, when arriving upon manhood, the young boys were made to eat the brains of the Rhesus monkey who were observed by the tribesmen to be always (um!) making babies. Therefore, the monkey became the symbol of manhood. Some of these monkeys though had the AIDS virus and humans contracted AIDS.

And another example from the Newfoundland data, this time involving direct transmission through blood:

> Monkey's blood was injected into [a] young adolescent's blood as a part of an African tribe's ritual of initiation into manhood. The virus originally came from monkeys. This is the theory speculated by many experts today.

Forms of transmission vary in the narratives, but all seem to recognize that the transfer of bodily fluids is prerequisite to HIV infection. As can be seen from the narrative examples already given, the means of transmission calls attention to exoticism through unusual sexual proclivities, "primitive" social customs, and exotic eating habits. Roger Abrahams sees a similar list as comprising the parts of what he calls the "deep stereotype" in that they refer to the general characteristics by which peoples throughout the world talk about strangers and enemies (1984:34). Here we must note, however, that by virtue of the necessary exchange of bodily fluids prerequisite to HIV infection, it is inevitable that sexual activities and food habits provide a natural theme for constructing otherness. The AIDS contamination narratives remind us of the very reason that our stereotypes are based on such factors.

In reference to monkeys, Abrahams notes, "Surely, our extreme ambivalence about the simian sort is conditioned by our actual identification with them and our feeling that eating them would be close to cannibalism; on the other hand, from the perspective of popular evolution, designating others as apes is judging them to be like us, but representative of our animal character that we have only recently been able to transcend" (1984:34). A similar ambivalence is reflected in the origin narratives. While monkey meat is ingested and thus becomes a means of transmission, it, most often, is contaminated with other food taboos—it is long dead, raw, or unclean. Perhaps most interesting of all, the meat ingested is often the monkey brain—internal organs being particularly sensitive to food taboos—and, in its image as the home of intelligence, the brain possibly acts to remind us of the evolutionary likeness suggested by Abrahams.

While monkeys are too like us to eat, they are simultaneously too different to engage in close contact. Occasionally, transmission is accomplished in the narratives through a monkey bite, but most often the exchange of bodily fluid is accomplished through sexual activity. This, however, is not as straightforward as it may sound. The simplest sexual explanation would appear to be direct sexual interaction between men and monkeys (bestiality), but a large number of the responses distance the sexual act, by using injected blood or organs, as discussed in the previous examples, or by framing the sexual act as a significant cultural practice or ritual.

One respondent stated, "It originally came from Africa where they have the ritual practice of natives having sex with apes." And another responded, "It came from central Africa where prostitutes sometimes perform sexual acts on animals in ceremonies." Like many of the other responses, these excerpts focus on the act of bestiality as one that finds ritual or tribal approval within the culture. The view, while bespeaking an offensive stereotypical image of African culture, is simultaneously, through its process of "fake ethnography," attempting to understand the behavior as exotic or tribal and as operating within a very different cultural frame. The act is not portrayed as simply deviant but, more sympathetically, as a primitive but culturally meaningful act.

A similar sympathetic, though less exotic, view is taken of transmission between sheep and men. Sheep origin theories surprised me initially when they appeared in the Newfoundland data. Most of the individuals interviewed seemed to believe in African origins for AIDS, and it seemed to me that sheep are not animals normally associated with African life. Sheep are, however, the main animals occasionally heard about in Newfoundland in narratives of local bestiality. *Blasons populaires* told about the nearby province of Nova Scotia often make reference to the old line, "where men are men, and sheep are nervous." A cycle of jokes about activities between men and sheep was extremely popular in the mid-1970s in St. John's, focusing on baymen (people who live outside of the city or "around the bay") as backward individuals who knew no better than to engage in intimate acts with animals. Bestial acts in Newfoundland constructions of AIDS transmission may simply fit into an already existing category of taboo but nevertheless recognized interaction between men and animals. This explanation is suggested by several of the responses that presented monkeys and sheep as alternative versions of the story. One said,

> I've heard many origin stories. The first one I heard was about a sailor who's ship stopped over in Africa and the sailor had intercourse with a baboon. The second story apparently happened in South America—Cuba I think, or in Mexico. A man had intercourse with his sheep. He was a Shepard.

While I could trace no coverage of sheep theories of AIDS origins in appropriate years of the local news sources, such a theory does exist in the medical literature. Several medical researchers have suggested that the human immunodeficiency virus closely resembles sheep and cattle viruses that cause wasting diseases with AIDS-like symptoms. A devastating sheep virus called Visna was successfully grown in human cell cultures in 1962 and has been the subject of a series of experiments in which subhuman primates were intentionally infected (Georgidis, Billiau, and Vanderschueren 1978). These experiments have been mentioned in relation to the possibilities for laboratory creation of the AIDS virus and figure occasionally in discussions of the plausibility of conspiracy theories (Burny et al. 1985; Gonda et al. 1985). While sheep have filled the culturally allotted slot for explanations involving transmission through bestiality in the popular tradition, they fill a different slot of plausible laboratory contaminants in the medical literature.

Forms of transmission that don't shake up our taboos quite as much are also discussed in the narratives. Insects distance the process of transmission between animals and humans: the mosquito bites the monkey then bites the human and transmits the virus with no need for direct interaction. Insects contaminate, but they do not break social rules. They cross boundaries, being simultaneously wild and yet making excursions into domestic spaces. Yet, while being equally at home on sheep, monkeys, or humans, they are capable of mediation between animals and men and, as such, become blameless transmitters. In the Newfoundland data, insects do not usually accomplish transmission on their own but rather ensure passage from animals to men. Commonly, the accounts state,

> A monkey in Africa had the virus and was bitten by a mosquito. The mosquito bit a human and from there the virus was transmitted through sexual intercourse and IV drug use.

The possibility of insect transmission was, of course, not ignored by the medical literature, forming some of the earliest medical research into animal transmission (Srinivasan, York, and Bohan 1987; Piot and Schofield 1986). Most researchers agree today that while the HIV virus can, in theory, be present in the blood extracted by an insect bite, its presence is likely to be too minimal to allow transmission.[4] One study noted that it would take ten million mosquito bites to pass on enough of the virus to cause infection.

Isolated-Case Theories

As noted earlier, isolated-case theories argue that the HIV virus has been around for a long time but went unnoticed either because it was confined to a small number of people or because it has only recently become virulent. While this theory takes many forms, its major focus is on the possibility that a small isolated ethnic group had the virus but also had an acquired immunity to it; and, thus, it is only when the virus spread outside the group (where there was no such immunity) that the disease gained the devastating effects that we now associate with AIDS. The pattern is one normally associated with the so-called white man's disease syndrome—European diseases such as measles and smallpox that were responsible for wiping out many previously unexposed native groups in the eighteenth and nineteenth centuries. In practice, the theory evokes reverse sympathies to the white man's disease pattern, however, since an emphasis

---

4.   When an insect bites a person, it does not inject its own or a previous victim's blood into the new victim. It injects saliva. Insect mouth parts do not retain large amounts of blood on the surface.

on Africa and Haiti as the disease source of HIV has provoked accusations of racism and self-serving science. Isolated-case theories
nevertheless are seen as scientifically desirable, since any group that
might be found to have an immunity to the virus also has the building blocks for the development of a vaccine.

Isolated-case theories have followed two main lines of research.
The most obvious line has been to establish the oldest cases of the
virus through the retrospective analysis of old medical records and
stored blood supplies. A second thread of research has been to locate the earliest areas of high concentration of the virus and test the
local population for antibodies.

Although AIDS appeared roughly simultaneously in the United
States, Europe, Africa, and Haiti, it was widely assumed by the medical profession that AIDS had originated in Africa, partly because of
African links to the cases initially reported and partly because it was
believed that such an unusual disease could not have gone unnoticed
in the United States (Sabatier 1988).

The first tests of African stored blood samples showed HIV antibodies in over 50 percent of the blood samples taken in Kenya
and Uganda in the 1960s and 1970s (Saxinger et al. 1985; Carswell
et al. 1986). These tests used procedures much less reliable than
those used today and have since been shown to indicate high percentages of false positives. The first erroneous test results, however,
implied that AIDS was endemic in Central Africa, and these results
received widespread attention in the media. Larger samples, using
better testing methods and indicating much lower levels of infection
(2 percent) were less well reported (Sabatier 1988:38). The early
false-positive results, like the early green monkey research, contributed to confusions and misunderstandings about the history of HIV
and its relationship to Africa but nevertheless set the stage for later
research.

Once again, the process of medical and media speculation became a storymaking activity, this time focusing on the small African
village or tribe carrying the virus for generations and unknowingly
becoming responsible for its spread. Stories of where this village
might be and who this tribe is became very popular, sending medical
researchers off to remote parts of Africa in search of hidden antibodies and reporters off in search of hidden information. One reporter
presented his narrative as follows:

Burundi is the very heart of central Africa, and at the core of the AIDS epidemic that stretches right across the continent. Some scientists believe that the AIDS virus originated somewhere among these majestic hills and lush valleys, mutated perhaps from the green monkey, possibly carried unwittingly for generations among the Hutu peasant farmers or the rival Tutsis who now rule Burundi. Over the past 20 years, as huge stretches of the land were exhausted by farming, many thousand of Burundians, among them those who may have been symptomlessly carrying the virus, drifted to the capital, Bujumbura, in search of work. (Prentice 1986)

The narrative continues, suggesting that once in the capital, the men became unfaithful, the women took to prostitution, two international hotels were built for traveling businessmen, and the world AIDS epidemic had begun (Chirimuuta and Chirimuuta 1987:91).

Similar narratives reported in the media cite spurious medical statistics to show the early incidence of HIV. Writing on Kenya, one reporter noted,

In 1980, some of the prostitutes were tested for AIDS at their local sexually transmitted disease clinic. At that time, none was HIV positive. Three years later, 53 percent were and now the figure is believed to be over 80 percent. (Murtagh 1987)

In response, African scientists pointed out that AIDS was recognized only in 1981, and the HIV blood test was not introduced until 1984. Unless Kenya had suddenly become a world leader in medical research, the statistics were completely false (Chirimuuta and Chirimuuta 1987:95). The statistical multiplication of AIDS cases in Africa remains, however, a very significant part of the narrative tradition, demonstrating enormous variation in numbers, resulting in intense exaggeration, and creating plausible-sounding details that ground the isolated-case narratives.

Searches through old medical records and stored blood samples were less controversial and more successful. After searching through past cases looking for instances of combinations of unusual opportunistic infections and, where possible, positive blood tests for HIV, investigators found a small number of possible cases spanning thirty years and three continents. The most publicized of these cases was a

British sailor with Kaposi's sarcoma and pneumocystis pneumonia, who died in Manchester, England, in 1959 (Williams, Stretton, and Leonard 1983). Another early case, less publicized, documents HIV in the Congo from plasma collected in 1959 (Nahmias et al. 1986). The earliest North American case found to date was traced from frozen tissue samples taken from an African American St. Louis teenager, who died in 1969 after reporting AIDS-like symptoms (Garry et al. 1988).

Popular tradition also concerned itself with isolated-case theory, with many of the Newfoundland respondents insisting that the disease had been around for a very long time but had been limited in its circulation. One student said,

> I've also heard a plausible rumor that its been around for centuries but was not discovered as AIDS until recently. I see this in tales of strange unexplained illnesses that were much like AIDS and [in] artwork.

Popular accounts, like the medical accounts, noted prevalence in a place as indicative of origin, particularly Africa, and also focused on cases in which there were extant stored blood samples. Note these excerpts:

> Since it is so prevalent among people in the countries of Africa, it is likely that it originated there and has been transmitted to Europe, Indonesia, North America, etc. through sexual transmission. How it developed in Africa is not certain. It may be possible that it was always present in members of their population but was limited.

And

> It has been recorded of a British sailor who was supposed to have had the symptoms of a person with AIDS 100 years ago but the medical technology at the time did not know this so it may have been [diagnosed] as something else.

Perhaps the most interesting isolated-case responses are formed as narratives concerning medical professionals who had encountered AIDS decades before anyone had heard of it. One of the students noted,

> I recently lived in England for three months, and I met a re-
> tired nurse there. After getting to know her, she asked me what I
> thought about AIDS. She told me that while working in England
> in the late 60's, she worked on a ward where many Jamaicans were
> dying of AIDS. So my opinion is that AIDS is not a new disease
> and has been with us for quite some time. Its progress has speeded
> up with the movements of people all over the world.

The implication in this narrative, as in many of the isolated-case
statements, is that AIDS has not only been around for some time
but has been kept quiet by the medical establishment. This belief
weaves these narratives together with conspiracy theories, which
form the most recognizable contemporary legend material in the
AIDS origins complex. The bulk of the conspiracy material concerns AIDS as a man-made virus—manufactured or caused either
accidentally or deliberately in a laboratory.

Laboratory-Virus Theory

Conspiracy theories of AIDS origins appear to have surfaced in
both scientific and popular sectors around 1986. Books dedicated
to the topic, such as Alan Cantwell's *Queer Blood: The Secret AIDS
Genocide Plot* (1993) and *AIDS and the Doctors of Death: An Inquiry
into the Origins of the AIDS Epidemic* (1988) cite 1986 and 1987 as
the pivotal point in the conviction that the disease was laboratory
engineered. Renee Sabatier (1988) traces the popularization of the
theory to a paper presented at a scientific conference in that year
by East German scientists Jacob and Lili Segal speculating that
a virus with the properties of HIV could have been created from
two other retroviruses, one that attacks sheep (which we have already discussed) and another that affects humans, such as leukemia. While the case was merely speculative, it was taken up by the
media and widely publicized. During that same year, the Segals
promoted their theory through a pamphlet entitled *AIDS: USA
Home-Made Evil*, which circulated extensively throughout Eng-
lish-speaking regions of Africa. The hint that AIDS could have
been laboratory manufactured was correlated with information
concerning the 1977 establishment of the first military institution
devoted to biological warfare in Fort Detrick, Maryland. International media exploded with articles focusing on the conspiracy

theory. On October 30, 1986, the Soviet publication *Pravda* published a cartoon showing a Pentagon scientist handing a soldier
the AIDS virus in return for money (Araeea 1986). An Indian magazine followed on February 7, 1987, with the headline "AIDS, A
U.S. Military Monster: Yankee Business, Not Monkey Business."
(*Blitz* 1987). In Nicaragua, a daily paper alleged that the United
States was using AIDS as a bacterial weapon to halt the population growth of Latin America and Asia (*El Nuevo Diario* 1987).
In June of 1987 at the Third International AIDS Conference, a
group called the United Front Against Racism and Capitalist Imperialism distributed a broadsheet claiming that AIDS was germ
warfare by the U.S. government against gays and blacks (Sabatier
1988:64).

The U.S. government responded. In July of 1987 the U.S. State
Department published a report arguing that the Fort Detrick hypothesis was part of a Soviet disinformation campaign designed to
discredit the United States prior to international arms negotiation
focusing on biological weapons (U.S. Department of State 1987).
Despite the assertions of the State Department, Soviet scientists
repeatedly argued that they rejected conspiracy theories that AIDS
was manufactured in a U.S. laboratory and the Soviet Academy of
Scientists refused to even respond to the accusations. The disinformation campaign idea never really caught the public imagination,
but the conspiracy theory had. Renee Sabatier, in a book entitled
Blaming Others: Prejudice, Race, and Worldwide AIDS, summed up
the African and Haitian interest in conspiracy theories as a kind of
counterblame:

> The asymmetry of AIDS origins research has left a breach into
> which conspiracy theories can march. If the Africans often see in
> Western discussion of an African origin of AIDS a wish to blame
> the epidemic on Africa, so many thirdworlders have found an at-
> tractive counter blame theory; that AIDS was unleashed on the
> world by Germ warfare experimentation in the US Defence De-
> partment Laboratory at Fort Detrick, Maryland. (1988:63)

In Africa and Haiti the notion of AIDS as a U.S. government conspiracy to exterminate blacks filled the local press, the works of local
artists, and the conversations of local people. Paul Farmer, writing
on AIDS and accusation in Haiti, quotes large numbers of Haitians

and Haitian Americans who believed in the U.S. conspiracy theory. One Haitian man Farmer interviewed said, "The Americans have always resented Haiti, ever since 1804. Being strong, they can punish us, humiliate us. The AIDS thing was the perfect tool" (1992:232). Farmer describes a group of Haitian teenagers attending Boston public schools who asked a teacher whether or not she thought U.S. officials had introduced AIDS to Haiti on purpose. The question was turned back to the teens. Of seventeen, sixteen replied, "On purpose"; one replied that he was not sure (233).

AIDS-conspiracy theories also pervaded popular culture. A song written by a Haitian group called the "Coordination of Progressive Artists" includes the refrain:

> The Americans made AIDS in their laboratories,
> Faithless, lawless scoundrels
> They made us carry the cross
> Together with the FDA
> and a bunch of other worthless people
> they nailed us upside down. (Farmer 1992:231)

Another song composed by two Haitian artists, titled "FDA, You're Crazy," contained this second verse:

> It's true our country has no money
> It's true our country's full of poor people
> But you know all too well that you're the cause of this
> You're the ones who brought us drugs
> You're the ones who invented AIDS to kill off black people
> To hold onto your power, rule all nations. (Farmer 1992:231)

African journals also reported high numbers of people who believed in the U.S. conspiracy theory, and the journals themselves continued to publish information, interviews, and ideas to support the theory. The journal *New Africa* published a special issue in April 1990 entitled "Africa and the AIDS Myth." It reports,

> In 1969, the US Department of Defence asked a budget committee of congress to allocate 10 million for research to produce an artificial virus which could destroy the human immune system. According to the Pentagon spokesman at the committee meeting,

consultations with outstanding scientists had already been held. All further details were declared secret. (Versi 1990:12)

While African and Haitian popular culture and presses clung to the U.S. conspiracy theories, most social scientists argued, as did Sabatier, that this was a form of counterblame, not popular outside of the developing countries initially blamed for origins. It was clear, however, that African American and gay presses in the United States were also interested in the conspiracy theories. In the African American community, Spike Lee, among others, continually voiced the theory that AIDS was an attempt by the U.S. government to kill off minorities. Likewise, gay periodicals continuously carried letters to the editor suggesting everything from transmission by a chemical agent sprinkled on the floors of bathhouses by government officials—where barefoot homosexuals would absorb it into their skin—to tainted KY jelly, contaminated by the Center for Disease Control (Altman 1986:43). Most of the authors writing about African and Haitian conspiracy-theory beliefs allow for the popularity of such beliefs in the African American and gay communities but generally noted that these communities also suffered accusations of responsibility for epidemic transmission. Farmer wrote,

> African Americans have also found such theories attractive, and they have received regular attention in the gay presses of NA and Europe. But it seems that the chief purveyors of the "conspiracy theory" initially attributed to *Pravda*, have been Haitians and Africans, in other words precisely those who have been themselves accused of introducing AIDS or HIV to the industrialized West. (Farmer 1992:234)

Paula Treichler, one of the first to write on popular beliefs about AIDS origins, notes that conspiracy theory beliefs make the most sense in developing communities:

> The notion that AIDS is an American invention is a recurrent element of the international AIDS story, yet one not easily incorporated within a Western positivist frame, in part, perhaps, because it is political, with discursive roots in the resistance of colonialism; the Western response, accordingly, attributes it to ignorance, state propaganda or psychological denial. (1989:43)

While Farmer and Treichler are most likely correct in their analysis of the conspiracy theory as gaining its greatest strength in the African and Haitian scenes, Treichler's assumption that it is not also incorporated into the general Western response to the disease is more questionable and, as mentioned earlier, appears to be an observation better suited to official and not necessarily vernacular discourses. The counterblame argument, asserted by Treichler, Sabatier, and Farmer, suggesting that the chief purveyors of conspiracy theories are those who have themselves been accused of responsibility for the disease, frames conspiracy belief as defensive, thereby diverting attention away from the more general message of medical distrust. Knowledge, belief, and attitude studies demonstrate, as Farmer and Turner (1993) suggest, a significant belief in AIDS conspiracy theories within the African American and Haitian American communities in North America, as well as in other communities disproportionately affected by the disease. Herek and Capitanio (1994), for example, found, in an extensive national telephone survey administered in the United States, that 20 percent of African Americans and only 4 percent of white Americans believed the government was using AIDS to kill off minority groups. Subsequent questions, however, revealed that nearly one-half (43 percent) of the African American respondents and over one-third of white respondents (37.1 percent) believed that information about AIDS is being withheld. While the difference in the two figures is attention grabbing, we should not let it obscure the startling information that more than one-third of those surveyed indicated a lack of trust in government and medical officials in relation to the AIDS epidemic. The Newfoundland data support these figures, revealing a not insubstantial number of reported conspiracy beliefs.[5]

In Newfoundland the unleashing of the virus is blamed occasionally on older enemies, such as Germany or Russia. Hitler stories, for example, are common among these. One woman said,

> It was one of Hitler's mad schemes gone astray. His scientists developed a virus to attack the enemy who in his opinion were full of

---

5.   The Newfoundland origins data do not lend themselves to statistical analysis as the data were collected in a number of formats over a long period of time; nevertheless, a conservative guess based on the more consistent questionnaire material would be that conspiracy beliefs are present in about a quarter to a third of the surveyed college-age population.

homosexuals. The virus would kill off the army. The plane used to transport the virus crashed in Africa.

But, the majority of the Newfoundland conspiracy theories blamed Western medical or government officials, particularly those from the U.S. Consider the following excerpts:

> I think it was a CIA plan that backfired to bring down the population of Africa thereby eliminating a threat to the USA.

> Some sick scientist invented it to curb the sexual activities of the populations of the world.

> I heard a friend remark that he thought AIDS was political control. He thinks that perhaps the [U.S.] government has a cure but will not release it because AIDS is acting as a population control. Economic situations are bad in many places and the government sees AIDS as a way to reduce the burden of a high population.

The Newfoundland versions of these narrative themes may be a form of counterblame as Sabatier and others would have it. While Newfoundlanders have at no time been accused of responsibility for the disease origins, the province has been pinpointed as having a disproportionate rate of infection, and scientific speculation over time has even suggested that there might be a localized strain of the virus (an idea which was later dropped). Treichler's suggestion of resistance to colonialism may also explain the popularity of the local AIDS conspiracy theories. Certainly, Canadians are sensitive to what they see as colonializing attitudes of our "neighbours to the south" (the United States). It is worth noting that the conspiracy narratives are most often targeted at the U.S. government or at political and medical power in general; the Newfoundland data included no versions that implicated the Canadian government specifically. Newfoundland itself has had a long history of colonialism and even now, over fifty years after confederation with Canada, continues to lack a full sense of belonging in its host country. Further, as a traditionally poor and isolated province, political alienation is rife. In this context, looking back at the corpus of origin narratives in a more holistic sense may be instructive in understanding the role of poverty and isolation in AIDS-origin beliefs.

Newfoundland responses concerning Africans and green monkey transmission were certainly heavily stereotyped and exoticized, like so many of the "scientific" speculations about African origins, but they were simultaneously sympathetic, often going out of their way to directly state concern. One woman followed her narrative concerning African isolated cases by saying,

> But I do not have any prejudices against my black brothers and sisters in Africa and feel sorry that they have such hardships because of poverty, lack of education and medical care and health products. We owe it to them to help because we have so much and so many things in our country to share.

Another said,

> You know it might have come from Africa, but I'm sure that they will find that vaccines or something, manufactured in the US put it there. You know, blame the poor, blame the little guy.

Africans clearly represent a foreign "other" in the narratives, but they are not nearly as foreign in their "otherness" as are the politically powerful. Government and medical officials, on the other hand, are depicted as evil, deceitful, and deranged; and their activities are described as devious and murderous. Despite the stereotyped racist undertones, the Newfoundland sympathies are clearly with their depiction of what they describe as the unsanitized, poor, and uneducated African, and their distrust clearly lies with the oversanitized, wealthy, and overeducated bureaucracy. As Treichler and Farmer suggest, these sympathies are based on some very real historical facts. Newfoundlanders are not strangers to the poverty, lack of education, and lack of health care they portray in their narratives of Africa. As noted in the introduction to this volume, in many Newfoundland communities access by road, electricity and plumbing, schools and hospitals are fewer than three decades old. In this sense it should not surprise us that the narratives portray a sympathetic view of the "primitive" African and a distrust of government and the academy. As Turner notes in her discussion of African American conspiracy beliefs, "the fact that some informants maintained that the intended targets of the conspiracy include others [not of their group] . . . suggests that a certain solidarity might

be emerging among groups traditionally at odds with the system"
(1993:162).

But even if Newfoundland supports Treichler's view of the conspiracy theory as resistance to colonialism, what can we make of
the popularity of conspiracy theories within majority American and
Canadian society? What, for example, about the distrust of AIDS
information reported by that one-third of the American population
in the Herek and Capitanio study? Trechler's argument, that the
narratives are grounded in resistance to colonialism, refers to a very
specific political experience; if broadened, the argument suggests
the simple prerequisite of insecurities concerning those in positions
of power. As political insecurities increase, conspiracy beliefs seem
to also increase, and a decrease should accordingly create fewer such
narratives. Likewise, partisan politics should locate the tradition in
specific pockets of society, those that are currently apprehensive of
the people in power.

But to stop there demedicalizes the problem. AIDS conspiracy
theories and their attendant beliefs are not solely about government
genocide but also about medicine as warfare, purposeful disinformation, and the withholding of drugs, treatment, and knowledge
by those who serve as gatekeepers of life and death. The theories
articulate substantial medical distrust, perhaps tied to the Tuskeegee
experiment (discussed in earlier chapters), perhaps tied to any number of ethically scandalous medical and scientific research projects
that have been reported in the news years after their damage has
been inflicted.

After the ARVC genetic study in Newfoundland[6] and due to
the publicity about the relative isolation of the gene pool, numerous stories about "medical vampires," intent on gaining samples of
Newfoundland blood for genetic testing, have entered circulation.
Medical experimentation is a local growing concern. Perhaps the
distrust is tied to the current consumer/business model of heath
care, a model that Canadians see as threatening social medicine.
Perhaps the distrust is linked to simple professional elitism, particularly in a place where employment has been ravaged by the death of
the fishery. The articulated insecurities expressed in the conspiracy
theories draw a frightening picture of medical professionals. That
picture is echoed in numerous contemporary health legends. When

---

6.   This study is described in chapter 1.

narratives depict the theft of kidneys for an organ-transplantation black market or individuals drugged by medical students for new cadavers, the overall concerns speak even louder. Legends are often best understood when taken together, as a series of dovetailed meanings. Medical distrust is a problem, not just in terms of origin beliefs but in terms of public health. The problem, as Herek and Capitanio note, is that "the effectiveness of a message depends, in part, on the credibility that recipients attach to its source" (1994:365). AIDS-education programs and risk-management programs are unlikely to have an effect if targeted populations doubt the veracity of medical experts. AIDS-origin narratives clearly depict a crisis of confidence.

Conspiracy theories are part of a larger complex of narrative blame for disease origins. Fully understanding a part of the complex requires understanding the whole, not so much as alternative narrative types and motifs, but as a collective indication of how disease discourse constructs and is constructed by concepts of cultural otherness. The conspiracy theory makes a different kind of sense if seen in historical and narrative context as a reaction of counterblame, but it also takes on new meanings when seen next to other origin narratives as part of a worldview that assigns characteristics of foreignness and trust.

5

Welcome to the Innocent
World of AIDS

Cultural Viability, Localization,
and Contemporary Legend

The headline on the front page of the St. John's *Evening Telegram* on April 22, 1991, announced "Bizarre AIDS Story Likely a Concocted Tale." The article went on to discuss a rumor about a person who knowingly transmitted the HIV virus and an inquiry into the rumor conducted by the Royal Newfoundland Constabulary's Criminal Investigation Unit. The story under investigation was not the bar pickup story extensively circulating around the world at that time. It was not the story of a man who meets a woman in a local bar, sleeps with her, and awakens to find the message "Welcome to the World of AIDS" scrawled in lipstick on the mirror. The message was the same, but the story itself was quite different. The story, according to the *Telegram*,

> involves a young woman who goes on vacation in the United States, has a one time affair, returns to Newfoundland, and some time later receives by mail a package containing a miniature coffin with a note "Welcome To The World of AIDS." (April 22, 1991)

While the *Telegram*'s synopsis gives an accurate basic description of the story circulating in Newfoundland, it left out some of the essential details—motifs that are crucial to understanding the narrative. The following text, collected from one of my students, gives a fuller sense of the story.[1]

> This girl needed a break and decided to go to Florida for a month or two holiday, I think. While she was there she met a man, who seemed to be . . . the man of her dreams. He had money, he treated her like gold and he gave her everything she wanted. She fell in love with him and . . . during her last night there they slept together. The next day he brought her to the airport for her return to St. John's. He gave her a small gift-wrapped box and told her not to open it until she got home. They . . . said goodbye and she left, hoping that someday they would be married and the gift would be an [engagement] ring. The suspense was killing her and . . . she decided to open the gift on the plane. It was a small coffin with a piece of paper saying "Welcome To The World of AIDS."

This fuller typical text gives an idea of the significance of the deviation of the new localized variation on "Welcome to the World of AIDS" from the bar pickup narrative, which was previously in circulation and which had been extensively written about by folklorists (Brunvand 1989; Fine 1987; Goodwin 1989). Although Smith (1990) noted variation in male and female role reversal and an occasional narrative coda in which the man stalks the woman for revenge in the "Lipstick on the Mirror" narrative, variation as extensive as the coffin version of this legend had not yet been reported by 1991. While personal communication[2] and the reports of two syndicated news features make it clear that the coffin variation of the legend existed

---

1.   Paul Smith, Carl Lindahl, and Bonnie O'Connor thoughtfully provided me with parallel versions of the narrative discussed here. Enormous thanks are owed to the students who assisted me with collecting. These include my graduate research assistants, Marie-Annick Deplanques and John Harries and several students in my Introduction to Folklore class, who made versions of the narratives they collected during the 1991 winter semester available to me for research and publication. Included in this latter group are April O'Grady, Heather Lilly, Shirley Harnum, Jerry Best, Cynthia Pye, Karen Hutchens, Jennifer Parsons, Bridie Mulrooney, Karen Osmond, Heather Keilly, Debbie Saunders, James Wheeler, Corrine MacDonald, Tina Collins, Darryl Keating, Rhonda Halbot, and four other collectors who wished to remain anonymous.

2.   Mark Glazer, Carl Lindahl, Bonnie O'Connor, Gary Butler, and Paul Smith indicated that they had encountered examples of similar versions of the narrative in Texas, Philadelphia, Toronto, and England. The coffin version appears, however, to be much less common than the "Lipstick on the Mirror" version even in those places where it has been occasionally reported.

beyond the confines of the Canadian province of Newfoundland in 1991, they also indicate different adaptation of the motifs and different patterns of adoption of the narrative in tradition from one place to another. To date, there has been no academic work done on regional and cultural variation in the legend. Clearly, however, "Welcome to the World of AIDS" is a narrative that by virtue of its messages about sexuality, trust, disease, intimacy, mortality, and morality will be molded and shaped in narrative tradition to reflect regional and cultural values. The narrative cries out for analysis in *cultural context* as a means of accessing local concerns and attitudes toward AIDS. In this chapter, I will focus on the legend "Welcome to the World of AIDS" as it took on shape and meaning in Newfoundland. In particular, I will look at the ways in which the specific Newfoundland variations of the narrative reflect the larger cultural concerns of Newfoundlanders.

Sometime around 1987 the "Lipstick on the Mirror" version of "Welcome to the World of AIDS" appeared in the St. John's rumor mill but was quite limited in circulation. A questionnaire I administered early in 1988 on the campus of Memorial University to approximately 300 students indicated that a very small number of respondents actually knew the narrative.[3] In 1989 the coffin variation entered the scene[4] and since then, has circulated very widely as evidenced by the constabulary investigation. Together with the help of several of my students at that time, I collected over 500 accounts of this narrative. A random sample of one hundred of these

---

3.   It should be noted here that this questionnaire did not ask specifically for this narrative but, rather, addressed the larger issue of AIDS folklore on campus. The specific question that resulted in reports of the narrative was as follows:

> Have you heard any stories about AIDS (e.g., anecdotes; true personal experience stories; made up stories)? Please relate the story as close to the way you heard it or tell it as you can.

This same question one year later indicated that virtually all respondents knew one version or the other and that nearly 80 percent of those who responded with a version knew the coffin narrative.

4.   It has been suggested that the Newfoundland coffin variation might be the earliest tracing of these motifs as associated with "Welcome to the World of AIDS." While the Newfoundland narratives may be the oldest recorded examples of the coffin variation, I have serious doubts that the variation originated in Newfoundland. My argument here is not one about origins but rather concerns the enormous popularity of this version in the province. The narrative clearly made greater sense to Newfoundlanders than the earlier version.

produced twenty-six accounts of the "Lipstick on the Mirror" story and seventy-four of the coffin story. By spring of 1991 the narrative's vitality had accelerated. Of seventy-five students in my Introduction to Folklore class that term, only three had heard the lipstick story, and seventy-two knew the coffin narrative.

The limited transmission of the more standard version of this narrative, combined with the wide circulation of the coffin variant, seems to be indicative of a process of cultural selection and correction in tradition, which replaced a narrative that was not culturally viable with a narrative that more accurately reflected the concerns and worldview of the culture. It created what folklorists call an *oicotype*, a term used today to refer to a localized narrative variant. The coffin version of "Welcome to the World of AIDS" is not only an oicotype in the contemporary sense but also in the original classical sense of "a special version of a . . . tale, developed by isolation in a certain cultural area, by which on account of special national, political or geographical conditions it takes a form different from that of the same tale in other areas" (Bødker 1965:220). It is my intention here to address the reasons why the lipstick version of "Welcome to the World of AIDS" was not viable in Newfoundland and precisely how the coffin variation more accurately reflects the beliefs, attitudes, and values of Newfoundlanders.

To facilitate this kind of discussion, certain reminders about the geographical context of Newfoundland might be helpful. As an island in the Atlantic, miles away from larger bodies of land, Newfoundland has always experienced a degree of geographical and cultural isolation. In recent years this isolation has lessened considerably with the building of roads and airports, increased access to technology and transportation alternatives, development in business, tourism and provincial resources, and developments in education. Newfoundlanders, however, are still island peoples, and part and parcel of living on an island is the simultaneous feeling, on the one hand, of geographical protection provided by the absolute boundaries of land and sea and, on the other, a zest for, and curiosity about, the mainland.

An important aspect of this island existence is the feeling that everyone on the island is known to you, either in terms of their social role, kinship status, and family name or by virtue of an extremely efficient and trustworthy social network. One of the AIDS narratives began,

> Well, there were these girls from Trepassey, that's a place close to
> home in St. Mary's. Anyway they went to Florida on a holiday. One
> of the girls, I believe she was a McNeil, met up with this guy.

This kind of introduction is quite standard in many Newfoundland narratives. You supply the community and follow it with the
family name. In this way anyone can identify the characters involved
(and it does seem that many people can identify connections to
virtually any name). In this context, the unknown deliberate transmitter of HIV present in the standard version of "Welcome to the
World of AIDS" makes little sense. The trust of Newfoundlanders
in traditional information networks simply does not allow for the
anonymity required for the narrative to work. Another local legend
about AIDS brings this point home. In the same year that the coffin
narrative became popular, a story cropped up in St. John's that one
of the students called "Top Forty."[5] In this story a St. John's resident
who is HIV positive is determined to infect a list of forty people. He
frequents the bars in order to pick up women and infect them; but,
according to the story, everyone knows who he is, and as a result
no one will accompany him home and his mission is thwarted. The
"Top Forty" narrative suggests a belief (at least on some level) that a
person is not likely to be hanging around the bars downtown picking
up partners and infecting them without everyone knowing who it is
and what they are doing. It simply makes no cultural sense. While
the notion is indeed dangerous, it reflects the faith in traditional information networks that are characteristic of traditional culture.

So the scene switches to Florida (sometimes Jamaica, Hawaii,
California, or Australia, but usually Florida) and most specifically St. Pete's (St. Petersburg). Since winters in Newfoundland are
long and hard, the development of easy air travel to the mainland
has provided an attractive alternative for winter vacationers. Newfoundlanders flock in droves in the winter to Florida; and due to
the establishment of charter flights, St. Pete's has become a particularly popular destination. As one of my students put it, "the streets
of St. Pete's are positively paved with Newfoundlanders."[6] Not an
attractive image, but one that certainly communicates the general

---

5.   I would like to thank John Harries for this appropriate title.
6.   Susan Vardy, a graduate student in folklore who has worked for some time with
      government tourism, came out with this apt characterization one day in response to
      my questions about the history of Newfoundland charter flights to St. Pete's.

understanding of this location as a regional favorite. Jeff Howard, past director of the Newfoundland AIDS Committee, responded to the AIDS legend by saying, "People head to glamorous resorts with the expectation of having Love Boat or Fantasy Island-type affairs for a couple of weeks while they're on vacation. The number who have contracted the AIDS virus in this way is very high" (*Evening Telegram* April 22, 1991).

The Florida dimension of "Welcome to the World of AIDS," however, is a bit more complicated than can be conveyed in a simple description of popular fantasy getaways. Florida is not just a warm sunny fantasy land for fun in the sun; it is the *mainland*—a place without the natural island protection of home, a place where anything could happen, and where the social controls of the island do not apply. It is, after all, a place beyond the protected boundaries of the sea. For Newfoundlanders, AIDS is a part of that world, the other world to the south and east of us. This image, however, is not simply based on the cognitive map of island peoples. It has its basis both in the initial facts and in the early mistakes of local public health and the news media.

It was 1986 before the first two cases of the HIV virus were diagnosed in Newfoundland. Until then, local newspapers continually printed headlines declaring "Newfoundland Low Risk for AIDS"[7] in an effort to quell AIDS panic. When the first two cases were finally reported, it was made clear that these were people who had contracted the virus on the mainland; HIV was essentially imported. This publicity was to have dire effects. Public health officials quickly discovered their mistake and launched a poster campaign that announced "AIDS, IT'S NOT JUST A MAINLAND DISEASE."[8] The message, however, never really got across. "Welcome to the World of AIDS," along with a host of other local AIDS folklore, continually depicts AIDS as a mainland disease. In the narratives, even in those

---

7. Articles and reports from the *Evening Telegram* carried the following headlines: "No AIDS Victim in Newfoundland" (May 13, 1985); "Risk of AIDS in Newfoundland Almost Zero, Says Doctor" (July 14, 1985); "One Case of AIDS So Far in Newfoundland" (August 8, 1985); "AIDS Kills Two in Low Risk Newfoundland" (October 10, 1986); and "AIDS Not a Major Concern in Province, Says Doctor" (October 31, 1986).

8. A version of this slogan was resurrected for use in the 1992 AIDS campaign and appeared on the bottom of some of the literature issued by the Government of Newfoundland and Labrador Department of Health. The newer pamphlets say "AIDS Is Not Just a Mainland Disease or a Gay Disease. Everyone Needs to Know the Facts about AIDS."

cases in which the victim did not go to the mainland and contract the virus, mainlanders came to them. When the story does take place in Newfoundland, narrators are frequently careful to introduce the antagonist in the story as a mainlander. It would typically begin as follows:

> I've heard a story about a guy here on campus. Actually, he's blond and he has blue eyes. We're told that he was of medium build. He goes by a lot of different names and he's from Vancouver or that area.

On other occasions the antagonist is black, which, since Newfoundland does not have an indigenous black population, marks the character as a "CFA" or "come from away."

Ultimately, the Newfoundland version of "Welcome to the World of AIDS" appears to be as much a story about the dangers of the world outside the island as it is about AIDS. Many of the legend tellers indicated that the story was told to them by mothers or friends as a warning when they were about to travel. Others distanced the victim in the narrative not just once from the island but twice, as indicated by this excerpt:

> This is a story, right, of a person from Newfoundland . . . well, Newfoundland originally. He moved to Ontario, where he grew up. He and a friend decided to go to Florida for a holiday. . . .

But the story is also about Newfoundlanders—Newfoundlanders as innocent victims. Great pains are taken by the narrators to portray the protagonist as pure, respectable, and proper. Consider these descriptions from the narratives:

1. Yes. There was this girl once, eh, I think she was from Corner Brook and she was a *hard worker*. She was working on the staff at the University there and she had a two week vacation.
2. The story I heard starts off with a girl in the Confederation Building. She is only a young girl, *pretty quiet*, everyone said. . . .
3. I heard this story about a year ago . . . 3 or 4 girls go down to Florida, they are students or something. One of the girls met a man, as *anyone would*. They date a bit and have a relationship. The guy seemed like a really nice person, very *sincere*.

As indicated by these descriptions, the protagonist is usually a professional person; generally a nurse, teacher, government worker, or a university student. She or he is portrayed as quiet, hardworking, innocent, pure, and upstanding. The girl normally travels with a group of friends or her parents, counteracting the notion of the woman who travels alone looking for trouble. She meets a man, often through a friend or in some other situation in which they are properly introduced. She acts responsibly in everything she does. He is also portrayed as the perfect man, he treats her well, and as several of the narrators said,

> They started dating and he was a real gentleman. He wined her and dined her and he gave her flowers and everything.

It is made clear by virtually every narrator who tells the story that the couple did not simply fall into bed and, further, that this was *not* a one-night stand. The length of time that they are together varies, but it is seldom less than two weeks and frequently exceeds two months. They were in love; and, in at least half of the narratives, they discuss marriage or things have gotten to the point where she has reason to think the gift is an engagement ring. In many of the stories she sleeps with him only after mention of marriage is made. In others she initially refuses his attentions, unsure of her feelings. Many of these elements are combined in the following excerpt:

> About a year ago there was this young girl and she must of been in her mid 20's and anyway she went to Florida . . . she was going on a trip with her parents. . . . so anyway she wanted to meet some friends so she met this really nice girl who introduced her to this young fella . . . so they were getting along. He took her out to dinner and he brought her flowers and everything like this and then [eventually] he asked her to go back to his place because he had his own place. . . . So that was alright, she went back. And anyway he wanted to make love to her and at first she said no because she didn't want to and she didn't want to really but anyway things started to get serious and finally she gave in and they started to make love. . . . So then, that was alright. . . . The girl really cared for him.

Other narrators use the airport scene to show, through a display of affection and emotion, her feelings for the man. One narrator put it this way:

> And so anyway when she was going home she got together with her man, and they were at the airport and they were saying good-bye to everyone. And she was all lovey dovey holding him going "Oh sweetheart I love you I'm going to miss you." And like, she was crying and he says, "Oh I'm going to miss you too." And he was being all sweet and all the girls were saying, "Oh, what a swell guy, what a hunk." And so he gave her a little gift. He said, "Now you're not allowed to open this gift 'till you're in the air." And she goes, "No, no, I want to open it now with you, I want to see the look in your eyes." He goes, "no, no, this is very serious." "This is from me to you," and he said, "don't open this till you're on the plane." So she said, "O.K." and she kissed him and they kissed and kissed.

While the Newfoundland protagonist who goes to the mainland in the story is portrayed as innocent and responsible, this is not the case for mainland protagonists. Mainlanders meet in bars and participate in one-night stands. Interestingly, they also find lipstick on the mirror, not coffins in boxes. Consider this story:

> There was this girl and she was from the mainland or something. And she went one night to this bar. While she was there, this guy came over and asked her to dance. And they started dancing to-gether a lot and had a few drinks and he came over to her table. So at the end of the night she went back to his hotel room. He was in town on business and he said he was leaving the next day. So she went back to the hotel room with him and they slept together and when she woke up the next day, he wasn't in the room. So she went to the bathroom and on the mirror written in lipstick was "Welcome To The World of AIDS."

The gender of the protagonist in these stories appears also to be intricately tied to the image of the innocent Newfoundland victim. In nearly all of these stories the victim is a woman. In the beginning of my work with these narratives I thought this was due to the actual facts of HIV infection on the island. Although incidence of

HIV infection was relatively low in the province at the time of narrative collection, it was *three times* the national average of percentages of women to men.[9] Despite the fact that the general population usually does not know these kinds of statistics, they have been very well publicized in Newfoundland; and most people will have at least noticed that recent local AIDS educational campaigns have been directed at women. Further, as Gary Alan Fine notes (1987), it is surprising that in the standard version of the narrative the perpetrator is a woman and the victim a male, when medical evidence indicates that the virus spreads from man to woman more easily than from woman to man. Initially, I felt that perhaps the local story had corrected the gender due to an increase in public awareness of the facts of HIV infection.

As I began to work more closely with these narratives, however, I began to see a set of patterns that indicate that traditional Newfoundland gender roles may account more accurately for the reversal. Newfoundland women, like women in many traditional communities, are expected to be the level-headed, controlling factor in sexual relationships. Men, on the other hand, are generally accepted as sexually active or even promiscuous. In cases of accidental pregnancy, for example, women's health educators continually note that the woman traditionally is seen as the one who lost control of the situation, while the man was simply "being a man." The image of the innocent Newfoundlander in the "Welcome to the World of AIDS" narrative requires a *woman* to gain the sympathy of the taleteller and audience. If you put a man into the role of victim, the protagonist loses innocence and credibility and therefore jeopardizes the image of the Newfoundlander tainted by the mainland. Such an argument requires a closer look at the narratives in which men do play the role of protagonist. Much to my amazement, such observation produced not only information about gender roles but further complications on Newfoundland notions of HIV infection.

In every case in which the protagonist was male, the narrative contained the "Lipstick on the Mirror" motif. The coffin motif

---

9. These statistics have been put forward by the Newfoundland and Labrador AIDS Committee. Since the statistics are based only on individuals tested in the province, the figures may be misleading. A study, however, of pregnant women tested anonymously for HIV throughout Canada showed a higher per capita level of positive tests among pregnant women in Newfoundland than anywhere else in the country. The first eight months of this two-year study put the level of infection for Newfoundland pregnant women at one in 900 (*Evening Telegram* July 23, 1992).

seemed to be reserved for local female protagonists. This made a certain amount of sense since in terms of traditional gender roles, gifts are expected to be given by men to women and seldom the reverse. But this proved to be an overly complicated observation. Eventually, I concluded that male protagonists don't receive coffins with messages because they don't go to Florida. Male protagonists generally get AIDS *at home*, sometimes through interactions with mainland visitors but sometimes without this information stated. The coffin provides a portable message, one that is not necessary if the interaction with the aggressor occurs at home.

So, the question then is why do men get AIDS at home and women go to the mainland to become infected? The answer, I believe, lies in the one-night stand seemingly always present in the "Lipstick on the Mirror" narrative. Newfoundland men engage in one-night stands in the narratives, Newfoundland women do not. The Newfoundland male, however, who participates in a one-night stand at home and encounters the message on the mirror has, in virtually every case, broken some other social taboo related to the encounter. The most common social violation in these narratives is the transgression of marriage bonds. For example,

> [this story] was about this man that cheated on his wife and he went out with a hooker. It was just one night. He had never done it before. And he woke up the next morning and the hooker had marked on the window, on the mirror with lipstick "Welcome to the World of AIDS."

Men who cheat on their wives in these narratives are, most often, straying for the first time. Their partner, the aggressor, as in the example just given, is a prostitute. But other social violations are also discussed in the narratives. In a few of the versions, the man has a fight with his wife, hits her, and stomps out of the house. Perhaps the most interesting of these violations is from a narrative offered as a second version heard by one woman. The teller volunteered the following:

> A priest had an extra-marital affair or extra-priestly affair, I guess. The same thing happened. He went to the bedroom to the bathroom in his hotel room and there was the same phrase "Welcome To The World of AIDS."

The taboo behaviors suggested in these narratives break local norms and violate local cultural values. As such, they place the protagonist in a position of liminality.

The variations on "Welcome to the World of AIDS" as found in the Newfoundland corpus of texts indicates quite specific cultural concepts of the disease and its relation to the social world of Newfoundlanders. If the question "Who gets AIDS?" is put to this material, the answer generates an interesting list—a list that includes (1) mainlanders; (2) innocent Newfoundlanders who go to the mainland; (3) Newfoundlanders who engage in intimate relations with mainlanders at home; and (4) Newfoundlanders who engage in taboo behavior and who might therefore be said to be "behaving as mainlanders." The process of selection in tradition has shaped a new narrative that makes sense locally and has manipulated the older narrative to facilitate localized commentary on social transgressions.

While reports of the coffin version of "Welcome to the World of AIDS" in other parts of North America indicate that the variation is not purely local, the specific constellation of motifs does appear to suggest a particular cultural shaping of the narrative. Syndicated columnist Judy Markey published a similar version of the narrative, which appeared in her newspaper feature in the *Houston Chronicle* in June 1990. Under the title "Teen-agers Remain Invincible," she summarized the story as follows:

> Becky's friend's friend, a college sophomore, apparently went to Florida for Spring Break. She met a guy and spent most of her time with him. And on the day that she left, he brought her a present and he said, "I hope this doesn't seem stupid but I got this for your parents." When her parents opened the box, they found a small plastic coffin with a note that said, "Congratulations. Your daughter has just been welcomed to the wonderful world of AIDS." The girl got herself tested last month and she apparently tested HIV positive. At least according to Joy, who got from her friend about a friend of hers. So for a few days I've been trying to check out this story.[10]

---

10.   The exact date of publication is unknown. The article was passed on to me by Carl Lindahl, who received it undated from a student. Efforts to find an exact date have proven fruitless, but we do know that the story ran in the *Houston Chronicle* (circulation 750,000) sometime before but close to June 24, 1990.

While Markey's version is similar to the Newfoundland story, it differs in emphasis, leaving out the extended courtship motifs, the Newfoundland theme of innocent love, and the focus on the good girl who meets with an evil foreign stranger. It is not clear from the column how popular this version is in Markey's experience since she comments only on the widespread nature of narratives with the same "punch line" but with variation in motif. She notes,

> It turns out that college kids from Connecticut to California all have heard a version of this story in the past few months. It's one of those tales that have come to be called an urban legend—a story that gets started (no one knows where) and then compounds and transmogrifies exponentially throughout thousands of American rumor mills.

Jan Harold Brunvand also reported a "coffin" version of "Welcome to the World of AIDS" in his syndicated column of February 1992, but in this case, "coffin" becomes "coffee maker." In the feature a thirteen-year-old girl writes in with her version of the story. She writes,

> A woman meets a man in a bar. They hit it off right away, and the man asks her to join him on vacation at his beach house in the Bahamas. She accepts and goes with him. They make love and the woman has never been happier. On the day she has to leave, the man sees her off at the airport. He gives her a present telling her not to open it until she gets home. Back home, she finds a coffee maker inside. A note on it says "this is for all the lonely nights you'll be facing. Welcome to the World of AIDS." (1992)

Brunvand cites spring of 1990 as the date for the variation, which he dubs "AIDS Harry." This variation he describes by highlighting the following:

> Usually the couple visited some tropical setting, after which the woman got the AIDS message. At first it was just a note in an envelope, but soon the note was described as found hidden inside a gift. (1992)

Brunvand's summary of the narrative as he has collected it, combined with the example he gives from the letter written in to his column, focuses on a couple who meet at home and travel together to the south—creating a different kind of antagonist from the Newfoundland example. Although Brunvand's antagonist is a stranger, he is nonspecific in terms of nationality or regional affiliation, and the implication is that he shares the background and affiliations of the protagonist. The cultural issues involved in the narrating context are different and, therefore, so are the motif patterns.

While the clustering of these motifs can be seen as an index to the cultural concerns of Newfoundlanders, the popularity of the specific narrative images remains to be explained. Why summer resorts, why planes, why coffins? The winter exodus south for Newfoundlanders suggests a local reason for the choices. But there are also parallel traditions and events that may help in arriving at an explanation.

In 1987, Randy Shilts published his best-selling book *And the Band Played On: Politics, People, and the Aids Epidemic*. The book described the sexual exploits of a twenty-eight year old Montreal man named Gaetan Dugas, dubbed "patient zero," who continued to have unprotected sex with a large number of lovers even after he was diagnosed with AIDS in 1980. The book argued that patient zero brought the disease to North America after having contracted it in Europe through sexual contacts with Africans. According to Shilts of the first nineteen cases of AIDS reported in Los Angeles, four had had sex with Dugas, and another four had sex with one of his partners. Shilts further reported that at least 17 percent of the first 248 AIDS cases diagnosed in the United States were linked to Dugas's exploits. As he is described in Shilts's book, Dugas bears a striking resemblance to the aggressor in our story. Shilts reports several of Dugas's sexual encounters ending in a message quite similar to "Welcome to the World of AIDS." Arranged chronologically, the book entry for June 18, 1982, notes,

> It was around this time that rumors began on Castro Street about a strange guy at the Eighth and Howard bathhouse, a blond man with a French accent. He would have sex with you, turn up the lights in the cubicle, and point out his Kaposi's sarcoma lesions.
> "I've got gay cancer" he'd say, "I'm going to die and so are you." (1987:165)

But the similarities between Dugas and our story don't stop there. Dugas worked as an Air Canada steward, and Air Canada was at that time the major sponsoring airline for charters between Newfoundland and Florida. Dugas also used his job and his flying benefits to travel to resort areas to meet potential lovers in clubs and on the beaches. The book follows his visits to these communities in his deliberate attempts to spread the disease.

Because Dugas was a Canadian, the press in Newfoundland latched onto this part of Shilts's book. The local newspaper printed four articles on Dugas in 1987,[11] and although I did not trace television coverage, we can probably safely assume that it matched the newspaper's interest. Two particular versions of "Welcome to the World of AIDS" from the Newfoundland corpus point to the Dugas story as a possible influence. In one the aggressor is an airline pilot; in the other the protagonist is a stewardess for Quantus Airlines in Australia. While Dugas's story bears a resemblance to the standard version of "Welcome to the World of AIDS," it has even greater similarities with the Newfoundland version and may help to explain the resort and airplane motifs popular in the corpus.

But the notion of going south and becoming involved with a contaminated sexual partner is not restricted in contemporary legend to this narrative or even to the AIDS epidemic. Jean-Noel Kapferer discusses this motif in relation to another contemporary legend: the "Spider Boil":

> In this story, a girl has been vacationing in some southern land (e.g., Africa or the West Indies), and when she comes back she has a boil on her cheek. The boil swells even larger and finally bursts one night; a lot of small spiders crawl out of the boil, covering her whole cheek. Interestingly enough Klintberg (152) found a gothic short story from the nineteenth century, Jeremias Gotthelf's "Die Schwarze Spinne" (1842), that is set in a medieval feudal community where villagers make a pact with the Devil, and a woman receives the Devil's kiss to seal the pact; when the villagers try to cheat the Devil out of his payment, a black boil starts growing on the woman's cheek. It eventually bursts, and poisonous spiders crawl out. Although the modern story is not identical to the Gothic

---

11.   For example, "Book Says Montreal Man Brought AIDS to America," October 6, 1987. Two years later the book again appeared in the press with an article entitled "Some Doubt Man First Carried AIDS to America," October 7, 1989.

one, the meaning of the black boil is similar. In the modern story, the girl has typically come back from vacationing in some southern land; she has met a dark southern man with whom she has a fling. The story typically targets women travelling south on vacation who have sexual relationships with black men (the equivalent of having commerce with Satan in the feudal plot). (1990:123)

While the story of Gaetan Dugas points to very specific kinds of motifs that may have influenced the Newfoundland version of "Welcome to the World of AIDS," the "Spider Boil" narrative indicates a wider legendary concern with the dangers of holiday relationships. Kapferer discusses this story in terms of a natural inclination for cultures to seek scapegoats who are taken to be responsible for the community's sins. He argues that "to designate a guilty party when one is confronted with an unexplainable crisis is to point to the cause of the problem" and that the "guilty party is always the same: foreigners, those who are not integrated into the collectivity, and those that do not share [their] beliefs."

The Newfoundland world of AIDS is perhaps a world of mainland scapegoats, but I believe the narratives tell us more than that. It is also a world that reflects the life and the complex culture of Newfoundlanders. It is a world of trust in home and trust in your own. It is a world that alters foreign messages that don't make sense and that creates local ones that do.

That world is not only about rumor and story. It points to crucial issues in AIDS education and risk perception and provides a clear example of the applied potential of contemporary legend. Clearly, the cultural notion of who gets AIDS is one central to educational endeavors, not just from the standpoint of understanding stereotypes of people with AIDS, but also from the perspective of perceived personal vulnerability. The upshot is that Newfoundlanders who stay home, don't get involved with mainlanders, and don't engage in the violation of cultural norms are not seen as "at risk" despite participation in risky behaviors. "Welcome to the World of AIDS" points to the possibilities for using selective tradition as a form of educational needs assessment. The narrative tradition speaks of a very specific world of AIDS, a world that might make bad health sense but that nevertheless makes good cultural sense.

6

"Billy Ray Virus"

The Folk Creation and Official Maintenance
of a Public Health Scapegoat

The cultural adaptation of the "Welcome to the World of AIDS" narrative, discussed in the last chapter, can be seen as instructive in terms of the articulation of local health attitudes otherwise not easily assessed or expressed in the survey forms normally used in knowledge, belief, and behavior studies. It stops short, however, of actually demonstrating the direct impact of the narrative on daily life and interaction. This chapter takes the story a step further, out into the community where the legend creates a kind of "master narrative" poised to leap into interstitial gaps in knowledge and comprehension (Wycoff 1996). The story that follows demonstrates the life of a legend as it wraps itself around day-to-day interactions, providing a script for action and interpretation when information is scant and realities are too harsh to contemplate. With this said, however, it is important to note that the image of recourse to legend when information and understanding are lacking is simultaneously too bold and too superficial to really capture the fragile borders between legend and reality. Legend rarely gets incorporated whole into those gaps, and gaps in information are rarely complete or visible. Realities are not singular or transparent but, rather, multiple and emergent. This chapter will demonstrate the more subtle and more complex interweaving of ideas that form the discursive traditions of health and illness.

The Events

In December of 1991, a twenty-eight-year-old man from the small Newfoundland community of Upper Island Cove was charged under the Common Nuisance Section of the Criminal Code of Canada for endangering the lives, safety, or health of the public through unprotected sex while knowingly carrying the AIDS virus. Ray Mercer was found guilty and sentenced to two and a half years in prison, later increased on appeal to a sentence of eleven years and three months (*R. v. Mercer* 1993).

While the Mercer trial provided Crown attorneys with a precedent-setting case in terms of long-term sentencing for the "purposeful" transmission of HIV, it simultaneously presented a case study for examining the interaction between rumor, legend, and reality. The Mercer case from its very beginning was plagued by confusion with narrative traditions about intentional infection, a confusion that was evident to lawyers responsible for the prosecution. Several weeks before the public announcement of Mercer's charges, I became involved in the case, albeit minimally. During that time, I was contacted by Senior Crown Prosecutor Tom Mills about events related to the Mercer trial. Mr. Mills expressed a concern that he might require a folklorist and then proceeded to fill me in on the bare essentials of the Mercer charges. In April of 1991 Ray Mercer's name was given to public health as a reported partner of someone who had tested positive for HIV. Ray was contacted, tested for the virus, and cautioned not to have unprotected sex while he waited for the results. Ray's tests came back showing that he was infected, and he was once again cautioned on the risks of engaging in sexual activity. At this second meeting with the public health officer, Dr. Catherine Donovan, Ray indicated that he understood the risks involved and asserted that he had had no partners since he was initially called in for testing. Nevertheless, in August of 1991 Dr. Donovan became aware through the rumor mill that Mercer was seeing a local girl, age sixteen (hereafter referred to as Susan).[1]

As a result of this rumor, Dr. Donovan contacted Susan and suggested that she submit to a blood test. Dr. Donovan also contacted

---

1.   Since one of the two women infected by Raymond Mercer requested a ban on publication of her name, I have chosen to use pseudonyms for both women.

Ray at this time, and he admitted that he was engaging in sexual activity with Susan and that he had not told her that he was HIV positive. The results of Susan's tests were inconclusive. A short time after the results were issued, Dr. Donovan attempted to serve Ray with a No-Sex[2] order but discovered instead that Ray had left the province, accompanied by Susan. By October, rumors reached the local RCMP detachment that a man had infected nine to twelve women in the Upper Island Cove area with the HIV virus. At this point it becomes difficult to trace the precise chronology of events because things began to happen simultaneously and rumors began to feed rumors. On October 15, Susan submitted to a second blood test in Toronto, which confirmed that she had indeed been infected with HIV. Susan did not at this time choose to press charges. Nevertheless, on December 5, 1991, Ray Mercer was arrested and charged by the police with committing a common nuisance in relation to his activities with Susan. The next day Ray was released on bail.

Later that day, December 6, 1991, the police received a call from a twenty-two-year-old single mother residing in Toronto (hereafter referred to as Catherine), advising them that she had also been infected by Ray Mercer in July while visiting her family in Newfoundland. In the fall, Catherine began being plagued by persistent illness; and after being informed by her mother that rumors were circulating in the community that Ray Mercer had AIDS, she visited a doctor in Ontario where she eventually tested HIV positive. Catherine's statement in December was actually the first direct evidence of Ray Mercer's involvement in knowingly transmitting the virus and resulted in a charge of criminal negligence causing bodily harm. Susan, who had refused to implicate Mercer, finally furnished the police with a statement on April 29, 1992, the eve of Ray Mercer's preliminary inquiry and nearly one year after the beginning of the public health investigation. Susan indicated in her testimony that Ray had feigned surprise when she received the call suggesting that she be tested; she also revealed in her statement that her relationship with Ray had led to a pregnancy, which she later terminated after being counseled that the baby would potentially be HIV positive.

Back in December of 1991, however, when I met with Mr. Mills, Susan had not yet given her statement; and in the absence of any

---

2.   This is a public health document ordering the recipient to refrain from sexual
      activity to protect the safety of potential partners.

direct charges, Ray had been charged more generally with the common nuisance section of the criminal code. Following Catherine's call to the police, things became confused. In Canada, police may press charges in lieu of a civilian complaint. And so they did. Two charges were brought against Ray Mercer—one from Catherine and the second representing Susan, by the police. The police, however, were intent on pressing another set of two charges—each representing rumors of an unknown female purposely infected by Ray Mercer. The charges, dated December 5, 1991, read as follows:

> On behalf of her Majesty the Queen the informant says that he/she has reason to believe and does believe that Raymond Mercer of Upper Island Cove, Newfoundland, between the 1st day of January AD 1991 and the 5th day of December AD 1991 at or near Bay Roberts and or Upper Island Cove and other places in the province of Newfoundland, did, knowing that his blood had previously been found to contain antibodies to the Human Immunodeficiency Virus, commit a common nuisance by endangering the lives, safety or health of the public, to wit, by having unprotected sexual intercourse with *a female person*, contrary to section 180 of the Criminal Code of Canada. (Ramsey 1991)

The charges were left ambiguous: the "informant" noted as pressing the charges was the RCMP Constable, the specific place of infection was local but very generalized, and the victim was identified as an unspecified "female person."

Mr. Mills's feeling that he "needed a folklorist" was based on his concern that the case had become so mixed up with rumor and narrative that charges based strictly on local stories were now being filed. As Crown lawyer responsible for prosecutions, Mr. Mills feared that unprovable charges would interfere with successful conviction on provable charges. What Mr. Mills wanted from a folklorist was information on AIDS rumor and narrative traditions in the province—information that might suggest a preexisting narrative tradition concerning an aggressor who knowingly transmits the HIV virus. Using this information, Crown prosecutors would try to convince the police that by pressing unspecified charges they were tapping into a larger tradition of AIDS folklore. And it certainly appears that they were. I provided Mr. Mills with folkloristic literature on the local "Welcome to the World of AIDS" tradition and other purposeful transmission narratives, and he ultimately convinced the police to drop the nonspecific charges.

Legend and the Law

While contemporary legends might, on the surface, appear to be "just stories," they are often so localized and compelling that they can have a significant effect on the beliefs and choices that govern human behavior. Legal case reports are full of legendary motifs, sometimes indicating ostensive enactment of legend (see chapter 2), other times indicating interpretations of events according to a pre-existing legendary tradition, and sometimes indicating polygenesis or multiple origins (where the narrative tradition and parallel events, despite their similarity, are actually separate and distinct and bear no relationship to each other). In a recent house robbery in Kingston, Ontario, for example, the burglar took the family dog, who began barking, and placed it in the microwave oven, setting the oven on five minutes. The similarity to the classic "poodle in the microwave legend," in which a lady unfamiliar with the technology attempts to blow dry her dog using the microwave, is immediately noticeable. As stories detailing the enactment of crimes, "Welcome to the World of AIDS" and other deliberate-infection narratives provide perfect templates for narrative-based criminal action. In 1990, for example, the "Welcome to the World of AIDS" story became the center of a murder case in Cincinnati, Ohio (Dennis 1991; Brunvand 1991). In that case, Mr. Jeffrey Hengehold was found guilty of the murder of Linda Hoberg. Attorneys for Mr. Hengehold argued for sentence reduction due to mitigating circumstances. Hengehold, defense attorneys told the courts, had picked up Ms. Hoberg at a bar, had sex with her, and then, as they parted, Ms. Hoberg allegedly said, "Welcome to the world of AIDS." Mr. Hengehold said that he responded to the comment in fear for his own life, losing control and hitting Ms. Hoberg repeatedly, eventually causing her death. Prosecutors in the case argued that the defendant had made up the story. The judge rejected the defense argument, sentencing Mr. Hengehold to life in prison.

The presence of the "Welcome to the World of AIDS" reference in the Hengehold murder trial suggests "ostension." Readers will recall (from chapter 2) that ostension involves situations where legend tradition bearers communicate narrative through action rather than narration (Dégh and Vázsonyi 1983:6). In other words, ostension occurs when individuals *act out* a story instead of narrating it or repeating it (Dégh 2001). In most cases ostensive action does not have a direct "playacting" kind of relationship to the story but rather suggests in a more subtle sense the way narrative provides an encoded cultural script for decision making and action.[3] In recent years, legend scholarship has been used in several criminal trials involving ostensive action, that is, in cases where criminal acts were informed by, or based on knowledge of, similar action in legend tradition (Ellis 1996). In these cases, the perpetrator places him- or herself in the role of the antagonist in a narrative and performs a crime previously known from legendary tradition (much like copycat crimes). Crimes involving food tainting, ritual abuse, and murder have been argued using expert testimony on legend tradition and ostension.

Since rumor and legend had become woven through the Mercer case, the possibility of ostensive behavior had to be considered. Were Ray Mercer's actions in some sense ostensive? Was he recreating through his actions the well-known "Welcome to the World of AIDS" narrative? I checked back through the questionnaire survey of AIDS folklore that I administered to students at Memorial University each year beginning in 1986. As I perused questionnaires responded to by people from Conception Bay North (CBN), where Upper Island Cove is located, I found that the "Welcome to the World of AIDS" legend was extremely well known in 1991 in that area. This was not surprising, as the story seems to have reached a peak in its popularity all over the province at that time. There was certainly a good chance that Ray Mercer knew the "welcome" story. Nevertheless, while it is very likely that Ray Mercer had heard the "Welcome to the World of AIDS" story and while Ray's actions did seem purposeful, they did not seem to reflect the narrative fully enough to indicate ostensive behavior. What did appear to be the case, however, was that the police and local residents had received the behavior as ostensive and perhaps had themselves acted ostensively.[4] Without doubt, the police in Conception Bay North allowed rumor and traditional narratives to shape their perception of what

---

3. Dégh and Vázsonyi (1983) describe different forms of ostensive behavior including pseudo-ostension and quasi-ostension, both of which are more subtle forms lacking in the direct narrative reproduction seen in full ostension.
4. Bill Ellis also notes the role of legend in helping to shape police expectations in a satanic cult investigation in Toledo, Ohio (Ellis 1996).

they were helping to uncover. While Susan and Catherine were the only cases of women infected by Ray Mercer found by the police, the officers were convinced that there were more and worked diligently at following up rumors, serving subpoenas to women reputed to have slept with Ray, and finally pressing their own rumor-based charges. It appears that their actions were based on their understanding of Ray Mercer as a perpetrator they recognized from narrative tradition, and it is clear that Mr. Mills also saw this potential narrative reflection in their actions.

Ultimately, truly understanding a behavior as ostensive requires insight into the psychological state of the actor at the moment of action.[5] This would, of course, be nearly impossible to know with certainty, particularly after the fact, but the relationship between legend and reality does not stop there. Ray Mercer's actions clearly fit with the already existing narrative tradition and were interpreted as such by subsequent narrative tellers. Upper Island Cove and its neighboring communities of Harbour Grace, Spaniard's Bay, Bay Roberts, and Carbonear became regularly woven into versions of "Welcome to the World of AIDS," as did facts from the Ray Mercer case. One man from St. John's told the following version typical of this merger:

> I heard about this guy from Carbonear or somewhere around there and he apparently knew he had AIDS but apparently he didn't seem to care and he'd be going around from place to place picking up girls and going back to their apartment and whenever a girl would wake up in the morning, on her bathroom mirror written in lipstick would be "Welcome To The World of AIDS" and it kept on going 'til the guy was eventually caught by the police.

Similarly, referring perhaps to Susan's pregnancy, a woman from St. John's wrote in response to a general narrative question in the AIDS questionnaire,

> I heard a story about a man from Bay Roberts who had infected a girl with HIV knowingly. She got pregnant by him and he found out and sent her a little coffin (similar to a matchbox) with a little note, "Welcome to the World of AIDS."

---

5.   I am indebted to Christina Barr for this observation.

While Ray Mercer may not have consciously thought he was the perpetrator in "Welcome to the World of AIDS," others clearly thought he was. And although the narrative may not have caused Ray to perform his actions, it is certainly resonant within them and likewise he is now resonant within the narrative tradition. There is no current evidence to support, with certainty, a contention that Mercer was aware of or concerned with the parallel legendary tradition that predated his actions;[6] there is, however, enormous evidence that the boundaries between legend and reality are continually tested and foregrounded in the Mercer case and in resulting legendary tradition. For this reason, it appears necessary to step away from the implicit notion of causality[7] found in the concept of ostension (where the narrative causes the pattern of events) and move on to try to understand the relationship between narrative and action intertextually, that is, as texts that must be read in relation to each other.

Intertextuality solves the causality puzzle intrinsic to ostension theory. It does not require us to know if the narrative provoked the action or if the action provoked the narrative; in some sense both may be the case. Rather, intertextuality focuses on the nonchronological and nongenetic reciprocal ties between texts, their "relationships of meaning, allusion, and connotation." As Lotte Tarkka notes,

> Intertextual relations are twodirectional and reciprocal: one text is not primary and the other secondary, neither in the chronological sense nor as an evaluation. The identity of a text, the boundaries between texts, their ends and their beginnings, become superficial, transparent and permeable. (1993:171)

Read intertextually, the problem is not whether one story causes or influences the other but, more correctly, that one story *and* the other are caused and influenced by the same *cultural imperative*. To demonstrate this, it is important to contextualize Ray Mercer in terms of AIDS in Conception Bay North; in terms of local beliefs,

---

6.   As noted earlier, interviews with Ray Mercer after the fact would not really have provided an evidential basis for establishing his state of mind at the time of the events, particularly because so much time had passed between his actions and the subsequent trial.

7.   Dégh and Vázsonyi do recognize this problem inherent in diagnosing ostension. They note, "We have to accept that fact can become narrative and narrative can become fact" (1983:29).

attitudes, and legends about AIDS and Ray; and in terms of the case itself. From an intertextualist perspective, however, it is equally important to recognize that contexts do not simply inform texts but rather that texts and contexts are relational: they structure each other and give meaning to each other (Bakhtin 1981). Conception Bay North did not simply create Ray Mercer and the Ray Mercer story; Ray Mercer also created and continues to create the Conception Bay North story. Few reciprocal relationships are as clearly visible as they are in this particular case.

AIDS in Conception Bay North

The area of Conception Bay North has a population of between forty and fifty thousand spread out over several communities along the coast. The area has the highest ratio of people with HIV and AIDS in the province, and the province had the highest ratio in the country in the years surrounding Mercer's trial. Conception Bay North, dubbed by some to be "the AIDS Capital of Canada" (Badcock 1995:5; Bailey 1995a:3), is believed by public health officials to have the sixth highest ratio of HIV infection per capita in North America, following behind cities like New York and San Francisco. Rates of infection are suspected to be as high as one in every 400 people.

Ray Mercer, referred to jokingly in the community as "Billy Ray Virus," is frequently blamed for this situation. One resident of Harbour Grace told me,

> Well, it seems that, that the AIDS that's in the area, probably ninety percent sprouted from him.[8] That's what it seems to be anyway. It seemed like that the people who eventually get AIDS there, you talk to them and go back through their, through their past

---

8.   This view of Mercer as the source of HIV infection in large numbers of women in the community also made it into literary circles. Canadian writer and broadcaster June Callwood, in her book about the trial of Charles Ssenyonga, an African immigrant to Ontario who allegedly infected a number of women with HIV, wrote of the Mercer case,

> The Mercer trial was quick and quiet, attracting little attention in the rest of Canada until his sentence was quadrupled. What Canadians did not know was that Mercer had infected many more women than court records show: a reliable source says at least nineteen women were infected by him. Like Ssenyonga, Mercer was a handsome, charming and tireless sexual predator. (1995:229)

histories, relationships, whatever, or one-night stands whatever, and [he] fits in the picture there.

Another girl from Harbour Grace said,

> There's all sorts of rumors that, people say that just about every-body in Conception Bay has AIDS, has contracted it from him and he went away and brought it back. They've put all the blame on him.

The scapegoating of Ray Mercer for the AIDS problem in Conception Bay North had also gone beyond the local lay community into official and media sectors. In April of 1995, the Canadian Red Cross withdrew all of its blood-donor clinics from the area arguing that the high ratio of HIV made the risks of blood collection too high. The following story came over the national wire service on April 3, 1995:

> The Red Cross has cancelled blood clinics in some communities near St. John's, Newfoundland, because the area has a high rate of HIV infection. About a dozen communities between Bay Roberts and Carbonear are covered by the decision, which was made about two weeks ago. Most of the 32 Newfoundlanders who have died from AIDS have been associated with the area, known as Conception Bay North. . . . No one is sure why the infection rate is so high in such a small area. Many believe it's related to the reck-less behaviour of Raymond Mercer, a former resident of Upper Island Cove, who was given a ground breaking 11-year sentence for knowingly infecting two area women with HIV in 1991. (CP News Wire, April 3, 1995)

The Red Cross announcement was received with a storm of pro-test centered around the segregating effect of the decision. Rumors once again abounded in the community: rumors of mandatory house-to-house blood testing, of individuals assaulted because of their as-sociation with Conception Bay North, and of taxi passengers refused a ride when they indicated where they were from. A lawyer from the

---

Catherine Donovan, in the final report of a community survey of AIDS in CBN, wrote "Although many of the cases have identified a common sexual contact, many have not" (Donovan 1995).

area took the Red Cross decision to the Human Rights Association,[9] and a local lounge owner produced buttons to be given away announcing "AIDS FREE: Like 50,000 other people in CBN."[10]

But feelings of AIDS discrimination or perceived discrimination in the community began much earlier, with the Mercer trial. In 1991, while having lunch with a colleague in the Memorial University student center, I was joined by a student from Upper Island Cove. I introduced her to my colleague, who asked her where she was from. She responded, "Placentia Bay" (an area quite far from Conception Bay North). When I asked her later why she had lied about her home community, she responded, "I don't say I'm from there any more; they think we all slept with Ray; they think everyone at home has AIDS." Virtually all of the female young people I know from the area have indicated that they regularly or occasionally lie about their community affiliation;[11] others have told me that they have not been able to get a date since the trial,[12] and several males

---

9.   The Human Rights Commission ultimately ruled that the regional operation of the Red Cross was acting in good faith when it cancelled blood-donor clinics in Conception Bay North (Bailey 1995b).

10.   Manager of the Cod Trap Lounge Lori Badcock indicated that she and several of her customers came up with the button shortly after the Red Cross decision. She noted:

> That was all our customers talked about. These people were really upset and they couldn't believe what was happening. . . . So one day we decided to do something that would be making a statement about how we felt. At first we considered selling T-shirts with the message "I live in Bay Roberts-Carbonear and I'm AIDS Free" but that would have been a little costly, so we decided to go with the buttons. (Flynn 1992:7)

11.   A personal advice columnist published the following letter in her column in the local newspaper.

> Dear Ruby, I'm so glad to see there's someone that we can write to for a word of advice. . . . The problem is this: I'm a young woman in my early 20's from Conception Bay North and as you know, this area is known for AIDS. I'm living in St. John's now but I soon realized my mistake when I would tell a new friend that I came from CB North. Some people raised their eyebrows! I could sort of foresee a problem after I met a very nice young man. I decided quickly to say I came from Windsor. This was OK until one evening he introduced me to another young woman at a club and she said "Oh, you are from Windsor . . . so am I!" You can imagine the embarrassment that followed. How do you think I can keep my reputation intact? Do you think I'm over-reacting to the AIDS situation in CB North? My name is written on the back of this letter. Please don't use it in print. Just sign me . . . Blind Date. (Ask Ruby 1996)

12.   One newspaper account (*Evening Telegram* April 5, 1995) reported that a woman from CBN was hired as a bartender in St. John's under the condition that she never tell customers that she was from Bay Roberts .

that I interviewed told me that they carry regular blood-donor cards to prove to women that they are HIV negative. One woman said,

> Even in our own Conception Bay area we tar the whole community. Like we say, [like] "Don't go out with anybody from Island Cove cause they all got AIDS, cause Ray gave it to them. Right? We associate it with Ray immediately.

Another person indicated that it is common to hear someone say, "Wear your gloves, you're going through Island Cove." In 1993 a joke started to make the rounds, which asked, "What's the new postal code for Conception Bay North? Answer: UIC-HIV": the prefix standing for both Unemployment Insurance Compensation *and* Upper Island Cove.

But Ray Mercer did not start the AIDS problem in Conception Bay North; nor is he responsible for the high rate of infection. In fact, to the contrary, Ray may be responsible for slowing the epidemic. Public health officials claim they knew in 1988 that Conception Bay North had a problem. In that year the first three cases of HIV were reported in the area. For a district so small, three cases signalled a problem. As the director of the Newfoundland and Labrador AIDS Association told me, in Newfoundland each case is multiplied by ten to arrive at a figure approximating contacts, and contacts of contacts, associated with an infected individual.[13] The resulting figure of thirty potential people with AIDS in the area was horrific. The same mathematical process just four years later would indicate close to 500.

Word of public-health concerns must have reached local churches and community organizations because, also in 1988, I was contacted by the United Church Council of Social Ministries and was asked if I would help them write a grant for a three-year AIDS education and hospice development project in CBN. The woman whom I assisted on this project would tell me only that the church

---

13. This in itself is interesting. Other sources figure more simply that for each person diagnosed there are estimated to be two others that have not been diagnosed (Morgan 1998:14). The social construction of statistics and the normative ways of counting not only that which is measurable but that which is potential deserve their own explorations as legend material. South African legend scholar Arthur Goldstruck has begun to address this issue in relation to beliefs surrounding what public health workers called "the doubling-time"—the length of time it takes for the number of infected people to double. (See Goldstruck 1993:231–233.)

had good reason to believe the area had a problem. Was it Ray's fault? Not likely. In 1988 Ray Mercer was living in Ontario and had been for sometime. Dr. Donovan, the Public Health Officer for Conception Bay North, however, has worked the Ray Mercer charges and trial into the variables she considers to be responsible for increasing public health awareness. The charges appear to have attracted attention to the disease, and the statistics for HIV-testing rose considerably in 1991 and 1992. Ray seems to have been a formative AIDS educator.

The Trial

So what did Ray do and why? While the police combed Conception Bay North looking for women infected by Ray, they never found the nine to twelve individuals rumored to exist. Despite a long series of inquiries and subpoenas, Susan and Catherine were the only victims ever located. Although Ray knowingly put Catherine and Susan at risk, the revenge motif central to "Welcome to the World of AIDS" does not really come through in the facts of the trial. The announcement of intent after infection—the punch line, central to the legend—is absent in Ray's reported actions; and in fact, Ray never did inform either woman of his HIV status. But Ray did lie to both women about the risks. Susan recounted,

> He was drunk and kept pressuring me to have sex with him. I did not want to but he kept saying that I could trust him . . . and finally I gave in to him. That was the first time I had sex with him and he did not use a condom. I asked him to use a condom but he told me there was no need to use one. If he thought he was with somebody before who was a slut, he would use one, but there was no need and I had nothing to worry about.

Catherine also asserted that when she suggested condom use, Ray indicated there was no need. Catherine, however, implies premeditation but not necessarily revenge:

> Mr. Mercer knew what he was doing when he, when we had sex, he knew that he was HIV positive and in my eyes he had some ultimate reason, I don't know why.

Two pieces of information from expert witnesses in the case suggest that Ray's disregard for responsible action may not have been premeditated. The forensic psychiatrist at the prison testified that Ray could not read or write, had only a grade-four education, and was of below-normal intelligence, implying that Ray may not have understood the full consequences of his disease. Dr. Donovan indicated at the trial in 1992 that Ray had only just begun to accept that he had AIDS, previously asserting that he felt fine[14] and was perfectly healthy. Both testimonies suggest the possibility that Ray either did not fully comprehend his condition or that he could not emotionally accept the seriousness of his situation.

Ray himself, in a letter dictated through a fellow prison inmate and addressed to the court, suggests another reason for his actions. He gave the following account of the facts of the case from his perspective:

> Raymond Mercer is a 29-year-old resident of Upper Island Cove, Nfld., Canada. In July 1992 the defendant pleaded guilty to two charges of having unprotected sex with two women, knowingly being HIV pos. The facts in the case is that these two women stated they were HIV pos also. Therefore what harm could come of people who are HIV positive having sex with one another. Charge number one *Susan*. Here is a girl I met in a night club in Harbour Grace the Piarts Cave [sic]. So naturally you assume that a person is nineteen years old to be in a club. Not so then to find out that this girl was sixteen at the time leave me to believe that I am being used as a scape goat in this case. This girl knew I was HIV pos at the time. So where are the facts in this case by the Crown that I infected her with this virus. Can Susan prove that I Raymond Mercer infected her with this virus. Therefore I ask this court that DNA tracing be done on me and her to see if she carry the same virus as me. The same thing must be done to Catherine to see if she carry the same virus as me.

DNA testing was requested by the court, and I was able to locate the laboratory order. The report of results of the tests, however,

---

14. Ray's comments suggest that he may not have been fully able to comprehend what asymptomatic seropositivity meant in terms of his ability to transmit the virus. This is consistent with the *Sexuality, AIDS, and Decision Making: A Study of Newfoundland Youth* survey, which found that 31 percent of grade-eleven youth were not aware that there were asymptomatic stages of HIV infection (Cregheur, Casey, and Banfield 1992).

was not traceable, but the Crown attorneys have indicated that if the report had provided new evidence, the case would have been recalled.

By all accounts in the trial, Ray's motives were somewhat milder than those of the aggressor in the "Welcome" legend. Community narrative tradition, however, has its own explanation for Ray's motives.

The Ray Corpus

Legends about what Ray did and why he did it abound in Conception Bay North. Revenge is a predominant theme in these stories—a general and wide-reaching revenge, explained nearly always in the same terms.

One man from Harbour Grace said,

> It wasn't made public that he did have it until, say, a few years ago, probably, . . . a year, year and a half before all this trouble came out with him. And he was just indiscriminately went out, and went out with other people, and from what they say he's been . . . he knew he had it and he says "I got it and you're gonna get it". Just that's the kinda attitude that . . . he had. Because he didn't, he just didn't care.

Another person from the area said,

> Well, they say his attitude about it is that: I'm sick and I'm dying so . . . I'm taking a couple of people with me, and I don't care.

A third person recounted,

> And the story then was after all this came out that he had spread it to these girls was that he had it in, that he caught it from the Armed Forces when he was in there . . . that's where he supposedly caught it, and he came out there with a vengeance and decided to take as many people as he wanted with him, which would be, obviously women.

Numerous stories indicate that the police asked Ray to write on a sheet of paper all of the women he slept with, and he was quoted as saying, "You better get me an exercise book" (a notebook—see the "number and names" game in chapter 2). Contrary to these narratives, the police reports indicate that Ray confessed only to sleeping with Susan, whom he intended to marry.[15]

A second significant theme in the narrative corpus attached to Ray is his efforts to infect people through purposeful, but casual, blood and saliva transfer. A man from Conception Bay North argued,

> Ray would do things, like he would get on the beer on a Friday night, Saturday night with the boys, you know get together with the boys. He'd get drunk and go home, he was then home with his parents and this is what I heard. He would cut his hand, some part of his arm or his hand and chase his Mom around and try to get the blood on her from the cut.

Another person from the area said,

> A friend of mine called me one day and he said, "Oh, Ray Nish [his local name][16] just slit his wrists and chased his mother up the road.". . . There was another story about how he was changing a flat or something at a local gas station there in Island Cove, on the main road, a GEO station. An RCMP officer stopped to talk to him when he cut his hand again and smeared the front of his uniform. I also heard how they arrested him for impaired one time and went to put him in the back of the police car and he threatened to do that. As far as I knew that was true. He said, you know, "You're not taking me anywhere, I'll cut my wrists," you know. Apparently that one was true.

15. It is not my intention to suggest here that the police would necessarily have located everyone infected by Ray or that it is impossible that Ray infected others. What is clear, however, is that it is unlikely that Ray infected the exponential numbers of women suggested by the narrative tradition (one account suggests 1500) and that the police certainly made an effort to locate as many contacts as possible.

16. While Ray Mercer's proper last name is Mercer, he is locally referred to as Ray Nish. Individuals from Upper Island Cove explained to me that the name Nish was given to the family by a local doctor, who found it difficult to deal with the limited number of family names in the area. There were so many families named Mercer that he devised new family names for each. The word "Nish" has its own meaning in Newfoundland. Interestingly, the *Dictionary of Newfoundland English* defines it as "Soft or tender; sore or inflamed; delicate" and "Of persons, delicate, lacking in hardiness" (Story, Kirwin, and Widdowson 1982:349).

Ray *was* arrested for impaired driving and assaulting a police officer sometime between being charged and his trial, but the police report indicates that he pushed the policeman with no mention of a blood-transfer threat. Most of the stories about casual transfer involve young children, emphasizing Ray's efforts to infect the innocent.

One man indicated,

> Yeah, [there were stories] . . . that were going around up there, that he cut his finger and was chasing the kids with it. Flicking the blood.

Another said,

> One evening at a hockey game, apparently he, at this point he knew he was already sick, he had been to court once already, and he spit in a young child's face, and he was saying things like y'know: I'm going and taking the women with me.

Many of the stories focus on Ray as simply evil. One of the members of the community said,

> Ray's parents used to sleep one at a time, afraid Ray would harm them. Ray had apparently told them if they ever did anything to piss him off, he'd burn them in their beds.

Ray's parents figure largely in the stories, generally though descriptions of them as loving adoptive parents, who gave him everything and who were afraid of their son. I collected several versions of the following story.

> Even before all this came about, a good many years ago, his mother would say, in particular now I'm just relating what someone, a woman told me, that [his mother said] "I don't know where the Christ we got you at. . . . I wished to Jesus you'd go back to wherever you came from, 'cause you're only the spawn of the devil," or something like that.

The most significant set of stories that I collected about Ray involves his continuous dares. The following narrative is a popular example.

Ray had blown the engine in his Trans Am. His father went to work one day. Ray took the engine out of his Dad's new pick up and put it down on his car, saying, "what are you gonna do about it."

The fact that Ray's illness was terminal gave Ray incredible power in the narratives and, like the Trans Am story, many of them focus on his actions as immune from consequence. In the narratives, Ray was going to die, and his evil powers came not only from his ability to infect but from his illness status, which placed him essentially outside of the law.

Crown prosecutor, Cathy Knox, in her closing statement in the trial shows a consciousness of this attitude:

> Your Honour, there were things that happened to each of us in life that are unfortunate and tragic but tragic circumstances visited upon us, does not give us the right to therefore respect less and afford less to the rights of others. . . .
>
> If we are advised that we have cancer and that we have, or that I have six months to live, I don't therefore become empowered to sit behind the wheel of my car, for example, and to run down the next person who passes in front of me on the street. Nor do I become empowered to get so upset because I know that I am going to die in six months that I go out and get drunk and while drunk behind the wheel I accidentally run down a person who is crossing the street in front of me. We do not become empowered by our own misfortune with a lesser degree of responsibility for others. . . . Your Honour, what Raymond Mercer did was took upon himself, a power that we cannot afford to give anybody in our Community. . . . If we listen to the evidence of the doctors, they did not say to him, "we are really sorry for you, we know that you are going to die, therefore we forgive you." And that is what you are being asked to do. (*The Queen v. Raymond Hayward Mercer* Appeal 1992:207)

While it is the power of impending death that gives Ray the strength of his evilness in the narratives, narrative tradition also recognizes one higher and fuller level of evil: the possibility that Ray might not die. One person said,

One of his, one of his friends stopped in on his, on his way up to Ontario to see him when he was in prison, and he . . . . its kind of, its kind of sad like he said that cause he, he never looked so good. And they like, well at the time, they say he had his own little place, and his own separate little living quarters. And they say he looked healthy, he's after putting on weight, and they say he seemed, the best he did in years. So I think its kind of, kind of sad now that he's been putting other people in that kind of predicament and he not . . . not sick yet himself.

This piece of information evolved into a real AIDS Mary story, where, like Typhoid Mary, Ray is a healthy carrier. Another individual argued,

I've heard other stories that, he doesn't have, he's just a carrier, and not a full-fledged AIDS patient as such, y'know he may live for another fifteen years and never develop the disease and just carry it and give it.

Public Health and the Stigmatized Community

Were the high rates of infection in Conception Bay North a reality? Unfortunately, they were. As mentioned in the introduction to this volume, Department of Health Studies done in the early 1990s across Canada collecting blood samples from anonymous pregnant women between the ages of fifteen and twenty-nine found that Newfoundland rates of seropositive blood samples were by far the highest in the country, with one in every 900 samples testing positive. These rates compared with one in 1,600 in Quebec, one in 3,700 in British Columbia, and one in 9,100 in Manitoba. Figures released from the study in 1992 indicated that Newfoundland had the highest number of pregnant women with HIV per capita in the country (Jackson 1992b). The anonymous study demonstrated that the number of Newfoundlanders infected with HIV was far higher than official non-anonymous numbers would suggest.[17] In 1993, the

17.   Previous numbers are based on diagnosis in the province. As noted earlier, numerous public-health workers have indicated concern that these figures in no way reflect actual cases of HIV/AIDS living in Newfoundland. Fear of small-town lack of confidentiality and inaccessibility of anonymous test sites around the province have meant that individuals "go away" to be tested. Their numbers are not registered.

Newfoundland and Labrador Prenatal Study of HIV Seroprevalence done by Sam Ratnam, director of the Newfoundland Public Health Laboratory, compared the pregnancy-study results for the Eastern Region, which includes Conception Bay North, to overall provincial results, finding that HIV prevalence in the Eastern Region was 26.6 in 10,000, far higher than the 8.7 in 10,000 found elsewhere in the province (Ratnam 1994).

So if Ray was not responsible for the high rates of infection in Conception Bay North, who or what was? Most epidemiologists agree that epidemic infection is rarely a result of one thing but rather stems from a cluster of events all coinciding to create perfect conditions for disease transfer. This, however, did not prevent medical researchers from attempting to find a laboratory explanation for the escalating number of infected individuals in the area. In 1995, Dr. Ratnam undertook a new study intended to explore whether the "outbreak" was associated with single or multiple strains of HIV and to compare HIV strains in the area with those found in other parts of the province and country. The prevalence of HIV infection among women in the area indicated that the virus was being transmitted through heterosexual contact. Ratnam focused his initial hypothesis that the strain might be significant on findings from Thailand, which suggested that the subtype of HIV found in North America and Europe (B) was more easily transmitted through "homosexual sex" (his term) and intravenous drug use, while the subtype (E) found in Thailand may be more easily transmitted through heterosexual intercourse. Ratnam theorized that the HIV strain found in Conception Bay North might be the same subtype found in Thailand, explaining the high ratio of women with HIV in the area. His hypothesis, however, proved to be wrong. The strain found in blood samples from Conception Bay North was the same as that which is typically found in North America. In the meantime, Ratnam's study created its own panic in the area as individuals speculated about a rare, highly infectious "special" form of HIV somehow brought into the community (*Express* 1995:19). Other medical researchers hypothesized that perhaps Ray Mercer had a "super" viral load (the quantity of HIV molecules present in the person's blood stream),[18] making him essentially the "superman" of HIV.

Local HIV/AIDS service providers argue that they have a patient base much higher than the official statistics reflect (see Jackson 1992b).

18. In the mid-1990s I sat on a Canadian national committee for AIDS research planning and priorities. A number of AIDS researchers at those meetings asked me if

Cultural issues are more likely to be responsible for the high rates of infection in the area. Risk-taking behaviors have always been reported to be high in Newfoundland. Survey studies done in the late1980s and early1990s (King 1989; Cregheur, Casey, and Banfield 1992) focusing on sexual behaviors among Canadian youth indicate that Newfoundland teens reported higher rates of sexual activity than anywhere else in Canada. They also reported strongly negative views on premarital sex, birth control, and protection from sexually transmitted diseases. While these studies suggest numerous reasons why HIV rates in the province would be high, little information is available to assess attitudes specific to this region. Catherine Donovan (1995) has attempted to survey knowledge, beliefs, and behaviors in Conception Bay North through a questionnaire made available at HIV test sites in the area. While the rates of response are low, the survey information is useful in highlighting certain issues.

Public health workers and physicians have always argued that chlamydia, genital warts, and other sexually transmitted diseases often go untreated in outport Newfoundland due to concerns about gossip and lack of medical confidentially. The presence of such pre-existing sexual disease conditions creates a predisposition for HIV due to the potential presence of skin lesions promoting transfer. In Donovan's 1995 study of 152 respondents who filled out questionnaires administered by the Community HIV Prevention Project at HIV test sites in Conception Bay North, 12 percent reported having had a previous STD. Keeping in mind that this figure is reliant on self-reportage, on the individual having made the choice to be tested for HIV, and on previous diagnosis of the earlier STD (which means one reported for initial medical care), it would appear that the percentage is substantial. The figure is consistent with earlier indications of misconceptions concerning other STDs. In the 1992 *Sexuality, AIDS, and Decision Making* study administered province wide, only 18 percent responded correctly to a question concerning whether or not chlamydia could lead to other health problems.

Further, the concern with community gossip and lack of confidentiality, combined with the strongly religious background of the area, discourages condom use. Numerous individuals interviewed

Ray Mercer's viral load had been tested. They asserted that there must be a scientific explanation for the high rates of infection. The super–viral load theory strikes me as the scientific version of the same superinfector concept behind the narratives.

for this chapter noted that they would never purchase condoms locally but rather would wait until they visited St. John's or other areas
of the province, for fear that store employees or observing patrons
would "talk." The 1992 province-wide study supports these observations. Forty-eight percent of grade-eleven youth indicated they
were too embarrassed to buy condoms and 66 percent responded
that "if you carry a condom, people will think you are having sex."
Donovan's area study found that 36 percent of respondents reported
never using condoms, and only 12 percent reported consistent condom use.

Most significant from Donovan's study is a set of statistics that
support anecdotal information on anal intercourse being used by
teens as a method of birth control. Donovan indicates that reports
of the prevalence of this practice in other areas had been conflicting
and thus health promotion campaigns had not focused on the issue.
The HIV testing site survey, however, reported that 24 percent of
respondents (22 percent of the males and 20 percent of the females)
engage in anal intercourse (Donovan 1995:4).

The risk factors discussed above are not peculiar to Conception
Bay North; to the contrary, they are found, with some variation, in
many parts of the province and elsewhere. These risk factors, however, combined with a few early cases of HIV in a small rural area,
act as a container for infection and sow the seeds for epidemic pro-
portions. The emphasis on Ray Mercer as the evil "patient zero" in
the area places the blame on one individual and denies the responsibility of all partners in self-protection. By so doing, it continues to
encourage risk.

Conclusion

From an intertextualist perspective, Ray Mercer—his reality and his stories—give us insight into "Welcome to the World
of AIDS" and other purposeful transmission narratives. The more
evil Ray Mercer becomes in the narratives, the more innocent his
victims (real or otherwise) become. Ray's evil absolves the members
of Conception Bay North of perceived guilt and yet explains the
devastation in the community. Without Ray, the stigma attached to
him since the trial attaches completely to Conception Bay North.
Like Ray, the aggressor in "Welcome to the World of AIDS" creates
the innocent victim of AIDS; that is not really a part of our thinking

about the disease. Guilt creates innocence, and the same cultural imperative created both "Welcome to the World of AIDS" and Ray Mercer. The struggle with guilt and innocence, the concern with the dying person's placement outside the law, the fear of one who may be treated without consequence and yet may survive the power given to that individual by impending death converge to give us insight into the human struggle with contagion and disease. Ostensive or not, it is the poignancy of that message that pervades these borders of narrative and reality.

Epilogue

In late 1999 Ray Mercer came up for parole. The parole board denied his applications on the basis that they felt that he would be likely to reoffend. A few months later, Canadian Blood Services decided to resume mobile blood clinics in the CBN area. On March 7, 2000, John Gushue, in an article in the *Medical Post* entitled "Blood Donation Ban Lifted from Tainted Nfld. Area," wrote of the original decision to withdraw the clinics: "The alarming increase [of HIV cases] in the early and mid-1990's was largely due to one person, Raymond Mercer, who is still serving a lengthy jail sentence for knowingly infecting his partners with HIV" (2000:1).

7

"Banishing All the Spindles
from the Kingdom"

Reading Needle-Prick Narratives as Resistance

On May 13, 1999, another AIDS legend made its way onto the pages of the *St. John's Evening Telegram* in an article entitled "HIV Cyber-hoax Spreading Concern." The so-called cyber-hoax in question was a narrative being forwarded by anonymous e-mails, warning of HIV-infected needles placed in movie theater seats, pricking unsuspecting moviegoers and infecting them with the virus. The news report quoted a portion of the e-mail message:

> For your information, a couple of weeks ago, in a movie theatre a person sat on something sharp in one of the seats. When she stood up to see what it was, a needle was found poking through the seat with an attached note saying, "You have been infected with HIV." (Lake 1999:1)

A spokesperson for the Regina (Saskatchewan) Police Department, whose name was on many of the warnings, told the *Canadian Press* that the e-mail was not sent by her department and furthermore that the message was causing small-scale panic in Regina, resulting in approximately thirty phone calls a day to the police and local government (Lake 1999:1). The situation was similar in Newfoundland. Patricia Murphy, executive director of the AIDS Committee of Newfoundland and Labrador, was also reported as saying that her office had been flooded with calls and e-mails from Newfoundlanders and

Labradorians concerned about the warning (Lake 1999:1). Other North American police departments, public health offices, and the American Center for Disease Control also reported a wave of public reaction to the narrative.

A few days before the *Evening Telegram* article, I received a phone call from the editor of the Newfoundland and Labrador AIDS Committee newsletter, *Reaching Out*, wanting to discuss the story. She noted, as had I, that this AIDS rumor was a bit different than the stories that had circulated previously. The story had no scapegoat, no sexual commentary, and no real construction of guilt or innocence. She wondered if the story was meant to implicate and condemn IV drug users. I didn't think so. The narrative didn't mention drug users; and, in fact, what made the story so unusual in the current legend climate, was that it didn't mention an antagonist at all. Like other pinprick narratives found in earlier and more limited circulation, anonymity was at the very core of the story. In those stories the sharp instrument was occasionally an intravenous needle but more often was thorns, straight pins, hat pins, and various other pointed objects and was almost always left by an anonymous, untraceable perpetrator. The big question, it seemed to me, was why the known scapegoated infector, so popular in recent AIDS legends, was replaced in this wave of tradition by a faceless anonymous infector, and why had the narrative taken on such currency now? Perhaps the nameless, faceless needle on the seat was a metaphor for new concerns about public vulnerability. Perhaps . . . , but what if these stories are not just about what we come to fear but also about the role of agency in those fears? In this chapter, I propose a counterreading of the needle narrative, a reading that suggests that the anonymous AIDS infector might be preferable to the one we know and that public danger is far more desirable than danger in our homes. On some level, I believe, needle-prick narratives can be read as a form of resistance—resistance to the modern construction of our homes as locations of risk and resistance to public health constructions of our loved ones as vectors of danger.

While contemporary-legend scholars have over the last ten years explored the deliberate sexual transmission of HIV characterized in so many of the narratives mentioned in this volume, such as "Welcome to the World of AIDS," "C. J. AIDS," or the "Irish Angel of Death" (Brunvand 1989; Fine 1987; Goodwin 1989; Smith 1990; Goldstein 1992; and others), *nonsexual* transmission legends have been virtually ignored. Largely absent from the legend literature is the narrative tradition about invisible infectors like those in our story, who make use of syringes, needles, pins, and other sharp or hollow instruments to contaminate condoms (see chapter 2), other objects, or food or to infect individuals with the HIV virus. With the exception of an anthology entry by Jan Brunvand (1989:206), two *FoafTale News* columns by Bill Ellis (1989b:5–6, 1990:9), and a few paragraphs in general contemporary legend readers (de Vos 1996:58), the scholarly record has not had a lot to say about needle-prick narratives, perhaps because the narratives themselves have been only loosely connected and borrow heavily from other legend constructs.

Certainly, the narratives make use of motifs we have seen before; they warn of public places, demonstrate fears of contamination, and indicate concerns about conspiracies to obliterate individuals or groups. While the stories all involve needle- or pinpricks and contamination with HIV, the narrative action differs: pins stuck in drugstore shelf condoms, lemons and oranges injected with HIV in the grocery store, raspberry pickers pricked by a thorn and bleeding on the fruit we buy, children stuck by sharp instruments in fast-food "ball rooms" or playgrounds, robbers armed with HIV-positive needles, pinpricks on buses, in bars, in theaters, and the list goes on.

The shared motifs in these stories predate AIDS and are familiar, not just from earlier needle crime narratives, but also from folktale and ballad tradition. While Sleeping Beauty comes immediately to mind, the *Motif Index*[1] is rife with tales of poisoned arrows (F831.3), sleep-bringing thorns (D1364.2), magic spindles (D1186), and murder by piercing with a pin (S115.3). Ballad tradition supplies analogous motifs in the "pulled a rose" formula, in which the victim is suddenly pierced by sharp growth from a plant, foreshadowing impending doom. In ballad tradition, the rose thorn-prick invariably signals some kind of bad news—usually rape or death—but not illness (Andersen 1985:116–119). But in both narrative and ballad tradition, piercing generally signals vulnerability, intrusion, invasion, or contamination. Both metaphorically and literally, the piercing leaves a hole that can be filled by all manner of evil.

The vulnerability and intrusion interpretations of pinprick legends do not require any great stretch of the imagination, but it would appear that the impetus for the nameless, faceless construction of

1. The *Motif Index* is a catalogue of narrative elements repeatedly found in international folklore (see Thompson 1955–58).

vulnerability is not quite as easily understood. Gail de Vos (1996) classifies pinprick panics as crime victim legends, noting, "crime victim narratives reflect society's fear of the anonymous criminal, the stranger lurking in a dark alleyway ready to pounce on an innocent victim" (49).[2] Pinprick narratives, however, and crime victim legends in general can also be read as a matter of agency—expressing preference for the *stranger* as antagonist rather than the familiar alternative. But let's begin with the story.

Contemporary Pinprick Narratives

AIDS pinprick narratives have been reported in legend and in the news since the mid-1980s (Ellis 1989b) but (as noted) with limited circulation, only recently exploding in popularity, largely in the form of needles that appear in public places, pricking the anatomy of an innocent individual, who simply wants to dance at a club, use a public phone, or watch a movie in a theater. In Canada, the most common version takes place in a dance club or at a party. One student at Memorial University noted,

> One of my friends informed me of a bar somewhere in Toronto or Ontario where people carried needles infected with the [AIDS] virus, [infected] directly from themselves, and while people would be getting drinks or dancing, whoever had these needles would prick the unsuspecting person. Another girl I know told me about a similar incident in which some legal aged young people "snuck" a younger sister, only 16, into a bar.[3] She ended up being the one stuck with an infected needle.

Like many needle-prick narratives, the dance club version frequently uses the "Welcome to the World of AIDS" tagline, which floats freely and attaches itself to any and all AIDS legends. Another student noted,

> I heard a story about a girl who was in a crowded bar in Toronto. She felt a prick in her side but ignored it. When she looked later

---

2.   See Wachs (1988) for a book-length treatment of crime-victim narratives.
3.   This narrative reveals a similar breaking of an initial taboo followed by the infecting action discussed in relation to the "Welcome to the World of AIDS" narrative, thus complicating the "innocent victim" picture (see chapter 5).

there was a syringe in her side with a tag on it that said "Welcome to the World of AIDS."

The nightclub and party version of the pinprick narrative occasionally also shares motifs with narratives of LSD-contaminated children's transfer tattoos,[4] but in this case the sticker is filled with HIV-infected needles. One Internet warning noted,

> Do any of you like to go clubbing? Well you might think twice after this message. Just in case you don't already know, there is a certain group of people with stickers that say "Welcome to our world." Once this sticker is stuck on you, you contract the AIDS virus because it is filled with tiny needles carrying the infected blood. This has been happening at many dance clubs (even DV8 and Beatbox) and raves. Being cautious is not enough because the person just chooses anyone, and I mean anyone, as his/her victim. So you could just be dancing the night away and not even realize the sticker has been stuck on you. It sounds too demented to be true, but it's the truth. In fact my sister's friend knows someone who just recently contracted the virus in this manner. The world isn't safe anymore. (Personal e-mail, 1998)

Interestingly, the dance club version of the pinprick narrative seems to have had a significant impact on the bar scene as it entered circulation. In Toronto and in San Diego popular dance clubs indicated in 1998 that the story had seriously affected their businesses. In August of 1998 one popular Toronto nightclub had estimated a drop in clientele of 50 percent as a result of the story (Rayner 1998).

While the nightclub narrative seems to be popular in Canada, the pinprick narrative that currently has the widest international circulation involves needles or pins hidden in movie theater seats, reported in 1999 in Canada, the United States, Germany, Finland, England, Scotland, Australia, India, Hawaii, Mexico, and Costa Rica.[5] The story typically resembles the following version, collected in Bombay in 1998:

---

4.   Sometimes referred to as "Mickey Mouse Acid" or "Blue Star Acid," the legend suggests that children's tattoo transfers are impregnated with LSD (see Brunvand 1984 and Kapferer 1993).

5.   These reports are from alt.folklore.urban, an Internet legend newsgroup with a substantial international subscriber base of legend enthusiasts.

There was a group of 6-7 college girls and they went to the theatre to see a movie. During the show one of the girls felt a slight pin prick but did not pay much attention to it. After some time that place began to itch. So she scratched herself and then saw a bit of blood on her hands. She assumed that she had caused it. At the end of the show, her friend noticed a sticker on her dress and read the caption. It read, "Welcome to the World of AIDS." She tried to pass it off as a practical joke but when she went for a blood test a couple of weeks later (just to be sure) she found herself HIV positive. When she complained to the cops, they mentioned that her story was one of the many such cases they had received. It seems the operator uses a syringe to transfer a bit of his or her infected blood to the person sitting ahead of him or her.

At about the same time as the movie theater pinprick narrative began making the rounds, another similar story began to circulate on e-mail. This story reflected little variation in electronic transmission, nearly always recounted through the Internet as follows:[6]

A very good friend of mine is in an EMT certification course. There is something new happening that everyone should be aware of. Drug users are now taking their used needles and putting them into the coin return slots in public telephones. People are putting their fingers in to recover coins or just to check if anyone left change. They are getting stuck by these needles and infected with hepatitis, HIV and other diseases. This message is posted to make everyone aware of the danger. Be aware. The change isn't worth it!

P.S. This information came straight from phone company workers, through the EMT instructor. This did NOT come from a hearsay urban legend source.[7]

6.   The needle-prick story is one of the best examples of the fluid movement of legend back and forth between print, electronic, and oral channels. The various channels appear to complement each other in moving the story quickly, efficiently, and persuasively from person to person. It should, however, be noted that while the fairly inflexible warning format quoted here is common, the narrative is also circulated on e-mail in a more traditional narrative form that has greater flexibility in content and variation, similar to oral narration.

7.   Later versions of the narrative place the needle in the trigger of gas pumps and warn the public to only use full-service gas stations, where handling the trigger is not necessary.

Within a very short time an Internet warning evolved that joined the movie theater version with the telephone narrative. The joining of the two stories did not take the usual merged form folklorists are used to seeing, in which one story is created out of motifs borrowed from two or more narratives. In this case the stories were used sequentially, one right after the other. Each, however, retained its original integrity. The following warning was forwarded to me in March 1998 from a student at the College of the North Atlantic here in St. John's:

> I thought this information is very important for all of you and your friends. Important F.Y.I Alert
> PLEASE CHECK YOUR CHAIRS WHEN GOING TO THE MOVIE THEATRE!!!!
> An incident occurred when a friend's co-worker went to sit in a chair and something was poking her. She then got up and found that it was a needle with a little note at the end. It said, "Welcome to the real world, you're now 'HIV POSITIVE.'" Doctors tested the needle and it was HIV POSITIVE. "BE CAUTIOUS WHEN GOING TO THE MOVIES!!!! IF YOU MUST GO TO THE MOVIES, PLEASE CHECK!!!!" One of the safest ways is NOT sticking your hands between the seats, but at least move the seat part way up and down a few times and REALLY LOOK! Most of us just plop down into the seats. . . . The following information was E-Mailed to all employees of the Metro Police Department on the morning of 11-03-98. Drug users are now taking their used needles and putting them into the coin return slots in public telephones. People are putting their fingers in to recover coins or just to check if anyone left change. They are getting stuck by these needles and infected with hepatitis, HIV, and other diseases. This message is posted to make everyone aware of this danger. Be Aware!!! The change isn't worth it!!!! This information came straight from phone company workers, through the EMT instructor. Make sure you share this information with your family, friends, and anyone else you can!!!!! E-MAIL IT TO PEOPLE YOU CARE ABOUT!!!!

The joint movie theater and telephone form of the narrative had incredible circulation on e-mail, through xerox, and by fax. The warning was all over the Internet, posted up outside schools and on workplace bulletin boards. I have received the warning from friends all over the world—from students and colleagues, from AIDS health-care workers, from AIDS lawyers and community activists. While many of these individuals forwarded the message having recognized it as a contemporary legend, others sent it out of concern, along with a note querying appropriate action. As could be predicted, the story has prompted all manner of ostension: police departments and phone companies launching investigations, loss of revenue for movie theaters, reports of seat cushions carried to the theater, heavy clothing and multiple layers worn for protection; and my own students reported that they no longer retrieve their change after a phone call.

Precursors

The narrative and its form of ostension triggered memories, among folklorists, of earlier needle crime narratives, particularly connected with fears of "white slavery." In his *FoafTale News* article of 1989, Bill Ellis recalls that his mother had recounted a story from the 1920s in Baltimore, Maryland, of a man attacking women on the street with a so-called poisoned needle used to sedate the victim so she could be sold into "white slavery":

> This rumor is at least as old as 1914, when the state of Massachusetts ordered an official investigation into 'the white slave traffic, so called' and recorded a number of contemporary legends about near abductions. One, the final report observed, "alleges the administration of a narcotic drug by the use of a hypodermic needle on his victim as he passes her on the street, or as he sits beside her in the street car or in the theater." (1989:5)

While the ultimate goal of the abductor mentioned by Ellis is to sell the young women into involuntary prostitution, reports from roughly the same period in Louisiana indicated abduction by medical students for cadavers. The book *Gumbo Ya Ya*, a Louisiana Writers Project WPA collection of folk tales, began chapter 4 with the following story (dialect transcription from the original):

> "No Sir!" declared Mamie Smith emphatically, . . . "I sure don't go out much at this time of year. You takes a chance just walkin' on

the streets. Them Needle Mens is everywhere. They always comes round in the fall, and they's 'round to about March. You see, them Needle Mens is medical students from the Charity Hospital tryin to git your body to work on. That's cause stiffs is very scarce at this time of year. But them men's ain't workin on my body. No, sir! If they ever sticks their needles in your arm you is just a plain goner. All they gotta do is jest brush by you, and there you is; you is been stuck. (Saxon, Dreyer, and Tallant 1945:75)

An earlier precursor for the pinprick narrative is discussed by Michael Goss in a book on the "Halifax slasher," chronicling the actions of a mystery assailant who inflicted cuts with a razor blade on women in Halifax, England, in 1938. Goss dates similar narratives back to a London assailant who, in the 1780s pricked ladies' thighs with a sharp knife. Like our current ostensive situation, Goss reported that women responded to the London slasher by wearing heavy, protective clothing (Goss 1987).

Barry Baldwin cites an ancient parallel to the pinpricks narratives from the Greek annalist (ca. AD 200) Dio Cassius, who indicated in his *History of Rome* (bk. 57, chap. II, par.6),

Some persons made a business of smearing needles with poison and then pricking with them whomsoever they would. Many persons thus attacked died without even knowing the cause, but many of the murders were informed against and punished. And this sort of thing happened not only in Rome but over virtually the whole world. (As cited in Baldwin 1999:51)

Between the needle-men narratives of the 1930's and the current narrative trend, the legend type appears to have surfaced actively in the early 1980's. In his discussion of the "attempted abduction" needle stories, Jan Brunvand notes that the legend became associated with the injection of heroine, cocaine, or LSD, sometimes administered through a seat in a darkened movie theater (Brunvand 1989:207). Ellis details a case in 1989 of a gang of teenagers in the Upper West Side of New York City who ran through the streets jabbing needles or pins into the backs and necks of randomly chosen females, ultimately totalling 41 victims. Television coverage suggested that the gang might be using syringes containing HIV-positive blood. Ten teenagers were ultimately arrested and charged. The teenagers indicated the needle pricks were a prank. HIV-infected needles were not involved (Ellis 1989).

Over the last ten years, numerous cases of HIV-needle robberies and virus infection attempts have been reported in the newspapers and tried in the courts. In June of 1996 the *Los Angeles Times* reported a robbery with an HIV-positive needle. In February of 1996 the *Miami Herald* reported a similar robbery. In August of 1995 an Israeli man confessed to robbing art galleries by threatening HIV infection. And in Australia in 1990 a prison guard was stabbed by a syringe containing HIV-positive blood.[8] HIV-needle-threat legal cases are too numerous to detail here, but Canada, twenty-eight states in the United States, Australia, Britain, and many other countries have enacted laws making it a crime to knowingly expose others to HIV through any of the methods of viral transmission (see Elliott 1997).

The statistical likelihood of needle-prick infection from a needle with a detached syringe, such as might be found in a pay phone or theater seat, is so low as to be negligible. Current statistics show that health-care workers who have suffered needlesticks involving HIV-positive blood have a rate of infection of only 0.3 percent.[9] What makes the situation risky for IV drug users is the attached syringe, which generally retains several microliters of blood around the tip even after the syringe is emptied. HIV cannot survive outside of the body unless it is sealed in a container. The small amount of blood left on a detached needle would quickly be exposed to oxygen and low temperatures, rendering the needle useless as a means of infection within roughly thirty seconds. Needles on buses, in theater seats, and in pay telephones would be largely ineffectual as a means of contact, while the reported legal cases involving syringes indicate a far more effective means of transmission.

Legend as Cultural Critique and Agency

Although contemporary legend scholarship has always seen legend in some sense as a critique of culture through the expression of

---

8.   For these and other related legal cases, see http://www.snopes.com/horrors/
      madmen/pinprick.htm (2002).
9.   These statistics are consistent from source to source. The CDC suggests that up
      to 5000 health-care worker needle exposures to HIV occur annually in the United
      States. See http://www.hivinsite.ucsf.edu/akb/1997/01hcw/index.html.

societal fears, concerns, and values, that critique is generally seen as consensual and complicitous and is rarely understood as potentially critical of dominant definitions or authoritative constructions of truth. While conspiracy narratives are the clearest example of the resistance and subversive potential of legend, it is possible we have been underreading the resistance voice in crime legends, health legends, technology legends, and others. I do not mean to suggest here that every legend is a "call to arms," and neither am I suggesting that it is the intention of each legend teller to subvert cultural authority. To do so would be to risk overreading and to fall into what Lila Abu-Lughod calls "the romance of resistance" (1990). Instead, I am suggesting that contemporary legends, like most expressive forms, can provide the means for resisting the imposition of dominating definitions, norms defining how we should behave, and official accounts of what has occurred in the world (Kleinman 1992). We resist, as Kleinman notes, "in the micropolitical structure of local worlds" (174).

Contemporary legend scholarship on deliberate-infection narratives generally assumes that the driving motive behind such stories is xenophobic fear of strangers, fear of urban crime, and fear of contamination. By broadening out the narrative context to include health-related data and then returning to the needle narrative itself for a closer reading, I would like to explore the possibility that the pinprick narrative actually reflects a disguised critique of medical authority and resistance (Scott 1990a) to what is seen as the inappropriate extension of biomedicine's reach into the domain of intimate experience. While this might initially appear to require a leap of faith, resistance reading is like a Salvador Dali painting—once you see the dog, the fruit bowl disappears.[10] In other words, the resistance reading tends to obscure earlier understandings of the material. Despite what happens to the visual field, the point is not that one interpretation exists to the exclusion of the other. Both readings are crucial to understanding the multivocal and multilayered nature of legend performance.

As argued in chapter 3, one of the most puzzling issues for AIDS public health education has been the relationship between risk knowledge and risk reduction. Findings from health interview

10.   The reference here is to a painting by the Spanish surrealist painter, Salvador Dali (1904–1989). The painting is entitled "Apparition of Face and Fruit-Bowl on a Beach" (1939).

surveys in Canada and the United States, we should remember, indicate that roughly 96 percent of adults know that HIV can be transmitted through sexual intercourse, from pregnant women to their babies perinatally, and by sharing needles with an infected person. Nevertheless, we will also recall that only 13 percent of Canadians report that they have changed their behavior because of AIDS, and surveys suggest the American situation is much the same. AIDS facts appear to be well known but not so easily acted upon.

Also argued in chapter 3 and generally agreed upon by health educators, AIDS decision-making models have not been successful in allowing for comprehension of the cultural understandings that influence the ability to personalize, internalize, and apply risk information to oneself. The challenge is in understanding the cultural meanings that surround the identification of personal susceptibility and vulnerability, including risk denial. Denying one's own risk generally involves asserting that others are at higher risk. Weinstein notes that even people who are aware of their own risk for AIDS tend to engage in biased comparisons that lead them to conclude that the behavior of others is more risky than their own (Weinstein 1989). In a related argument, Sobo suggests that AIDS educational messages are seen by women as reflecting negatively on themselves and their partners. To admit to risk is to deny that they or their partners are monogamous and to suggest that they do not have the wisdom or ability to choose a partner wisely. Sobo argues that individuals construct patterned narratives of monogamy and wisdom to protect self-esteem. The result is the construction of a set of narratives that reinforce the practice of unsafe sex (1995:113–120). Perhaps most interestingly, Sobo suggests that these narratives function not only in our external narrative performances but internally, as narratives we tell ourselves that reinforce risk-related choices and behaviors.

Sobo's work and that of others writing on risk denial are instructive for understanding the pinprick narrative phenomenon. Virtually all populations associated with AIDS since its discovery have been represented by members of the dominant population in some way as alien, antisocial, unnatural, dangerous, or immoral. To move then to locate risk in the ordinary home is to import all of those meanings. The resistant response is to externalize the risk—to cast it out of the bedroom (where we don't want it) and back into the outer world (where we will take our chances). By doing so, we simultaneously move medical authority out of our bedrooms and resist the encroachment of increasing medicalization on our lives. By externalizing risk, creating an external threat, the narrative renders personal internal risk reduction measures to be insignificant and therefore unnecessary. In other words, a condom won't help me in the bedroom if the real risk is hiding in a movie theater, on a bus, or in a pay phone. This form of resistance may be dangerous or self-defeating, but it does provide a challenge to dominating definitions and a bid for medical and sexual autonomy. Pinprick narratives, kidney-theft stories, and cadaver legends all address, in quite a powerful way, resistance to the dominating authority of medicine. James Scott notes, "While folk culture is not coordination in the formal sense, it often achieves a 'climate of opinion' which, in other more institutionalized societies, would require a public relations campaign" (1990b:443).

What I am suggesting here is that resistance to the quotidian definition of AIDS, the cultural connotation that we or our partners are sites of danger, and rejection of the medicalization of intimacy have prompted a lay redefinition of the site of danger, a reclamation of the home, and a community-based retheorizing of the shape and nature of risk. Legend becomes, as Scott has articulated it, one of the "weapons of the weak" in "everyday forms of resistance" (1985). In their introduction to the book *Feminist Messages*, Radner and Lanser note, "in the creations and performances of dominated cultures, one can often find covert expression of ideas, beliefs, experiences, feelings and attitudes that the dominant culture . . . would find disturbing or threatening if expressed in more overt forms" (1993:4).

For this reason, resistance messages are often coded, making use of strategies of covert contestation. One of these strategies, evident in the pinprick narrative corpus, is the appropriation of the voice and structures of dominating medical culture. By appropriating elements normally associated with medicine, the narrative reshapes legend performance into a public health message. In contemporary legend scholarship the appropriation of voice is interpreted as a pedigree, the source that argues for the plausibility of the narrative. With the pinprick narrative, the initial friend-of-a-friend pedigree was quickly replaced by the voices of dominant culture: the police, the military, emergency medical personnel, and eventually government officials responsible for disease control. By borrowing the voice and reshaping the message, the narrative defines the location of risk seemingly from within the seat of power.

Following immediately on the heels of the friend-of-a-friend warning, the movie theater story appeared as a notice from a local police department. In Dallas, Texas, the warning noted,

> The previous information was sent from the Dallas Police Department to all local governments in the Washington area and was interdepartmentally dispersed.

In Denver, Colorado, the warning said,

> Please take a moment to read this. . . . From the Denver Police Department (if it is happening in Denver, it is probably happening elsewhere also).

In Germany, the notice cited the OSI—Office of Special Investigations. The warning read,

> The following information has been validated and passed on to us by the OSI as a Germany wide alert.

In the United States and Canada, a further pedigree attached itself to the story citing the Center for Disease Control in Atlanta, Georgia. The new version said,

> The following information was sent from the Dallas Police Department to all of the local governments in the Washington area and was interdepartmentally dispersed. We are all asked to pass this to as many people as possible.
>
> Two weeks ago, in a Dallas movie theater, a person sat on something sharp in one of the seats. When she stood up to see what it was, a needle was found poking through the seat with a note attached saying, "you have been infected with HIV."
>
> The Center for Disease Control (CDC) in Atlanta reports similar events have taken place in several other cities recently. All of the needles tested HAVE BEEN POSITIVE for HIV.
>
> The CDC also reports that needles have been found in the coin return areas of pay phones and soda machines.
>
> Everyone is asked to use extreme caution when confronted with these types of situations. All public chairs should be thoroughly

inspected prior to any use. A thorough visual inspection is considered the bare minimum. Furthermore, they ask that everyone notify their family members and friends of the potential dangers as well.

What is remarkable about the CDC version of the narrative is the softening of the warning and the constrained conservation of words intended to mimic public health rhetorical style. The CDC received so many queries about the notice that on March 17, 1999, they posted a denial on their Web site and released a press announcement. I include this denial here not just to show the CDC response to the narrative but to demonstrate the incredible similarity in rhetorical structure between the legendary notice and the actual voice of the CDC. The CDC wrote,

> CDC has received inquiries about a variety of reports or warnings about used needles left by HIV infected drug users in coin return slots of pay phones and movie theater seats. These reports and warnings are being circulated on the Internet and by e-mail and fax. Some reports have falsely indicated that CDC "confirmed" the presence of HIV in the needles. CDC has not tested such needles nor has CDC confirmed the presence or absence of HIV in any sample related to these rumors. The majority of these reports and warnings appear to have no foundation in fact.
>
> CDC recently was informed of one incident in Virginia of a needle stick from a small-gauge needle (believed to be an insulin needle) in a coin return slot of a pay phone. The incident was investigated by the local police department. Several days later, after a report of this police action appeared in the local newspaper, a needle was found in a vending machine but did not cause a needle-stick injury.

The press release continues:

> Needle stick injuries can transfer blood and blood-borne pathogens (e.g., hepatitis B, hepatitis C and HIV) but the risk of transmission from discarded needles is extremely low. . . . CDC is not aware of any cases where HIV has been transmitted by a needle-stick injury outside a health care setting. (CDC Update 1999)

The earlier warning had not only borrowed the organizational name and rhetorical structure but had also evolved a series of signatures by people in official-sounding positions: Sgt. T. L. Paullin, Press Officer for Okinawa Marine; Judith Baker, Region IX Hemophilia Program of the Children's Hospital of Los Angeles; Barbara Gaskins Wallace of the National Naval Medical Center Patient Administration, and others. Internet searches for these individuals were fruitless, and in at least one of these cases the name appears to have been constructed from a combination of words and names cited in articles on HIV displayed on the Web. Nevertheless, the appropriation of voice was persuasive enough that subscribers to HIV law and the ACT UP AIDS-activist discussion lists responded to the CDC warning with concern. In both cases, the list membership is fully familiar with not only the mechanisms of HIV transmission but also the rhetorical style of public health messages. A friend of mine involved in ACT UP[11] sent me the warning with an attached note saying, "Is this just one of those scares, or should we be concerned?"

The most interesting part of the needle-prick warning from a resistance point of view is the sequential use of the telephone and theater narratives. While the narratives retain a cut-and-paste appearance, their coexistence without motif blending has survived extensive circulation and alteration of other parts of the narrational structure. The stories seem to want to stay together, forming a joint message. While the sequential telling of two separate contemporary legends is relatively common in oral contexts, it is rare in Internet or written form. As a message of resistance though, the joint narration has a significant effect. Radner and Lanser note,

> Because interpretation is a contextual activity, the ironic arrangement of texts, artifacts or performances can constitute a powerful strategy for coding. An item that in one environment seems unremarkable or unambiguous may develop quite tendentious levels of meaning in another. (1993:13)

The telephone and theater narratives are juxtaposed to create a context for each other. That juxtaposition forms what I believe to be the

---

11.   The AIDS Coalition to Unleash Power (ACT UP) is an AIDS-activist group in the United States, founded in March 1987 (see Crimp 1988). They describe themselves as "a diverse, nonpartisan group united in anger and committed to direct action to end the AIDS crisis" (Crimp and Rolston 1990).

subversive core of the story. Ewick and Silbey, in an article on hegemonic and subversive legal narratives, argue that when narratives efface the connection between the particular and the general, they help sustain hegemony. Conversely, when narrativity helps bridge particularities and makes connections across individual experiences and subjectivities, it can function as a subversive cultural practice (Ewick and Silbey 1995:200). By providing two stories that relocate risk, the pinprick narratives bridge the particular and demonstrate that the unusual is not so unusual after all. While the general experience of public health asserts one coordinated narrative of risk factors, the particular experiences narrated in the warning suggest a world of numerous particulars all existing together in tension with the dominant construction. If needles are in phones and needles are also in theaters, these are no longer isolated cases. The two stories working together create a counterargument for the location of risk. Further, individual tellers or users of the narrative continue to mount affirming particulars onto the story. One person circulating the narrative wrote,

> I remember a few years back this had happened to a man in Toronto who rented a car and found a needle wedged in the seat.

Another added this to the narrative:

> This reminds me of when my husband worked at Burger King several years ago. . . . An employee was mashing down garbage by hand and got stuck by a used needle.

The particular narratives aggregate to constitute a larger social reality, a reality that flies in the face of dominant constructions of risk.

As we know, narrative is not just a form that captures social life. It is also constitutive of what it represents. As such, narratives have significant subversive and transformational potential. The resistances that I have discussed in this chapter are not the pitched battles of collective action normally associated with power struggles; nor are they as overt as some of the minor acts of defiance discussed as *everyday* forms of resistance. There is no one resistor here and no recognizable group of performers conscious of responding to an oppressive situation.

Instead, using the subtle power of narrative to reconstitute reality, the legend resists when we tell it, when we act on it, and when we think about it. Statistics show that the vast majority of violent crimes occur between people who know each other. In that respect, the resistant and reconstitutive power of narrative to protect our sense of safety in our homes is as much an issue in all anonymous crime narratives as it is in the needle stories. Perhaps what we have always taken to be an articulation of fear in contemporary legend is actually an articulation of choice.

8

Once Upon a Virus

Public Health and Narrative as a Proactive Form

The stories told on the pages that precede this chapter are not just entertaining tidbits of dinner conversation but rather the incredibly powerful narrative core of personal and collective action. This is not to say that we are slaves to the stories we hear, going out and enacting each narrative plot or including all narratives uncritically in the body of information we hold to be true. But the narratives we hear and tell dovetail with our cultural life, becoming slotted in holes in information, explicating unresolved issues, challenging unpopular dominant constructions, asserting the importance of cultural truths in the construction of health truths, and forming the basis of crucially important health choices.

The health-related choices that arise from the narratives are numerous and are even sometimes unquestionably positive. Rumors concerning C. J. AIDS, the writer of the letter to *Ebony* magazine who asserted that she was deliberately spreading the disease throughout Dallas, Texas (discussed in chapter 2), inspired a flurry of public health activity. Following the *Ebony* story and the interview on a local radio talk show (both of which proved to be hoaxes), there was an incredible increase in males in the area seeking AIDS tests and attending educational seminars. One local health official was quoted as saying, "I look at what happened with C.J. as a fire drill, something that has made people aware of danger and risk" (Ellis 2001:161).

Paralleling the situation with C.J., rumors of Ray Mercer infecting large numbers of women in Conception Bay North were followed by a significant acceleration in the rate of visits to local CBN AIDS clinics. The Ray Mercer stories, however, may have motivated other critical health actions, some positive and some more disturbing. One public health nurse indicated that she feared that the Mercer stories would inspire individuals to take risks, feeling safe in their knowledge that they had not slept with Ray and therefore were invulnerable and, further, that Ray would become a true scapegoat in the sense that HIV-positive individuals who wished to protect themselves or their partners from contact tracing would untruthfully assert Mercer as the source of their infection. The Mercer narratives played a role in both the closing and reopening of blood clinics, in the local understanding of and reaction to AIDS, and in partner selection. Through the stories and their tellers, we can infer the potential for other legend-inspired health choices: that some individuals might take greater care with pay phones, movie theater seats, gas pumps, cars, and fast food than they do with condom use (especially if condoms are believed to contain holes punched through them on drugstore shelves and thus are believed fallible anyway); that sex at home might be seen to require less safety than sex away or with strangers; that people who are HIV positive are perhaps understood as socially recognizable and therefore avoidable; that lack of promiscuity might equal safety; and the list goes on. But as we have said, these stories don't simply promote wrong ideas, wrong choices, and wrong behaviors, they emerge out of and articulate ideas, concerns, and attitudes that are already present and that are acceptable and viable within the culture. This chapter will explore the messages about vernacular risk perception hidden in these narratives and what they mean for public health. Before dealing with specific issues that arise out of these narratives though, a number of general areas of significance in the construction of risk and the relationship between vernacular culture and medical culture should be addressed.

The "Know Your Partner" Message

The legend material discussed in this volume underlines the possibility that the statistics on low rates of condom use despite widespread knowledge of the literature on risk activities might actually be being misread by health educators. Continually, these statistics are taken as a sign that the general population is not protecting itself and is disregarding safe-sex messages. But a different reading, one based on Farmer's hermeneutic of generosity, is also possible. Perhaps those who are understood as demonstrating a flagrant disregard for safe-sex messages are actually hearing the messages and engaging in what they understand culturally to be a type of *safer* sex. The following quote from a teenage male, for example, demonstrates an understanding of safer sex as involving both protection from pregnancy and knowledge of the partner but not necessarily condom use.

> Well, obviously, my opinion is unsafe sex is somebody who you just meet, you don't talk about things and you don't use any kind of contraception, birth control or prevention against STDs. Okay, the girl that I'm seeing right now, we practice safe sex for contraception. She's on the birth control pill and that's all we practice. Whether or not, you know, we have never been tested for HIV. (Lear 1995:1319)

As Metts and Fitzpatrick note, "Many sexually active people do not use condoms but assume they engage in safer sex because they have intercourse only with persons they believe to be safe" (1992:1). Canadian AIDS researcher Eleanor Maticka-Tynedale found in her interviews with heterosexual college students that the most popular prophylactic was the selection of a noninfected partner (variously ascertained) (1991). These findings are consistent with those of Cindy Patton, briefly mentioned in chapter 3, who found that sex workers were more likely to use condoms at work than they were in their personal relationships and that condom use would decline as the sex worker established a regular relationship with the client. Patton noted, "the better one knows a partner—paying or not—the less appropriate it seems to enforce condom use" (Patton 1994:53).

We should not be surprised by these assertions that knowledge of a partner, or what is seen as wise partner selection, provides safety from risk of infection. Public health, initially, although to some extent inadvertently, suggested that this was the case. In 1988 when the American Surgeon General's office sent its brochure, "Understanding AIDS," around to every household in the United States, it solidified the "know your partner" public health strategy. The brochure instructed readers to ask several questions about a potential partner's background before engaging in a sexual relationship. Among the questions were these: Did the individual experiment with drugs? Had the potential partner ever had a sexually transmitted disease? How many people had the partner slept with? The idea behind the campaign was to help individuals evaluate the risk of intercourse with each new partner. But the campaign was a mistake. It told the public that individuals infected with HIV were somehow distinguishable from "safe" partners and that rather than initiating indiscriminate condom use, one simply needed to avoid unsafe sexual liaisons.

In Canada, the campaigns contained similar messages. In 1988 the Ontario Ministry of Health created a brochure for mass mailing called "AIDS, Let's Talk." The brochure emphasized the importance of abstinence and monogamy and once again asserted the "know your partner" philosophy. The phrase "safe sex" was never mentioned in the brochure, and condoms were mentioned only once in a sentence that said, "If you have sexual intercourse with someone whose past you're not sure of, use latex condoms" (cited in Kinsman 1991:50).

In many ways "know your partner" strategies form the very basis of the attitudes voiced by those interviewed for this project and found within the AIDS legend corpus. Clearly, Ray's reported comment when his partner queried condom use ("If I had slept with any 'sluts' I would tell you"), the practice of showing a blood-donor card to potential partners, and the "Welcome to the World of AIDS" and "Top Forty" legends all operate on a "know your partner" principle. Later public health campaigns in both the U.S. and Canada tried to undo the damage. Health Canada subsequently issued several brochures and posters that focused on the impossibility of detecting infected partners. One poster, for example, announced, "If Mr. Right Won't Wear a Condom, He's Wrong." Another used a foil mirror to indicate that even the reader could potentially have the face of an HIV-positive person. But the idea of practicing "safer" sex through "know your partner" strategies made sense to much of the heterosexual public and seemed a far less difficult option than consistent condom use.

Knowing your partner as a strategy for safety fit nicely with the negative attitudes toward condoms continually reported in North American knowledge, belief, and behavior studies (see, for example,

Kelley, St. Lawrence, Hood, and Brasfield 1989). These studies generally found that respondents reported lack of use due to reduced
sensitivity, loss of spontaneity, discomfort, unpleasant odor, and
messiness (Kelley, St. Lawrence, Hood, and Brasfield 1989). Further, as condoms became increasingly associated with HIV protection, they began to take on a connotation of guilt; individuals would
introduce a condom into sexual activity if they had reason to believe
that either they or their partners were HIV positive. The result was
an association of condom use with the suggestion of promiscuity,
drug use, uncleanliness, and lack of care.

More abstractly, the "know your partner" strategy worked well
with the natural distancing mechanism, which searches for ways to
demarcate differences and boundaries between ourselves and disease.
Basing his argument on physician surveys, Sander Gilman asserts
that entrenched in our culture is the notion that you can *see* disease:

> Young physicians often see beautiful patients as exemplary or
> "good" patients, patients who will follow doctor's orders and
> therefore will regain health. The aged or poor patient, on the
> other hand, is seen even by the trained physician, as one who is
> a "bad" patient, a patient who will probably "make trouble" and
> whose health will not improve. Indeed "lower-class" patients were
> often diagnosed as being more gravely ill and were given poorer
> prognoses than those of other social classes when, in fact, they
> differed from the patients only in terms of the visible (or stated)
> criteria of class. Cultural differences concerning gender also play a
> major role in constructing those groups understood as being more
> at risk. Obesity, while statistically more frequent in males than
> females, was used as a criterion twice as often for women as for
> men. (1988:4)

If, as Gilman argues, even physicians correlate beauty, outward
impressions of class, and weight with health, one can only assume
that equivalent notions of health and disease as visible and easily
distinguishable exist within the general population.

Added to these reasons for the cultural preference for "know
your partner" strategies is a general governing natural sense that
those whom you "know" (variously defined) are unlikely to hurt you,
while strangers—those who exist apart from you and "out there in
the world" (variously defined)—are less trustworthy. Legend scholars

call this phenomenon "stranger danger" (Conrad 1998; Whatley and Henken 2000:76), the common notion expressed in contemporary legends, including those not about AIDS, that evil lurks outside of one's social group while known individuals provide relative safety. It is the governing ethic of "stranger danger" that places so many legends away from home, in the company of cultural "others," and creates the foreign or culturally distant antagonist. "Know your partner" advice makes great sense within the "stranger danger" ethic. In Newfoundland, the rural and island distrust of those who "come from away" and the dependence on social networks that made so much sense in outport communities dovetail nicely with both the "stranger danger" and "know your partner" ideologies. In many ways, knowing your partner is possible in outport Newfoundland in a way that would not be possible in larger centers. One might remember in this context that news of Ray's infection travelled quickly through the community, ultimately motivating one of the infected women to seek testing. Comments such as "if anyone I had slept with was infected I would have heard" are not uncommon in Newfoundland or for that matter throughout North America. But in Newfoundland they take on a different resonance, meshing with the common belief (and considering the isolated gene pool, the fact) that nearly everyone on the island is intimately connected.

As mentioned above, an unfortunate consequence of the "know your partner" strategy is a resulting notion of discernable innocence and guilt associated with HIV. The strategy provided questions that are easily construed as a quiz or test for innocence—the right answers cleared one enough to allow sexual interaction. The flip side of the strategy's "low vs. high risk" / "innocence vs. guilt" message was a prevailing notion of an identifiable HIV-positive bad guy, an AIDS outlaw. In some sense the "know your partner" brand of "safer sex" could be taken as the ability to find the bad guys and avoid them. C. J. AIDS, the "Irish Angel of Death," "Welcome to the World of AIDS," Ray Mercer, "Top Forty," and numerous other AIDS legends all depict the knowable, distinguishable, AIDS bad guy. While that notion is devastating when considered in relation to the treatment of persons with HIV/AIDS, it also, of course, conveys the message that if one stays away from the AIDS bad guy, safety is assured. The public's job then is to devise increasingly sophisticated ways of assessing guilt or innocence (Patton 1994:83), new and better ways of spotting the bad guys. The legends and legend tellers do exactly that. After all, public health told them to.

Lay Risk Assessment and the Problem of Perceived Susceptibility

The rationalistic models of risk-related behavior discussed in chapter 3 (the Health Belief Model, the Theory of Reasoned Action, and the AIDS Risk Reduction Model) all contain an inherent assumption that knowledge of risk factors will relate directly to the informed estimation of one's own risk. As we have argued, where the models have not been successful is in their lack of allowance for the cultural associations and meanings that feed individuals' abilities to internalize and apply notions of risk to themselves. The various knowledge, belief, and behavior studies suggest that the correlation of knowledge of risk factors, perception of susceptibility, and risk-reducing behavior is not a simple one. The problematic part of these models is our lack of understanding of the components of perceived susceptibility. Separate studies by Landesman (Nichols 1990) and Lindsay (with others, 1989) of large samples of seropositive women, for example, found that over 70 percent of those who tested positive for HIV did not acknowledge *any* participation in risk activities. As discussed in the previous chapter, Weinstein addresses the issue of unacknowledged risk by asserting that most individuals engage in what he calls "an optimistic comparison bias," which preserves self-esteem by asserting that others are at higher risk (1989). As a result, the more stigmatized the condition, the more likely one is to underestimate personal risk. Sobo's subsequent analysis (1995) puts both a cultural and narrative spin on Weinstein's findings by asserting that women continually tell stories to the outside world and to themselves concerning their participation in what they see to be the ideals of heterosexual relationships, particularly wisdom in partner choice and the monogamous nature of their actions and those of their partners. To suggest risk then, Sobo argues, is to suggest that one or one's partner has at some point not chosen wisely. Likewise, to suggest condom use implies that either the individual has not been monogamous or accuses the partner of infidelity (Sobo 1995). According to both Sobo and Weinstein, the need for preserving self-esteem makes it highly unlikely that one will recognize potential participation of either partner in risk activities or take protective action. Deeply entrenched in our cultural response to the "know your partner" advice is the belief that a partner who has been chosen wisely will not hurt us, and that is the very stuff of the optimistic bias.

The diminishment of one's own risk, inherent in the optimistic bias and the wisdom and monogamy narratives, corresponds naturally, however, to the *exaggeration* of risk outside of one's primary relationship, home, or community. AIDS crime legends and panics reinforce notions of diminished risk at home by constructing the image of the "foreign" or "named" deliberate infector with murderous intent who is responsible for high rates of infection. The scapegoated deliberate infector creates sharp contrasts of guilt and innocence that feed directly into optimistic bias and pinpoint risk as existing primarily with identified externalized individuals. Legal cases of nondisclosure of HIV-positive status fan the flames of externalized risk belief, appearing (especially through the media's handling of such cases) to suggest that once specific individuals are incarcerated (or dead) the public will be safe from disease. Risk is "out there," not in one's home or personal relationships. The needle and pinprick stories discussed in the last chapter convey a similar message, making the external world and the behavior of others the "real" location of risk. Stories of garbage collectors handling bags and receiving needle pricks, individuals finding discarded needles on a lawn, and other more mundane pin-prick stories combine with the legendary needle narratives to externalize risk by collecting unusual risk factors and making them appear usual. As noted, the effect is to make the external world riskier than any risks that might obtain in personal behavior.

Also present in the AIDS legends is a message concerning the *futility of risk management*. Primary among the arguments related to futility assessments are narratives concerning the fallibility of risk-reduction measures. Stories of condoms that break or that are reported to have holes deliberately placed in them and narratives of lack of care with body fluids by HIV-positive individuals outside of the bedroom provide the data for futility assessments by suggesting that no matter what one does to reduce risk, efforts of self-protection will be rendered insignificant or useless. Futility assessments also take the narrative form of conspiracy and fatalistic beliefs, suggesting release from personal responsibility for self-protection by placing viral control in the hands of corrupt government or medical bureaucrats or in the hands of a higher power.

While Weinstein and Sobo tend to take a sociopsychological view of the optimistic bias, monogamy, and wisdom arguments, their findings are parallel to the concerns and attitudes expressed continually in AIDS legendary forms. For Weinstein and Sobo, however, these are mechanisms of denial: a refusal to grant the truth of one's risk. The denial argument is indeed one way of understanding lack of perceived susceptibility, but it moves toward a line of argument that reflects perspectives focused on "real risks" as a nondialogic form, that is, as a singular one-way communication of messages. Similar to the cultural understanding of "safer sex" as careful *partner choice* despite lack of condom protection, optimistic forms of risk denial can also be understood as the weighing of cultural truths over public health truths. In this understanding, risks are not denied, they are ultimately weighed as less significant than the risks to self, partner, and relationship implied in a perception of personal susceptibility.

Despite my small quibble with Weinstein and Sobo on the framing of these narratives and attitudes as "denial," they address the issue of diminished internal risk assessment in a way that provides clarity for understanding a series of risk-assessment mechanisms expressed in the legend corpus, including the expanded external risk and futility arguments discussed above. Through diminished internal risk assessment, exaggerated external risk assessment, and an assessment of the futility of risk prevention, the narratives reinforce the decision not to comply with condom-use advice. These mechanisms and their corresponding narrative forms are portrayed in the following table.

Mechanisms for Risk Assessments

Diminished Internal Risk Assessments	Expanded External Risk Assessments	The Futility of Risk-Prevention Assessment
Optimistic Comparison-Bias narratives (Weinstein 1989)	Deliberate Infection Narratives	The Fallibility of Risk-Reduction Measures Narratives
Monogamy Narratives (Sobo 1995)	The Collection of Multiple-Unusual-Risk-Factor Narratives	The Fatalistic/God's Will Risk-Assessment Narratives
Wisdom Narratives (Sobo 1995)	AIDS Crime Narratives	The AIDS Conspiracy Narratives
"Know Your Partner" Advice	Nondisclosure Legal Cases in the Media	

The diminished internal risk, expanded external risk, and futility mechanisms continually feed into and out of the narrative tradition, affecting health choices and asserting the importance of cultural values in the construction of risk.

The Question of Authority

The tellers of these stories and their audience are actors in a world that combines the traditional reliance on narrative for life's instruction and news with a new kind of medical consumerism, lay activism, and questioning of medical authority. More than any other disease, AIDS has challenged the construction of health expertise, questioned the credibility and claims of scientists, physicians, and others in positions of power, and brought to the forefront the view of a thinking, researching, credible, political, and active layperson. As Steven Epstein has argued, "the interventions of lay people in the proclamation and evaluation of scientific claims have helped shape what is believed to be known about AIDS—just as they have made problematic our understanding of who is a 'layperson' and who is an 'expert'" (1996:3). The reasons for the incredible impact of AIDS in the promotion of lay expertise are complex but arise largely from the populations first associated with the disease and the moment in history at which it arrived. As Epstein notes, the disease affected young people in their twenties and thirties, who were disinclined to "lie down and wait to die" (10), and it initially appeared in the gay community among people who had become used to identity management and knew how to mobilize and to challenge social norms, organizations, and institutions. It is also not insignificant that the gay community was comprised in part of white, middle-class men with political clout, education, money, and fund-raising abilities. But AIDS also benefited from what Epstein calls "social movement spillover" (12), coming as it did after the feminist health movement of the 1970s, which critiqued patriarchical medical institutions, argued for women to take back their bodies, and promoted the creation of self-help and support groups. It also followed the activism of the antinuclear and "green" movements, which actively challenged scientific authority, and the New Age movement, which rejected much of the scientific way of knowing and argued for the importance of other kinds of epistemological structures (Epstein 1996). While lay activism is generally discussed in relation to the control of treatment and clinical trial issues, it can also be seen in less obvious and perhaps less political ways in resistance to medical authority and moral regulation, defiant reactions to constructions of safety, distrust of and noncompliance with public health information and expertise, and an overall assertion of cultural ideologies rather than scientific/ medicalizing ideologies.

The spectacular successes of AIDS activism also came at a time when the economic structures of health care were shifting in ways that were seen as threatening to patient-practitioner relationships and the continued quality of health care. The corporatization of the American health-care system, continual threats of privatization in Canada, and the growing power of third-party hospitalization and care payment systems to define treatment strategies were increasingly creating lay dissatisfaction with medicine and a heightened sense of alienation. As O'Connor states,

> The shift in perspective from medicine-as-service to medicine-as-business transforms patients into "consumers" of health care. The business model embodies a fundamental change in moral view: while the classical patient-physician relationship was based on an ethic of trust and service, the consumer-provider relationship is based on savvy, skepticism, self-protection (on both sides) and the directives of the "bottom line." Ironically, it has also placed patients in a relatively more powerful position ideologically with respect to the system, for it has heightened their sense of their right to choose. Consumerism is based on choice. Consumers compare and critique, and they bring their own standards and preferences to bear in evaluating their purchase options. They continue to patronize (and help to advertise) only those providers of goods and services who satisfy their needs within the framework of an adequate cost-to-quality ratio. Consumers decide both what they perceive their needs to be and how well they feel those needs are met by specific products and services. (1995:167–168)

The new medical consumer no longer "bought" what physicians said "on spec." Medicine was a new ball game from the lay perspective and one that required greater public accountability and less arrogance and authoritarianism on the part of health care systems.

In addition to the activism created by lay reactions to the epidemic and the business model of health care, the Worldwide Web and Internet were also busy creating a new kind of medical consumer in North America—one who had access to a proliferation of information and ideas. Researching your own syndromes and treatments on the Web, becoming knowledgeable about ever more sophisticated ways to protect yourself,[1] communicating with others through Internet health-support groups, passing on warnings about products, conspiracies, and misinformation are all part of the rise of lay uses of computer technology. Not long ago such a statement might have been true only of privileged populations, and to some extent this is still the case; but increasingly Internet accessibility has worked its way out into the community, available in public locations such as free libraries and through schools, community centers, and other social services.[2] The new, technologically assisted health consumer was no longer forced to be a passive receptor of physician's advice. The result is a (generally) more-educated lay consumer but also one who processes information and ideas from a variety of sources, including those that medical professionals might not wish to encourage or support. Conspiracy sites, hoax sites, alternative-science sites, as well as natural communication in chat rooms, e-mail, and discussion lists—all are seen as potential purveyors of misinformation. As a result, Health Canada and the Center for Disease Control have both created medical rumor and hoax Web sites dedicated to dispelling popular information which they see as inaccurate and risky. The United States Information Agency (USIA) also employs a Program Officer for Countering Misinformation and Disinformation, charged with responding to false stories considered to pose a risk to the United States and its citizens, many of which are health related (Castañeda 2000:137).

Despite official stereotypical views to the contrary, lay readers of Internet health materials have not, however, been passive receptors of the information they contain. In fact, many Internet health-support groups and discussion lists exist, in part, as a mechanism

---

1.   This is not to say that lay people have not always asserted considerable knowledge about their health and treatment. Certainly vernacular health practices and beliefs have always coexisted with the use of more-official medical resources. The new activism, consumerism, and access to information through the Internet, however, represents a higher degree of interaction between systems than has been previously the case in Western cultures.

2.   When I once asserted too strongly to an American colleague that ready access to computer communication was class based, she took me to the public library in her city to witness the number of homeless individuals "surfing the Web." While I admit that access may be more widespread than I had once thought, it is worth noting (with caution) that literacy in general is still, to some extent, an artifact of privilege. Nevertheless, the increased access for some means, in a sense, increased access for many, due to the speed with which lay health information is shared by word of mouth.

for sifting through the proliferation of studies and information now available to both health care workers and the lay population (see Goldstein 2000). The cooptation of the C.D.C. voice, and therefore C.D.C. authority, in the circulated "needles in movie theater seats" warning indicates that lay users of the health Internet do not only sift through and carefully process the content they find there but also react to the legitimization structures encountered on the Web. In other words, they are cognizant of the source and the relative hierarchy of authority. While they may not agree with that source or agree with its place in authoritative structures, they are aware of its officialness, and one would assume they are equally aware of official hierarchical attitudes toward less-legitimated sites. As is the case with all forms of health information, lay users of the Internet may weigh subjective experience and vernacular knowledge over education, training, and professional status in their own concept of what creates an authority. Lay health Internet users, in other words, are not indiscriminate readers.

Access to the Internet, proactive medical consumerism, and epidemic activism have, in the eyes of some public health practitioners, created a lay health monster. Lay knowledge is considered to be dangerous, creating innumerable obstacles to the management of the health of the population. Irving Zola provides a classic example of this attitude in the anecdote recounted below.

> Recently, in a European country, I overheard the following conversation in a kidney dialysis unit. The chief was being questioned about whether or not there were self-help groups among his patients. "No," he almost shouted, "that is the last thing we want. Already the patients are sharing too much knowledge while they sit in the waiting room, thus making our task increasingly difficult. We are working now on a procedure to prevent them from ever meeting one another." (1972:501)

Concerns about patients knowing too much reflect the philosophical premise that the public should submit uncritically to the claims of experts who know better and who can act on behalf of the common good. These experts in part gain and preserve their authority through claims of dispassionate objectivity, which allows them to weigh information and make decisions without psychological, social, or cultural issues clouding their judgement (Hufford 1991).

The patient population and the educational target groups are seen in this formulation as too subjective, too "in the moment," and too self-interested to process health information and address larger medical needs. Within this framework, situated or vernacular knowledges are seen as unacceptable, trivial, chaotic, misleading, and fragmented.

In this essentially positivist construction, all information and all knowledges concerning health require mediation by experts, who translate the relativistic and probabilistic logic of science into statements of certainty and fact (Adam and Loon 2000:4). While these statements of fact appear to be objective and authoritative, they are all too often ridden with value judgements dressed up as expert knowledge. In a process that David Hufford calls the "bloating of cultural authority," scientists move beyond the boundaries of their expertise, presenting authoritative statements that are actually intensely moralistic and doctrinal but that are nonetheless presented *as expertise*. Hufford explains,

> Our professional authorities have set the boundaries of their expertise far beyond the limits that can be rationally defended. When experts in radiation and health tell us what increase in cases of leukemia is likely as a result from a given release of radiation, they are within the legitimate boundaries of their expertise. They may be wrong; they may even be biased in their calculations. But this is their territory. Ordinary citizens do not expect to be able to do such calculations. However, when those same experts state how many such cases of leukemia constitute an acceptable risk given the value of nuclear power, they have no grounds for claiming authority. The people around the power plant are not obliged to suspend their personal judgement about this issue, and the experts have no special knowledge that is pertinent. The same is true when a physician goes beyond telling you how painful a procedure may be and how likely it is to be successful, to telling you how much pain you should be willing to bear or how desirable such a success may be to you or what one chance in ten is worth. The physician has no more grounds for telling you these things *than you have for making that determination yourself*. The physician may disagree with your decision, but the physician cannot show such a decision to be wrong. (1991:13–14)

A number of the legends and narrative motifs discussed in this volume demonstrate vernacular response to both the rise of the educated lay person and the bloating of medical authority. The resistant redefining of risk, fears of medicine's role in the manufacture of disease, belief in the withholding of drugs and treatment, concerns about government health conspiracies, and distrust of both the giving and receiving of public health information all point to a crisis in confidence concerning the social institution of medicine. The primary concerns arise out of a very particular set of authority issues: a perception of a *lack of accountability* on the part of medicine and suspicions about the medicopolitical power of government and special interests groups (clearly articulated in the origin narratives); *the extension of medicine into areas of life seen as outside of medical jurisdiction*, including intervention into areas of personal intimacy and moral regulation (articulated in the origin and needle narratives, stories of mandatory house-to-house testing, contact list narratives); and *the excessive control over access to and withholding of information* (seen in relation to narratives about withheld treatments, suspicions about noninfectious and infectious body fluids, healthy carrier narratives, condom fallibility, and a number of other motifs).

Concerns about medical authority expressed in the narratives also demonstrate a consciousness of the expert dismissal of lay knowledge and expertise. Even when vernacular knowledges are taken into consideration by health experts, it is generally with a sense of "we must know what it is that we are combatting" and rarely with a sense that disembodied information can be understood only as incomplete. Numerous narratives, such as the "Holes in Condoms," "Needles in Movie Theater Seats," and "Top Forty," assert the strength and power of subjective experience and local observations over medical cautions. In these narrative constructions, medical authority is diminished through an assertion of the superiority of vernacular reasoning.

What the Taletellers Know That Public Health Does Not

The very strength of vernacular knowledge is in its understanding of the individual context of health information and in the subjective experience of disease constructions. In other words the greatest asset of lay expertise is in precisely those areas of thinking and relating to information most criticized by medical authorities.

Scott Rushforth, in his work on Athapaskan knowledge and authority, distinguishes between primary and secondary ways of knowing:

> Primary knowledge denotes fully justified beliefs that an individu-
> al acquires through his or her experiences, including social inter-
> actions. Primary epistemic evidence is the foundation of primary
> knowledge. People employ the former as warrant for the latter.
> Secondary knowledge is based only indirectly on primary evi-
> dence. Non-epistemic factors such as a speaker's credentials can
> provide the salient reasons for believing in secondary knowledge.
> (1994:336)

The existence of health legends and health narratives should indicate to those who are concerned about public health and who are
listening to lay responses that all information requires placement in
cultural context. Narratives provide just that. Through narration,
health information comes to life, exploring, affirming, rejecting, and
sometimes replacing information that is offered by powerful outsiders without true cultural contextualization. Narratives take truth
claims and hegemonic constructions and make them a culture's own
(or not), twisting them and turning them in ways that force them to
make cultural sense. Sometimes that sense is consistent with what
the claim's makers wish, sometimes it is discordant and risky, and
other times it improves on those claims in remarkably positive ways.
But while health educators might recognize some responses to information as positive and others as negative based on results in terms
of changed risk behaviors, this formula is in and of itself based on
cultural misunderstanding. Responses that imply negative "uptake"
of health messages are gifts of cultural insight, moments to understand health truths that may not be compatible with cultural truths.
The accommodation of that new information about lack of "fit" has
the potential to result in not only greater cultural understanding but
also potentially greater medical understanding.
    So what do the tale tellers know that public health might have
missed, forgotten, or been unable to see based on lack of primary
knowledge?
    1. Public health messages must get more sophisticated as the
target audience itself becomes more sophisticated in its processing
of the problem. Much of the legend material, particularly with regard to origin and contamination legends, is based on vernacular

understandings of the nature of body fluids and viral shelf life. Insect transmission, semen in food products, and car or home contamination narratives are not unreasonable or lacking in logic, and the stories create the opportunity for dialogue on the nature of various apparent inconsistencies in the role of types of contact. Participation in that dialogue is missing at the official levels. Public health has failed to clarify the reasons why some modes of bodily fluid exchange are riskier than others and the quantity and magnitude of the detectable virus needed for efficient transmission. Legal regulations further complicate this situation, enforcing in some jurisdictions laws against the importation of used clothing, real estate regulations that require disclosure of the HIV status of previous homeowners, and criminal prosecution for spitting by HIV-positive individuals. Information from official sources is in this sense inconsistent and contradictory. The public wants the information necessary to assess situations for themselves—not simply announcements of the safety of casual contact, which are then thrown into question through the punitive actions of other official sectors of society.

2. The inconsistent and contradictory nature of AIDS information has fueled a preexisting fire of North American distrust in medicine. Public announcements of mistaken sources for the disease, such as the use of "poppers" in the gay community or speculation about the role of Haitian voodoo, create an environment that casts into question the competence of medical authority and the role of cultural bias. While conspiracy narratives provide the most direct evidence of medical distrust, other legends demonstrate sharp discomfort with the handling of information coming from and going to medical and institutional sources. Narrative concerns about the withholding of drugs and AIDS-related genocide sit side by side with narratives about contact tracing, naming of HIV-positive individuals, testing anonymity, and the management of private information. One of the most interesting differences between the 1988 (King) survey of attitudes toward AIDS found among Newfoundland Youth and the 1991 (Cregheur, Casey, and Banfield) follow-up study, which focused on the same questions, was a significant decline in reported trust in AIDS information from public health and government sources and a rise in trust in parental information about AIDS. As noted earlier, it is both a sociolinguistic and a public health dictum that the effectiveness of a message depends on the credibility recipients attach to its source. Public health and medicine are in dire

need of both restructuring and public relations focused on gaining the trust of the population.

3. While public health is losing trust, it is simultaneously asking that communities reverse their trust in local information networks. The insistence on a single (official) source for information is not a workable prospect, particularly in closely knit communities. If forced to make a choice between local information sources and hegemonic sources, community members will most often choose "their own people," those who through primary experience are known to be trustworthy." Top Forty," "Pinholes in Condoms," needle narratives, and deliberate infection stories all suggest a strong attachment to local information sources. It is foolish for any organization to operate on the principle that individuals will trust outsiders over those they know, particularly in the context of eroding medical authority. Peer-education programs recognize the importance of local community members but still tend to work on a nondialogic, one-way, risk-relating basis that upholds the hierarchal nature of medicine and negates the discursive nature of primary knowledge.

4. AIDS theorists have written about concerns of moral regulation (Kinsman 1996) and the policing of desire (Watney 1987) in relation to gay activist responses to AIDS messages, but the issue has received less attention in relation to heterosexuality. Abstinence messages and health constructions of HIV-positive and gay bodies as deviant continue to suggest that sex itself is problematic or that specific types of sex are responsible for transmission of the virus rather than the practice of unprotected sex. This context of apparent condemnation creates a perception of medicine and public health as keepers of the moral good. Gay activist efforts to create erotic guides to safer sex have tried to remedy these negative sexual messages by AIDS educators, but less has been done in addressing heterosexual sexuality in a way that recognizes intimacy and eroticism. Reactions to the punitive infiltration of medicine and public health into areas of sexuality and intimacy are, however, addressed by the legends. Numerous conspiracy narratives refer to government creation of AIDS to control teenage sexuality or to limit procreation through condom use. The concern with privacy expressed through legend also indicates a sensitivity to public health's role in moral regulation. Narratives of mandatory house-to-house testing and contact lists, while not specifically about sexual policing, certainly suggest a fear of intrusion. This perception of medical intrusion and sexual

policing makes it impossible for individuals to discuss their actual sexual behaviors (such as the heterosexual practice of anal sex to avoid pregnancy—see chapter 5), thus further burying those areas of post-safe-sex education that might warrant further dialogue. Resistance readings of much of the legend material push not only risk but also regulation out of the bedroom.

5. The legends point out the continued promotion by public health of risk as related to groups and individuals, despite the lip service paid to the movement away from notions of risky people to the concept of risky behaviors. In a sort of tag-team demonization, the vernacular tradition and the actions of official sectors in Conception Bay North continually constructed a location for risk—a person, a people, a place. Despite motives of concern, the legal trial and the removal of area blood clinics pointed to the isolation of individuals as a solution to the spread of the virus rather than highlighting the need for universal precautions. The result is a stigmatized community, a stigmatized individual, and a public-health message that is both unclear and contradictory.

6. The narratives recognize the boundary-making activities that are a natural part of dealing with an imposing threat. Association of safety and risk fall predictably along the lines of "home" and "away," "familiar"and "foreign," "moral" and "immoral." "Know your partner" advice espoused the same ideal, creating an identifiable risk, which simply required knowledge of the boundary and avoidance. The narratives create an AIDS bad guy so that it will be easier to see the AIDS good guy. But the narrative tradition also recognizes that not all people who are HIV positive are bad or foreign or immoral. The narratives of high numbers of HIV tests at high school blood drives and the stories of long lists of contact partners submitted to public health also suggest a realization that the virus can affect anyone. The narratives are not strictly about externalizing risk but also about fears of having to own those risks. While the AIDS bad guy is scary, the AIDS good guy is an even scarier prospect—for both the community and official sectors.

Once Upon a Virus

The aim of this volume has been to use the rich tradition of AIDS legends, as they are situated in cultural context, to explore vernacular perspectives on risk. While many of the narratives discussed here are reported all over the world, they *mean* at home—finding, in their telling, the nuances that give them local life and import. Few of the issues discussed here are significant only in this culture. The relationship between AIDS messages and cultural life, the concerns of rural communities, and the sense of distrust of medical officials are all issues likely to be expressed in many places—but not as they relate to this particular past, this culture, this moment in history. The little and large nuances of a tradition of outsider doctors re-naming families to tell them apart (in chapter 5), badly managed resources and genetic mining (chapter 1), poverty and the collapse of the fishery (chapter 1), a health care system that struggles with rural access (chapter 1), a dependence on the mainland for every-thing from refrigerators to bone-marrow transplants—all of these issues and many more make these stories what they are, give them meaning and depth. Indeed, the Newfoundland world of AIDS is unlike any other. As is the Haitian world of AIDS or the Chicago world of AIDS.

I believe that it behooves public health officials to be aware of these narratives—not just as an indication of the rumors they need to combat, but also as a resource for understanding risk, local perspectives on public health efforts, and areas for improvement. But being able to interpret what the narratives are saying requires a degree of respect for the narratives and their tellers, a willingness to relinquish sole expert status, and a recognition of lay authority. It requires moving on from thinking about communities as target groups and narratives as ephemeral quaint stories.

It is not uncommon in the current intellectual climate to read studies directed at strengthening risk communication that argue, as does Dana Lear, "We have proceeded with assumptions about the way people behave and with whom they identify that have too often proved incorrect" (1995:1312). And yet, a few sentences earlier in the same article, Lear writes, "Public reaction toward AIDS has moved universally through stages of denial, scapegoating and blame before any constructive response to the epidemic has occurred" (1312). The simultaneous concern for understanding lay communication and condemnation of that communication for what it contains are both extremely common and problematic. Understanding the cultural conception of risk requires being prepared for its divergence from the understandings of public health while recognizing that that very divergence is instructive. Denial, scapegoating, and blame are not dismissible, and neither are the narratives that express those ideas. The very fact that the ideas and the narratives affect health choices and decision making means that they, at the very least, must be taken seriously as expressions of cultural values and health worldviews. These narratives produce and support assertions of truth and claims about the nature of reality, sometimes literally, but more often as a way to test that reality, to find out more about it, to shake it up. As Bill Ellis says, "Legend telling is often fundamentally a political act" (2001:xiv). The coherency and logic of the legend discourses are keys to frames of local awareness, to the ways that reasonable and intelligent people make use of information—how they selectively assign importance to issues and how they turn health truths into cultural truths and cultural truths into health truths.

In the best of all worlds, in the land of fairytales and not legends, the story would go like this: Once there was a virus. No one got sick. No one was stigmatized. They all lived happily ever after. Unfortunately, the world of fairytales is not the world of legends. People are getting sick and getting stigmatized and dying, and it is time to listen to what the storytellers have to say about that.

Editorial cartoon by KT from *The Evening Telegram*, St. John's, Newfoundland, April 7, 1995.

Appendix

Legends Index

References Cited

Abrahams, Roger. 1984. Equal Opportunity Eating: A Structural Excursus on Things of the Mouth. In *Ethnic and Regional Foodways in the United States: The Performance of Group Identity*, ed. Linda Keller Brown and Kay Mussell, pp. 19–36. Knoxville: University of Tennessee Press.

Abu-Lughod, Lila. 1990. The Romance of Resistance: Tracing Transformations of Power through Bedouin Women. *American Ethnologist* 17:41–55.

Adam, Barbara, and Joost van Loon, eds. 2000. *The Risk Theory and Beyond: Critical Issues for Social Theory*. London: Sage Press.

Adam, Barry D., Alan Sears, and Glenn E. Schellenberg. 2000. Accounting for Unsafe Sex: Interviews with Men Who Have Sex with Men. *The Journal of Sex Research* 37(1):24–36.

AIDS around the World. 2002. http://www.avert.org/aroundworld.htm.

Ajzen, L. Icek, and Martin Fishbein. 1980. *Understanding Attitudes and Predicting Social Behavior*. Englewood Cliffs, N.J.: Prentice-Hall.

Altman, Dennis. 1986. *AIDS in the Mind of America*. New York: Anchor Press/Doubleday.

Andersen, Flemming-Gotthelf. 1985. *Commonplace and Creativity: The Role of Formulaic Diction in Anglo-Scottish Traditional Balladry*. Odense, Denmark: Odense University Press.

Araeea, P. 1986. Editorial cartoon. *Pravda*, 30 October.

Ask Ruby. 1996. AIDS Stigma Spurs Teen to Lie about Hometown. *St. John's (Nfld.) Evening Telegram*, May 7, p. 16.

Badcock , Stephen. 1995. Red Cross Decision Unfairly Brands CBN as AIDS Capital. *St. John's (Nfld.) Evening Telegram*, April 15, p. 5.

Bailey, Ian. 1995a. Local Doctor Fears "AIDS Capital" Label. *St. John's (Nfld.) Evening Telegram*, April 5, p. 3.

———. 1995b. CBN Blood Ban Not Discriminatory, Says Ruling. *St. John's (Nfld.) Evening Telegram*, September 30.

Baker, Houston. 1987. *Blues, Ideology, and African American Literature: A Vernacular Theory*. Chicago: University of Chicago Press.

Baker, Melvin. 2001. Fish, But No Cod. In *Newfoundland and Labrador: Insiders Perspectives*, ed. Elke Dettmer, pp. 9–11. St. John's, Nfld.: Johnson Family Foundation.

Baker, Melvin, and Robert H. Cuff. 1993. "Down North": A Historiographical Overview of Newfoundland Labrador. *Newfoundland Quarterly* 88(2):2–12.

Bakhtin, M. M. 1981. *The Dialogic Imagination: Four Essays*. Austin: University of Texas Press.

Baldwin, Barry. 1999. Some Old Pricks. *Fortean Times* 129:51.

Barin, F., S. M'Boup, F. Denis, P. Kanki, J. G. Allan, T. H. Lee, and M. Essex. 1985. Serological Evidence for Virus Related to Simian T-lympotropic Retrovirus III in Residents of West Africa. *Lancet* 21–28:1387–1389.

Bartlett, Steve. 2001. Fighting a Stigma: Educating the Province about HIV and AIDS Is an Uphill Battle. *The Aurora* 34(1):24–25.

Bayer, Ronald. 1995. AIDS Prevention vs. Cultural Sensitivity. *Responsive Community: Rights and Responsibilities* 6(1):20–27.

Bella, Leslie. 2002. *Newfoundlanders: Home and Away*. St. John's: Greetings from Newfoundland Ltd.

Bennett, Gillian. 1985. What's "Modern" about the Modern Legend? *Fabula* 26:219–229.

———. 1997. Bosom Serpents and Alimentary Amphibians: A Language for Sickness. In *Illness and Healing Alternatives in Western Europe*, ed. Marjswijt-Hofstra, Hilary Marland, and Hans de Waardt, pp. 224–242. London: Routledge.

Bennett, Gillian, and Paul Smith, eds. 1996. *Contemporary Legend: A Reader*. New York: Garland Publishing.

Berer, Marge, and Sunanda Ray, eds. 1993. *Women and HIV/AIDS: An International Resource Book*. London: Pandora Press.

Best, Joel. 1990. *Threatened Children: Rhetoric and Concern about Child Victims*. Chicago: University of Chicago Press.

———. 1991. Bad Guys and Random Violence: Folklore and Media Constructions of Contemporary Deviants. *Contemporary Legend* 1:107–121.

Best, Joel, and Gerald T. Horiuchi. 1985. The Razor Blade in the Apple. *Social Problems* 32(5):488–499.

Bird, S. Elizabeth. 1996. C.J.'s Revenge: Media, Folklore, and the Cultural Construction of AIDS. *Critical Studies in Mass Communication* 13:44–58.

Blitz (India). 1987. AIDS, a U.S. Military Monster: Yankee Business, Not Monkey Business, 9.

Bødker, Laurits. 1965. *International Dictionary of Regional European Ethnology and Folklore*, vol. 2. Copenhagen: Rosenkilde and Bagger.

Broadhead, Robert S., Douglas D. Heckathorn, Jean-Paul C. Grund, L. Synn Stern, and Denise L. Anthony. 1995. Drug Users Versus Outreach Workers in Combatting AIDS: Preliminary Results of a Peer-Driven Intervention. *The Journal of Drug Issues* 25(3):531–564.

Bronner, Simon. 1990. Left to Their Own Devices: Interpreting American Children's Folklore as an Adaptation to Aging. *Southern Folklore* 47(2):101–115.

Brunvand, Jan Harold. 1981. *The Vanishing Hitchhiker: American Urban Legends and Their Meaning.* New York: W. W. Norton.

———. 1984. *The Choking Doberman and Other "New" Urban Legends.* New York: W. W. Norton.

———. 1989. *Curses! Broiled Again! The Hottest Urban Legends Going!* New York: W. W. Norton.

———. 1991. AIDS Mary Murder. *FoafTale News* 22(June):9.

———. 1992. AIDS Legend Brews a New Variation. United Feature Syndicate, February 10, 1992.

Bureau of HIV/AIDS/Health Canada. 1999. HIV and AIDS Among Youth in Canada. LCDC: Health Canada.

Burke, Kenneth. 1945. *A Grammar of Motives.* New York: Prentice-Hall.

Burny, A., C. Bruck, Y. Cleuter, J. Deschamps, D. Couez, J. Ghysdael, and J. Gregroire, D. Kettman, R. Mammerick, and M. Marbaix. 1985. Bovine Leukemia Virus, a Distinguished Member of the Human T-lymphotropic Virus Family. In *Retroviruses in Human Lymphoma/ Leukemia*, ed. Miwa, M., pp. 219–227. Utrecht: VNU Science Press.

Callwood, June. 1995. *Trial without End: A Shocking Story of Women and AIDS.* Toronto: Random House of Canada Ltd.

Calnan, Michael. 1987. *Health and Illness: The Lay Perspective.* London: Tavistock.

Campion-Vincent, Véronique. 1990. The Baby-Parts Story: A New Latin American Legend. *Western Folklore* 49:9–25.

———. 1997. *La légende des vols d'organes.* Paris: Les Belles Lettres.

Canadian Press. 1995. Red Cross Cancels Blood Clinics. Newswire, April 3.

Cantwell, Alan, Jr. 1988. *AIDS and the Doctors of Death: An Inquiry into the Origins of the AIDS Epidemic.* Los Angeles: Aries Rising Press.

———. 1993. *Queer Blood: The Secret AIDS Genocide Plot.* Los Angeles: Aries Rising Press.

Carswell, J. W., N. Sewankambo, G. Lloyd, and R. G. Downing. 1986. How Long Has the AIDS Virus Been in Uganda. *Lancet* May:1217.

Castañeda, Claudia. 2000. Child Organ-Stealing Stories: Risk, Rumour, and Reproductive Technologies. In *The Risk Society and Beyond: Critical Issues for Social Theory*, ed. Barbara Adam and Joost van Loon, pp. 137–153. London: Sage Publications.

Catina, Joseph.A., Susan.M. Kegeles, and Thomas Coates. 1990. Toward an Understanding of Risk Behavior: An AIDS Risk Reduction Model. *Health Education Quarterly* 17(1):53–72.

CDC Update. 1999. Fear of Needles Needless. *CDC HIV/STD/TB Prevention News*. http://www.cdc.gov/hchstp/hiv_aids/pubs/faq/faq5a.htm.

Chandler, Marilyn. 1991. Voices from the Front: AIDS in Autobiography. *Autobiography Studies* 6(1):54–64.

Chavis, William M., and Gwendolyn Norman. 1995. A Survey of Knowledge, Attitudes, and Beliefs about AIDS in a Medical School Student Population. *Journal of Sex Education and Therapy* 21(3):167–173.

Chirimuuta, Richard C., and Rosalind J. Chirimuuta. 1987. *AIDS, Africa, and Racism*. Derbyshire, Eng.: Bretby House.

Chirimuuta, Richard C., Rosalind Harrison, and Davis Gazi. 1987. AIDS: The Spread of Racism. *West Africa* 9(Feb): 260–262.

Cohen, Stanley. 1973. *Folk Devils and Moral Panics: The Creation of Mods and Rockers*. Great Britain: Paladin/Granada.

Conrad, Joann. 1998. Stranger Danger: Defending Innocence, Denying Responsibility. *Contemporary Legend: New Series* 1:55–96.

Cregheur, L. A., J. Casey, and H. G. Banfield. 1992. *Sexuality, AIDS, and Decision Making: A Study of Newfoundland Youth*. St. John's, Nfld.: Department of Education.

Cresswell, Tim. 1997. Weeds, Plagues, and Bodily Secretions: A Geographical Interpretation of Metaphors of Displacement. *Annals of the Association of American Geographers* 87:330–345.

Crimp, Douglas, ed. 1988. *AIDS: Cultural Analysis, Cultural Activism*. Cambridge: MIT Press.

Crimp, Douglas, and Adam Rolston. 1990. *AIDS Demographics*. Seattle: Bay Press.

Czubala, Dionizjusz. 1991. AIDS and Aggression: Polish Legends about HIV-Infected People. *FoafTale News* 23(September):1–5.

Danielson, Larry. 1979. Folklore and Film. *Western Folklore* 38:209–219.

Davis, Cindy, Mariam Beth Noel, Shui Fun Fiona Chan, and Law Siu Wing. 1998. Knowledge, Attitudes, and Behaviors Related to HIV and AIDS among Chinese Adolescents in Hong Kong. *Journal of Adolescence* 21(6):657–665.

Davis, Donna. 1995. Women in An Uncertain Age: Crisis and Change in a Newfoundland Community. In *Their Lives And Times: Women in Newfoundland and Labrador: A Collage*, ed. Carmelita McGrath, Barbara Neis, and Marilyn Porter, pp. 279–295. St. John's, Nfld.: Killick Press.

Dean, Ruth Grossman. 1995. Stories of AIDS: The Use of Narrative as an Approach to Understanding in an AIDS Support Group. *Clinical Social Work Journal* 23(3):287–304.

deCock, Kevin M. 1984. AIDS: An Old Disease from Africa? *British Medical Journal* 4(289):306–308.

Dégh, Linda. 2001. *Legend and Belief: Dialectics of a Genre*. Bloomington: Indiana University Press.

Dégh, Linda, and Andrew Vázsonyi. 1983. Does the Word Dog Bite? Ostensive Action: A Means of Legend Telling. *Journal of Folklore Research* 20:5–34.

Denison, Julie. 1999. Behavior Change: A Summary of Four Major Theories. AIDSCAP Behavioral Research Unit, Family Health International. http://www.fhi.org.

Dennis, Debra. 1991. Judge Rejects AIDS Defense in Murder Case. *Cincinnati Post*, January 30.

Des Jarlais, D. C., S. R. Friedman and D. Strug. 1986. AIDS and Needle Sharing within the IV Drug Use Subculture. In *The Social Dimensions of AIDS: Method and Theory*, ed. D. A. Feldman and T.M. Johnson, pp. 111–125. New York: Praeger.

Dettmer, Elke. 2001. *Newfoundland and Labrador: Insiders Perspectives*. St. John's, Nfld.: Johnson Family Foundation.

de Vos, Gail. 1996. *Tales, Rumors, and Gossip: Exploring Contemporary Folk Literature in Grades 7–12*. Englewood, Colo.: Libraries Unlimited Inc.

Dinham, Paul S. 1977. *You Never Know What They Might Do*. St. John's, Nfld.: Institute for Social and Economic Research.

Donovan, Catherine. 1995. *Community HIV Prevention Project Final Report April 1995*. HIV/AIDS Division, LCDC and the AIDS Education and Prevention Unit of Health Canada.

Doolittle, Russell F. 1989. Immunodeficiency Viruses: The Simian-Human Connection. *Nature* 339:338–339.

Douglas, Mary. 1966. *Purity and Danger*. London: Routledge.

———. 1992. *Risk and Blame: Essays in Cultural Theory*. London: Routledge.

Durdle, Jodi. 2001. How Women Cope in a Rural Newfoundland Community. In *From Red Ochre to Black Gold*, ed. Darrin McGrath, pp. 133–145. St. John's, Nfld.: Flanker Press.

Early, Evelyn A. 1982. The Logic of Well Being: Therapeutic Narratives in Cairo, Egypt. *Social Science and Medicine* 16:1491–1497.

Ebony Magazine. 1991. Letter signed C. J. AIDS, Dallas Texas. 46(Sept.):90.

Elliott, Richard. 1997. *Criminal Law and HIV/AIDS: Final Report.* Montreal: The Canadian HIV/AIDS Legal Network and the Canadian AIDS Society.

Ellis, Bill. 1989a. Death by Folklore: Ostension, Contemporary Legend, and Murder. *Western Folklore* 48:201–220.

———. 1989b. Needling Whitey. *FoafTale News* 16(December):5–6.

———. 1990. Mystery Assailants. *FoafTale News* 19(October):9.

———. 1996. Legend Trips and Satanism: Adolescents' Ostensive Traditions as Cult Activity. In *Contemporary Legend: A Reader,* ed. Gillian Bennett and Paul Smith, pp. 167–187. New York: Garland.

———. 2001. *Aliens, Ghosts, and Cults: Legends We Live.* Jackson: University Press of Mississippi.

El Nuevo Diario. 1987. Managua, July 6.

Epstein, Steven. 1996. *Impure Science: AIDS Activism and the Politics of Knowledge.* Berkeley: University of California Press.

Evening Telegram. 1985. No AIDS Victim in Newfoundland. St. John's, Nfld., May 13, p. 1.

———. 1985. Risk of AIDS in Newfoundland Almost Zero, Says Doctor. St. John's, Nfld., July 14, p. 1.

———. 1985. One Case of Aids So Far in Newfoundland. St. John's, Nfld., August 8, p. 1.

———. 1986. AIDS Kills Two in Low Risk Newfoundland. St. John's, Nfld., October 10, p. 1.

———. 1986. AIDS Not a Major Concern in Province, Says Doctor. St. John's, Nfld., October 31, p. 3.

———. 1987. Book Says Montreal Man Brought AIDS to America. St. John's, Nfld., October 6, p. 4.

———. 1989. Some Doubt Man First Carried AIDS to America. St John's, Nfld., October 7, p. 9.

———. 1991. Bizarre AIDS Story Likely a Concocted Tale. St. John's, Nfld., April 22, p. 1.

———. 1992. HIV Stats Startling: Six Pregnant Women Carry AIDS Virus. St. John's, Nfld., July 23, p. 1.

———. 1992. Cause for Alarm. St. John's, Nfld., July 25, p. 1.

———. 1995. Vengeful Woman Spread HIV. St. John's, Nfld., September 13, p.32.

Ewick, Patricia, and Susan Silbey. 1995. Subversive Stories and Hegemonic Tales: Toward a Sociology of Narrative. *Law and Society Review*
29(2):197–227.

Faris, James. 1972. *Cat Harbour: A Newfoundland Fishing Settlement.* St
John's, Nfld.: Institute for Social and Economic Research.

Farmer, Paul. 1992. *AIDS and Accusation: Haiti and the Geography of Blame.*
Berkeley: University of California Press.

———. 1994. AIDS-Talk and the Constitution of Cultural Models. *Social
Science and Medicine* 38(6):801–809.

Fasting, U., Christensen, J., and S. Glending. 1998. Children Sold for
Transplants: Medical and Legal Aspects. *Nursing Ethics* 5(6):518–526.

Fine, Gary Alan. 1987. Welcome to the World of AIDS: Fantasies of
Female Revenge. *Western Folklore* 46(3):192–197.

———. 1991. Redemption Rumors and the Power of Ostension. *Journal
of American Folklore* 104:179–181.

———. 1992. *Manufacturing Tales: Sex and Money in Contemporary Legend.*
Knoxville: University of Tennessee Press.

Firestone, Melvin. 1969. Mummers and Strangers in Northern New-
foundland. In *Christmas Mumming in Newfoundland*, ed. Herbert
Halpert and G. M. Story, pp. 62–75. Toronto: University of Toronto
Press.

———. 1980. *Brothers and Rivals: Patrilocality in Savage Cove.* St. John's,
Nfld.: Institute for Social and Economic Research.

Fishbein, Martin, Susan E. Middlestadt, and Penelope J. Hitchcock.
1994. Using Information to Change Sexually Transmitted Disease-
Related Behaviors. In *Preventing AIDS: Theories and Methods of Behavioral Interventions*, ed. Ralph J. DiClemente and John L. Peterson, pp.
61–78. New York: Plenum.

Fiske, John. 1993. *Power Plays Power Works.* London: Verso Books.

Fitzpatrick, Ray, John Hinton, Stanton Newman, Graham Scambler, and
James Thompson. 1984. *The Experience of Illness.* New York: Tavistock.

Flynn, Mike. 1992. AIDS Buttons Tell How CBN Feels. *St. John's (Nfld.)
Evening Telegram*, April 2.

FoafTale News. 1992. 25(March):11.

Foster, George. 1965. Peasant Society and the Image of Limited Good.
American Anthropologist 67:293–315.

Foucault, Michel. 1980. Two Lectures. In *Power/Knowledge: Selected Interviews and Other Writings 1972–1977*, ed. and trans. Colin Gordon, pp.
78–108. New York: Pantheon.

Fox, Kathryn J. 1991. The Politics of Prevention: Ethnographers Combat AIDS among Drug Users. In *Ethnography Unbound: Power and Resistance in the Modern Metropolis,* pp. 227–249. Berkeley: University of California Press.

Frazer, James G. 1959 (1890). *The Golden Bough: A Study in Magic and Religion.* Ed. T. H. Gaster. New York: McMillan.

Garro, Linda. 1992. Chronic Illness and the Construction of Narratives. In *Pain as Human Experience,* ed. Mary Jo DelVecchio, P. Brodwin, B. Good, and A. Kleinman, pp. 100–137. Berkeley: University of California Press.

Garry, Robert F., Marlys H. Witte, Arthur A. Gottlieb, Memory Elvin Lewis, Marise S. Gottlieb, Charles L. Witte, Steve S. Alexander, William R. Cole, and William L. Drake, Jr. 1988. Documentation of an AIDS Virus Infection in the United States in 1969. *Journal of the American Medical Association* 260(14):2085–2087.

Gaudet, Marcia. 1990. Telling It Slant: Personal Narrative, Tall Tales, and the Reality of Leprosy. *Western Folklore* 49:191–207.

Georgidis, J. A., A. Billiau, and B. Vanderschueren. 1978. Infection of Human Cell Cultures with Bovine Visna Virus. *Journal of General Virology* 38:375–381.

Gilman, Sander L. 1988. *Disease and Representation: Images of Illness from Madness to AIDS.* Ithaca: Cornell University Press.

Gilmore, Norbert, and Margaret A. Somerville. 1994. Stigmatization, Scapegoating, and Discrimination in Sexually Transmitted Diseases: Overcoming "Them" and "Us." *Social Science and Medicine* 39(9):1339–1358.

Goldstein, Diane E. 1991. *Talking AIDS: Interdisciplinary Perspectives on Acquired Immune Deficiency Syndrome.* ISER Research and Policy Papers #12. St. Johns, Nfld.: Institute for Social and Economic Research.

———. 1992. Welcome to the Mainland, Welcome to the World of AIDS: Cultural Viability, Localization, and Contemporary Legend. *Contemporary Legend* 2:23–40.

———. 1993. Not Just a Glorified Anthropologist: Medical Problem Solving through Verbal Art. *Folklore in Use* 1:15–24.

———. 1998. Positive Perspectives: Folk Medical Worldview and Legal Cases of Deliberate Infection. Unpublished paper, presented at the American Folklore Society meeting.

———. 2000. "When Ovaries Retire": Contrasting Women's Experiences with Feminist and Medical Models of Menopause. *Health* 4(3):309–323.

————. 2001. Competing Logics and the Construction of Risk. In *Healing Logics*, ed. Erika Brady. Logan: Utah State University Press.

Goldstein, Diane E., Cindy Patton, and Heather Worth, eds. Forthcoming. *Reckless Vectors: AIDS and the Infecting "Other" in Law, Policy, Ethics, and Narrative. Sexuality Research and Social Policy: Journal of NSRC* special issue.

Goldstruck, Arthur. 1993. *The Leopard in the Luggage: Urban Legends from Southern Africa.* Middlesex, Eng.: Penguin.

Gonda, Matthew A., Flossie Wong Staal, Robert C. Gallo, J. E. Clements, O. Narayan, and R. V. Gilden. 1985. Sequence Homology and Morphological Similarity of HTLV-III and Visna Virus, A Pathogenic Lentivirus. *Science* 227:173–177.

Good, Byron. 1994. *Medicine, Rationality, and Experience: An Anthropological Perspective.* Cambridge: Cambridge University Press.

Good, Mary-Jo DelVecchio, Paul E. Brodwin, Byron J. Good, and Arthur Kleinman. 1992. *Pain as Human Experience: An Anthropological Perspective.* Berkeley: University of California Press.

Goodwin, Joseph P. 1989. *More Man Than You'll Ever Be: Gay Folklore and Acculturation in Middle America.* Bloomington: Indiana University Press.

Goss, Michael. 1987. *The Halifax Slasher: An Urban Terror in the North of England.* London: Fortean Times.

Government of Newfoundland and Labrador. 2003. Provincial Economy. http://www.gov.nf.ca/nfld&lab/economy.htm.

Greco, Ralph S. 1983. Haiti and the Stigma of AIDS. *Lancet* 27:515–516.

Green, J., and D. Miller. 1986. *AIDS: The Story of a Disease.* London: Grafton.

Grider, Sylvia. 1984. The Razor Blades in the Apple Syndrome. In *Perspectives on Contemporary Legend: Proceedings of the Conference on Contemporary Legend*, ed. Paul Smith, pp. 128–140. Sheffield, Eng.: CECTAL Conference Papers Series No. 4.

Gushue, John. 2000. Blood Donation Ban Lifted from Tainted Nfld. Area. *The Medical Post* 36(9):1–2.

Hanrahan, Maura. 1993. *Uncertain Refuge: Lectures on Newfoundland Society and Culture.* St. John's, Nfld.: Breakwater.

Haraway, Donna. 1991. The Biopolitics of Postmodern Bodies: Constitutions of Self in Immune System Discourse. In *Simians, Cyborgs, and Women: The Reinvention of Nature*, 203–230. New York: Routledge.

Heath, Linda, Marvin Acklin, and Catherine Wiley. 1991. Cognitive Heuristics and AIDS Risk Assessment among Physicians. *Journal of Applied Social Psychology* 21:1859–1867.

Henrickson, Roy V., D. H. Maul, K. G. Osborn, J. L. Sever, D. L. Madden, L. R. Ellingsworth, J. H. Anderson, L. J. Lowenstein, and M. B. Gardner. 1983. Epidemic of Acquired Immunodeficiency in Rhesus Monkeys. *Lancet* 19:388–390.

Herek, Gregory, and John P. Capitanio. 1994. Conspiracies, Contagion, and Compassion: Trust and Public Reactions to AIDS. *AIDS Education and Prevention* 6(4):365–375.

Hines, Robert. 1991. AIDS, the Disclosure Dilemma. *Missouri Realtor*, May/June, pp. 4, 9–10.

House, J. Douglas. 2001. From Fish to Oil: The Economy in 2000. In *Newfoundland and Labrador: Insiders Perspectives*, ed. Elke Dettmer, pp. 15–16. St. John's, Nfld.: Johnson Family Foundation.

Hufford, David J. 1982. Traditions of Disbelief. *New York Folklore Quarterly* 8(3/4):47–55.

———. 1984. *American Healing Systems: An Introduction and Exploration*. Hershey: Pennsylvania University Medical School.

———. 1991. AIDS, Culture, and Authority. In *Talking AIDS: Interdisciplinary Perspectives on Acquired Immune Deficiency Syndrome*, ed. Diane E. Goldstein, pp. 7–22. ISER Research and Policy Papers. St. John's, Nfld.: Institute for Social and Economic Research.

Jackson, Craig. 1992a. Lack of HIV Screening a Worry in Delivery Room. *St. John's (Nfld.) Evening Telegram*, July 28, p. 1.

Jackson, Craig. 1992b. No Confidentiality Biggest AIDS Fear. *St. John's (Nfld.) Evening Telegram*, August 12, p. 2.

Janz, Nancy K., and Marshall H. Becker. 1984. The Health Belief Model: A Decade Later. *Health Education Quarterly* 11(1):1–47.

Kane, Stephanie C. 1993. National Discourse and the Dynamics of Risk: Ethnography and AIDS Intervention. *Human Organization* 52:224–228.

———. 1998. *AIDS Alibis: Sex, Drugs, and Crime in the Americas*. Philadelphia: Temple University Press.

Kanki, P. J., J. Alroy, and M. Essex. 1985. Isolation of T-lymphotropic Retrovirus Related to HTLV-III/LAV from Wild-Caught African Green Monkeys. *Science* 230(4728):951–954.

Kapferer, Jean-Noel. 1990. *Rumors: Uses, Interpretations, and Images*. New Brunswick: Transaction Publishers.

———. 1993. The Persuasiveness of an Urban Legend: The Case of Mickey Mouse Acid. *Contemporary Legend* 3:85–101.

———. 1996. A Mass Poisoning Rumor in Europe. In *Contemporary Legend: A Reader*, ed. Paul Smith and Gillian Bennett, pp. 245–260. New York: Garland Publishing.

Kelley, J. A., J. S. St. Lawrence, H. V. Hood, and T. L. Brasfield. 1989. Behavioural Intervention to Reduce AIDS Risk Activities. *Journal of Consulting and Clinical Psychology* 57:60–67.

Kimmel, Alan, and Robert Keefer. 1991. Psychological Correlates of the Transmission and Acceptance of Rumors about AIDS. *Journal of Applied Psychology* 21(19):1608–1628.

King, A. 1989. *Canada Youth and AIDS Study: Newfoundland Report*. Kingston, Ont.: Queens University.

Kinsman, Gary. 1991. Their Silence, Our Deaths: What Can the Social Sciences Offer to AIDS Research. In *Talking AIDS: Interdisciplinary Perspectives on Acquired Immune Deficiency Syndrome*, ed. Diane E. Goldstein, pp. 39–60. ISER Research and Policy Papers. St. John's, Nfld.: Institute for Social and Economic Research.

———. 1996. Responsibility as a Strategy of Governance: Regulating People Living with AIDS and Lesbians and Gay Men in Ontario. *Economy and Society* 25(3):393–409.

Kippax, S., and J. Crawford. 1993. Flaws in the Theory of Reasoned Action. In *The Theory of Reasoned Action: Its Application to AIDS Preventative Behavior*, ed. D. J. Gallois and M. McCamish, pp. 253–269. New York: Pergamon.

Kleinman, Arthur. 1975. Explanatory Models in Health Care Relationships. In *Health of the Family*, pp. 159–172. Washington D.C.: National Council for International Health.

———. 1992. Pain and Resistance: The Delegitimation and Religitimation of Local Worlds. In *Pain as Human Experience: An Anthropological Perspective*, ed. Mary Jo DelVecchio Good, Paul Brodwin, Byron Good, and Arthur Kleinman, pp. 169–198. Berkeley: University of California Press.

Koenig, Fredrick. 1985. *Rumor in the Marketplace: The Social Psychology of Commercial Hearsay*. Dover, Mass.: Auburn House.

Kotarba, Joseph A. 1990. Ethnography and AIDS: Returning to the Streets. *Journal of Contemporary Ethnography/Special Issue: Ethnography and AIDS* 19(3):259–269.

Krawczyk-Wasilewska, Violetta. 2000. *AIDS: Studium Anthropologiczne (An Anthropological Study)*. English Summary, pp. 109–118. Lodz, Pol.: Wydawnictwo Uniwersytetu.

Labov, William, and Joshua Waletsky. 1967. Narrative Analysis: Oral Versions of Personal Experience. In *Essays on the Verbal and Visual Arts*, ed. June L. Helm, pp. 12–44. Seattle: University of Washington Press.

Lake, Holly. 1999. HIV Cyber-hoax Spreading Concern. *St. John's (Nfld.) Evening Telegram*, May 13.

Langlois, Janet. 1991. Hold the Mayo: Purity and Danger in an AIDS Legend. *Contemporary Legend* 1:153–172.

Lear, Dana. 1995. Sexual Communication in the Age of AIDS: The Construction of Risk and Trust among Young Adults. *Social Science and Medicine* 41(9):1311–1323.

Lindsay, M., H. Peterson, T. Feng, B. Slade, S. Willis, and L. Klein. 1989. Routine Antepartum Human Immunodeficiency Virus Screening in an Inner-City Population. *Obstetrics and Gynecology* 76(3):289–294.

Lock, M. 1982. Models and Practice in Medicine: Menopause as Syndrome or Life Transition. *Culture, Medicine, and Psychiatry* 18(7):361–380.

MacKinnon, Joanne. 1993. *Towards the Development of a Comprehensive HIV/AIDS Strategy for Newfoundland and Labrador*. Government of Newfoundland and Labrador Department of Health.

Markey, Judy. 1990. Teen-agers Remain "Invincible." United Feature Syndicate, June.

Martin, Emily. 1994. *Flexible Bodies: Tracking Immunity in American Culture—From the Days of Polio to the Age of AIDS* . Boston: Beacon.

Maticka-Tyndale, E. 1991. Sexual Scripts and AIDS Prevention: Variations in Adherence to Safer Sex Guidelines by Heterosexual Adolescents. *Journal of Sex Research* 28:45–66.

Mattingly, Cheryl. 1998. *Healing Dramas and Clinical Plots: The Narrative Structure of Experience*. Cambridge: University of Cambridge Press.

Mayor, Adrienne. 1995. The Nessus Shirt in the New World: Smallpox Blankets in History and Legend. *Journal of American Folklore* 108(427):54–77.

McDonnell, Kathleen. 1994. *Kid Culture: Children and Adults and Popular Culture*. Toronto: Second Story.

McGrath, Carmelita, Barbara Neis, and Marilyn Porter, eds. 1995. *Their Life and Times: Women In Newfoundland and Labrador: A Collage*. St. John's, Nfld.: Killick.

McGrath, Darrin. 2001. *From Red Ochre to Black Gold*. St. John's, Nfld.: Flanker .

McGrath, Janet W., Charles B. Rwabukwali, Debra A. Shumann, Jannie Person-Marks, Sylvia Nakayiwa, Barbara Namande, Lucy Nakyobe, and Rebecca Mukasa. 1993. Anthropology and AIDS: The Cultural Context of Sexual Risk Behavior Among Urban Baganda Women in Kampala Uganda. *Social Science and Medicine* 36:429–439.

McKinnon, Joanne. 1993. *Towards the Development of a Comprehensive HIV/AIDS Strategy for Newfoundland and Labrador: Report of the Working Groups on Prevention and Education, Testing and Treatrment, Care and Home Support.* St. John's, Nfld.: Government of Newfoundland and Labrador Department of Health.

McLaughlin, Thomas. 1996. *Street Smarts and Critical Theory: Listening to the Vernacular.* Madison: University of Wisconsin Press.

Metts, Sandra, and Mary Anne Fitzpatrick. 1992. Thinking about Safer Sex: The Risky Business of "Know Your Partner" Advice. In *AIDS: A Communication Perspective*, ed. T. Edgar, M. Fitzpatrick, and V. Freimuth, pp. 1–19. Hillsdale, N.J.: Lawrence Earlbaum Association.

Mikkelson, Barbara, and David Mikkelson. 2001. *Urban Legends Reference Pages.* http://www.snopes.com/horrors/parental/bloodtst.htm.

Miller, James, ed. 1992. *Fluid Exchanges: Artists and Critics in the AIDS Crisis.* Toronto: University of Toronto Press.

Morgan, Tansy. 1998. Fewer New HIV Cases in CBN. *Express*, September 16–22, p. 14.

Murtagh, Peter. 1987. AIDS in Africa. *Guardian*, February 3.

Nahmias, A. J., J. Weiss, X. Yao, F. Lee, R. Kodsi, M. Schanfield, T. Matthews, D. Bolognesi, D. Durack, and A. Motulsky. 1986. Evidence for Human Infection with an HTLV III/ LAV–Like Virus in Central Africa 1959. *Lancet* 31:1279–1280.

Nemeroff, Carol, Alana Brinkman, and Claudia Woodward. 1994. Magical Contagion and AIDS Risk Perception in a College Population. *AIDS Education and Prevention* 6(3):249–265.

Nemeroff, Carol, and Paul Rozin. 1994. The Contagion Concept in Adult Thinking in the United States: Transmission of Germs and of Interpersonal Influence. *Ethos* 22(2):158–186.

Nichols, Margaret. 1990. Women and Acquired Immune Deficiency Syndrome: Issues for Prevention. In *AIDS and Sex: An Integrated Biomedical and Behavioral Approach*, ed. B. Voeller, J. Reinisch, and M. Gottlieb, pp. 375–392 (New York: Oxford University Press, 1990).

Nicoll, Angus, U. Laukamm-Josten, B. Mwizarubi, C. Mayala, M. Mkuye, G. Nyembela, and H. Grosskurth. 1993. Lay Health Beliefs Concerning HIV and AIDS: A Barrier for Control Programmes. *AIDS Care* 5(2):231–241.

Noireau, F. 1987.Transmission from Monkey to Man. *Lancet* 27:1498–1499.

O'Brien, Patricia. 1994. Tuberculosis. In *Encyclopedia of Newfoundland and Labrador*, vol. 5, ed. Cyril F. Poole, pp. 430–434. St. John's, Nfld.: Harry Cuff.

O'Connor, Bonnie Blair. 1995. *Healing Traditions: Alternative Medicine and the Health Professions.* Philadelphia: University of Pennsylvania Press.

Opie, Iona, and Peter Opie. 1985. *The Singing Game.* Oxford: Oxford University Press.

Organista, Pamela Balls, Kurt C. Organista, and Pearl R. Soloff. 1998. Exploring AIDS-Related Knowledge, Attitudes, and Behaviors of Female Mexican Migrant Workers. *Health and Social Work* 23(2):96–103.

Parker, Richard G., and Manuel Carballo. 1990. Qualitative Research on Homosexual and Bisexual Behavior Relevant to HIV/AIDS. *Journal of Sex Research* 27:497.

Patton, Cindy. 1988. Inventing African AIDS. *City Limits* 15–22:85.

———. 1994. *Last Served? Gendering the HIV Pandemic.* London: Taylor and Francis.

———.1996. *Fatal Advice: How Safe Sex Education Went Wrong.* Durham, N.C.: Duke University Press.

Piot, Peter, and C. J. Schofield. 1986. No Evidence for Arthropod Transmission of AIDS. *Parasitology Today* 2:294.

Pitt, Janet E. Miller. 1984. Health. In *Encyclopedia of Newfoundland and Labrador,* vol. 2, ed. Joseph R. Smallwood, pp. 864–889. St. John's: Newfoundland Book Publishers.

Powell, Douglas, and William Leiss. 1997. *Mad Cows and Mother's Milk: The Perils of Poor Risk Communication.* Montreal: McGill-Queens University Press.

Prentice, Thomson. 1986. Africa's New Agony. *Times,* October 27.

Pucey, William Allen. 1933. *The History and Epidemiology of Syphilis.* Springfield, Ill.: C. C. Thomas.

Radner, Joan N., and Susan S. Lanser. 1993 Strategies of Coding in Women's Culture. In *Feminist Messages: Coding in Women's Folk Culture,* ed. Joan Newlon Radner, pp. 1–30. Urbana: University of Illinois Press.

Ramos, Reyes, Rochelle N. Shain, and Leonard Johnson. 1995. "Men I Mess With Don't Have Anything to Do with AIDS": Using Ethnotheory to Understand Sexual Risk Perception. *The Sociological Quarterly* 36(3): 484–505.

Ramsey, Constable J. N. 1991. Police Charges against Raymond Harword Mercer. Filed December 5.

Ratnam, Sam. 1994. *The Newfoundland and Labrador Prenatal Study of HIV Seroprevalence.* Final Report to National Health and Research Development Program.

Rayner, Ben. 1998. Clubs Suffer as Needle Rumour Persists. *Toronto Star.* August 17.

Rogers, John Davenport. 1911. *Newfoundland.* Oxford, Eng.: Clarendon Press. Cited in G. M. Story, Newfoundland: Fishermen, Hunters, Planters and Merchants. In *Christmas Mumming in Newfoundland,* ed. Herbert Halpert and G. M. Story, p. 10. (Toronto: University of Toronto Press, 1990).

Rosenberg, Matt. 2003. Province of Newfoundland and Labrador Name Change. *About Geography.* http://geography.about.com/library/weekly/aa022303a.htm.

Royko, Mike. 1992. Blood Test "Results" Already Legendary. *Chicago Tribune,* May 15, p. C3.

Rozin, Paul, Maureen Markwith, and Carol Nemeroff. 1992. Magical Contagion Beliefs and Fear of AIDS. *Journal of Applied Social Psychology* 22 (14):1081–1092.

Rushforth, Scott. 1994. Political Resistance in a Contemporary Hunter-Gatherer Society: More About Bearlake Athapaskan Knowledge and Authority. *American Ethnologist* 21(2):335–352.

R. v. Mercer. Newfoundland Supreme Court, Court of Appeal (Goodridge, CJN, Mahoney and Marshall, JJA July 19, 1993) 110 Nfld. & P.E.I.R. and 346 A.P.R. 41–58.

Sabatier, Renée. 1988. *Blaming Others: Prejudice, Race, and Worldwide AIDS.* Paris: Panos Institute.

Sachdev, Paul. 1998. AIDS/HIV and University Students in Delhi, India: Knowledge, Beliefs, Attitudes, and Behaviors. *Social Work in Health Care* 26(4):37–57.

Sanchez, Roberto. 1995. County Jailers Fear That Inmate-Prepared Meals Are Tainted. *Phoenix Gazette.* May 4, p. A1.

Sanderson, Stewart. 1969. The Folklore of the Motor-car. *Folklore* 80:241–252.

Saxinger, W. Carl, P. H. Levine, A. G. Dean, G. de The, G. Lange-Wantzin, J. Moghissi, F. Laurent, M. Hoh, M. G. Sarngadharan, and R. C. Gallo. 1985. Evidence for Exposure to HTLV-III in Uganda before 1973. *Science* 227:1036–1038.

Saxon, Lyle, Edward Dreyer, and Robert Tallant. 1945. *Gumbo Ya-Ya: A Collection of Louisana Folk Tales.* New York: Bonanza.

Schechter, Harold. 1988. *The Bosom Serpent: Folklore and Popular Art.* Iowa City: University of Iowa Press.

Scheper-Hughes, Nancy. 1996. Theft of Life: The Globalization of Organ-Stealing Rumours. *Anthropology Today* 12(3):3–11.

Schoenborn, C., S. Marsh and A. Hardy. 1994. AIDS Knowledge and Attitudes for 1992: Data from the National Health Interview Survey. In *Advance Data from Vital and Health Statistics* 243. Hyattville, Md.: National Center for Health Statistics.

Scott, James C. 1985. *Weapons of the Weak: Everyday Forms of Peasant Resistance*. New Haven: Yale University Press.

———. 1990a. *Domination and the Arts of Resistance: Hidden Transcripts*. New Haven: Yale University Press.

———. 1990b. Everyday Forms of Peasant Resistance. In *Customs in Conflict: The Anthropology of a Changing World*, ed. Frank Manning and Jean-Marc Philibert, pp. 414–447. Peterborough, Ont.: Broadview

Segal, Jacob, and Lili Segal. 1986. *AIDS: USA Home-Made Evil*. N.p.

Sherman, Josepha, and T. K. F. Weisskopf. 1995. *Greasy Grimy Gopher Guts: The Subversive Folklore of Childhood*. Little Rock: August House.

Shibutani, Tomotsu. 1966. *Improvised News: A Sociological Study of Rumor*. Indianapolis: Bobbs-Merrill.

Shilts, Randy. 1987. *And the Band Played On: Politics, People, and the AIDS Epidemic*. New York: St. Martin's.

Sinclair, Peter R. 2001. Sustainable Development in Fisheries-Dependent Regions? Reflections on the Unsustainable Newfoundland Cod Fisheries. In *From Red Ochre to Black Gold*, ed. Darrin McGrath, pp. 166–182. St. John's, Nfld.: Flanker.

Smith, James Monroe. 1996. *AIDS and Society*. Upper Saddle River, N. J.: Prentice-Hall.

Smith, Paul. 1990. 'AIDS—Don't Die of Ignorance': Exploring the Cultural Complex. In *A Nest of Vipers: Perspectives on Contemporary Legend*, vol. 5, ed. Gillian Bennett and Paul Smith, pp. 113–141. Sheffield, Eng.: Sheffield Academic Press.

———. 1992. "Read All about It! Elvis Eaten by Drug-Crazed Alligators": Contemporary Legend and the Popular Press. *Contemporary Legend* 2:41–70.

———. 1998. Legend, Contemporary. In *Folklore: An Encyclopedia of Beliefs, Customs, Tales, Music, and Art*, vol. 2, ed. Thomas A. Green, pp. 492–495. Oxford: ABC-CLIO.

Sobo, Elisa J. 1993. Inner City Women and AIDS: The Psycho-Social Benefits of Unsafe Sex. *Culture, Medicine, and Psychiatry* 17(4):445–485.

———. 1995. *Choosing Unsafe Sex: AIDS Risk Denial among Disadvantaged Women*. Philadelphia: University of Pennsylvania Press.

Sobo, Elisa J., Gregory D. Zimet, Teena Zimmerman, and Heather Cecil. 1997. Doubting the Experts: AIDS Misconceptions among Runaway Adolescents. *Human Organization* 56(3):311–320.

Sonnex, C., J. G. Hart, P. Williams, and M. W. Adler. 1989. Condom Use by Heterosexuals Attending a Department of GUM: Attitudes and Behavior in Light of HIV Infection. *Genitourinary Medicine* 65:248–251.

Srinivasan, A., D. York, and C. Bohan. 1987. Lack of HIV Replication in Arthropod Cells. *Lancet* 1:1094–1095.

Stanley-Blackwell, Laurie C. 1993. The Mysterious Stranger and the Acadian Good Samaritan: Leprosy Folklore in 19th Century New Brunswick. *Acadiensis* XXII(2):27–39.

Staples, Sarah. 2000. Human Resource: Newfoundland's 300-Year-Old Legacy Has Triggered a Gold Rush. *Report on Business Magazine* 17(3):117–18,120.

Statistics Canada. 2003. Population by Religion. www.statcan.ca/english/Pgdb/demo30a.htm.

Statistics Canada. 2003. Population. http://www.statcan.ca/english/Pgdb/demo.

Stevenson, Howard C. Jr. 1994. The Psychology of Sexual Racism and AIDS: An Ongoing Saga of Distrust and the "Sexual Other." *Journal of Black Studies* 25(1):62–80.

Stevenson, Howard, Kristin McKee Gay, and Laura Josar. 1995. Culturally Sensitive AIDS Education and Perceived AIDS Risk Knowledge: Reaching the "Know-It-All" Teenager. *AIDS Education and Prevention* 7(2):134–144.

Stillwaggon, Eileen. 2003. Racial Metaphors: Interpreting Sex and AIDS in Africa. *Development and Change* 34 (5):809–832.

Stoffle, Richard, Michael Traugott, John Stone, Paula McIntyre, Florence Jensen, and Carla Davidson. 1991. Risk Perception Mapping. *American Anthropology* 93(3):611–635.

Story, G. M., W. J. Kirwin, and J. D. A. Widdowson. 1982. *Dictionary of Newfoundland English*. Toronto: University of Toronto Press.

Surgeon General. 1988. *Understanding AIDS*. Washington, D.C.: Government Printing Office.

Szwed, John. 1966. *Private Cultures and Public Imagery : Interpersonal Relations in a Newfoundland Peasant Society*. St John's, Nfld.: Institute for Social and Economic Research.

Tarkka, Lotte. 1993. Intertextuality, Rhetorics, and the Interpretation of Oral Poetry: The Case of Archived Orality. In *Nordic Frontiers: Recent*

Issues in the Study of Modern Traditional Culture in the Nordic Countries, ed. Pertti Anttonen and Reimund Kvideland, pp. 165–195. Turku, Fin.: Nordic Institute of Folklore.

Tarr, Chou-Meng, and Peter Aggleton. 1999. Young People and HIV in Cambodia: Meanings, Contexts, and Sexual Cultures. *AIDS Care* 11(3):375–384.

Taylor, F. K. 1979. Penis Captivus, Did It Occur? *British Medical Journal* 20(2):977–978.

The Compass. 2001. 15,000 People across the Country Are HIV Positive and Don't Know It. 33(16).

The Express. 1995. Study Answers Questions about Strain of HIV in CBN Outbreak. December 6, p. 19.

The Guardian. 1995. AIDS Revenge Shocks Ireland. December 13, p. 2.

The Queen v. Raymond Hayward Mercer Appeal. *Transcript of Evidence*, Province of Newfoundland, District of Harbour Grace. Court dates: June 25, 1992; July 3, 1992; July 10, 1992. Pp. 1–233.

Thomas, Stephen B., and Sandra Crouse Quinn. 1991. Public Health Then and Now: The Tuskegee Syphilis Study, 1932 to 1972: Implications for HIV education and AIDS Risk Education Programs in the Black Community. *American Journal of Public Health* 81(11):1498–1505.

Thompson, Kenneth. 1998. *Moral Panics.* London: Routledge.

Thompson, Stith. 1955–1958. *Motif-Index of Folk-Literature.* Bloomington: Indiana University Press.

Timmo, Lazaro. 1988. One Wife? You Must Be Joking! In *Blaming Others: Prejudice, Race, and Worldwide AIDS*, ed. Renee Sabatier, pp. 125–127. Philadelphia: New Society.

Treichler, Paula. 1988. AIDS, Gender, and Biomedical Discourse: Current Contests for Meaning. In *AIDS: The Burden of History*, ed. Elizabeth Fee and Daniel Fox, pp. 190–266. Berkeley: University of California Press.

———. 1989. AIDS and HIV Infection in the Third World: A First World Chronicle. In *Remaking History*, ed. Barbara Kruger and Phil Mariani, pp. 31–86. Seattle: Bay.

———. 1999. *How to Have Theory in an Epidemic: Cultural Chronicles of AIDS.* Durham, N.C.: Duke University Press.

Turner, Patricia A. 1991. The Atlanta Child Murders: A Case Study of Folklore in the Black Community. In *Creative Ethnicity: Symbols and Strategies of Contemporary Life*, ed. Steven Stern and John Allan Cicala, pp. 75–86. Logan: Utah State University Press.

————. 1993. *I Heard It through the Grapevine: Rumor in African American Culture*. Berkeley: University of California Press.

United States Department of State. 1987. *The USSR's AIDS Disinformation Campaign*. Washington, D.C.: State Department Reports.

Vanlandingham, Mark J., Somboon Suprasert, Nancy Grandjean, and Werasit Sittitrai. 1995. Two Views of Risky Sexual Practices among Northern Thai Males: The Health Belief Model and the Theory of Reasoned Action. *Journal of Health and Social Behavior* 36:195–212.

Versi, Anver. 1990. Africa and the AIDS Myth. *New African* 271:9–12.

Victor, Jeffrey S. 1993. *Satanic Panic: The Creation of a Contemporary Legend*. Chicago: Open Court.

Wachs, Eleanor. 1988. *Crime Victim Stories: New York City's Urban Folklore*. Bloomington: Indiana University Press.

Waldby, Catherine, Annette Houlihan, June Crawford, and Susan Kippax. Forthcoming. Medical Vectors: Surgical HIV Transmission and the Location of Culpability. In *Reckless Vectors: AIDS and the Infecting "Other" in Law, Ethics, Policy, and Narrative*, ed. Goldstein, Diane E., Cindy Patton, and Heather Worth. *Sexuality Research and Social Policy: Journal of NSRC* special issue.

Walters, Jennifer, Renee Canady, and Terry Stein. 1994. Evaluating Multicultural Approaches in HIV/AIDS Educational Material. *AIDS Education and Prevention* 6(5):446–453.

Warren, Ted. 1992. AIDS Education Policy Crucial to the Province. *St. John's (Nfld.) Evening Telegram*, July 25, p. 3.

Watney, Simon. 1987. *Policing Desire: Pornography, AIDS, and the Media*. London: Comedia/Methuen.

————. 1989. Missionary Positions: AIDS, "Africa," and "Race". *Differences* 1(1):83–100.

Weinstein, Neil. 1989. Perceptions of Personal Susceptibility to Harm. In *Primary Prevention of AIDS: Psychological Approaches*, ed. V. Mays, G. Albee, and S. Schneider, pp. 142–167. Newbury Park, Cal.: Sage.

Whatley, Mariamne H., and Elissa R. Henken. 2000. *Did You Hear about the Girl Who . . .?: Contemporary Legends, Folklore, and Human Sexuality*. New York: New York University Press.

Williams, George, T. B. Stretton, and J. C. Leonard. 1983. AIDS in 1959? *Lancet* November:1136.

Wycoff, Donna. 1996. Now Everything Makes Sense!: Complicating the Contemporary Legend Picture. In *Contemporary Legend: A Reader*, ed. Gillian Bennett and Paul Smith, pp. 363–380. New York: Garland.

Zola, Irving. 1972. Medicine as an Institution of Social Control. *Sociological Review* 20(4):487–504.

Index